History Flows through Us

History Flows through Us introduces a new dialogue between leading historians and psychoanalysts and provides essential insights into the nature of historical trauma. The contributors – German historians, historians of the Holocaust, and psychoanalysts of different disciplinary backgrounds – address the synergy between history and psychoanalysis in an engaging and accessible manner. Together they develop a response to German history and the Holocaust that is future-oriented and timely in the presence of today's ethnic hatreds. In the process, they help us to appreciate the emotional and political legacy of history's collective crimes.

This book illustrates how history and the psyche shape one another and the degree to which history flows through all of us as human beings. Its innovative cross-disciplinary approach draws on the work of the historian and psychoanalyst Thomas Kohut. The volume includes an extended dialogue with Kohut in which he reflects on the study of German history and the Holocaust at the intersection of history and psychoanalysis. This book demonstrates that the fields of history and psychoanalysis are each concerned with the role of empathy and with the study of memory and narrative.

History Flows through Us will appeal to general readers, students, and professionals in cultural and German history, Holocaust and trauma studies, sociology, psychoanalysis, psychotherapy, and psychology.

Roger Frie is Professor of Education at Simon Fraser University and Affiliate Professor of Psychiatry at the University of British Columbia, Vancouver, and Psychoanalytic Faculty and Supervisor at the William Alanson White Institute of Psychiatry, Psychoanalysis, and Psychology in New York. He is the author of *Not in My Family: German Memory and Responsibility after the Holocaust* (2017).

Psychoanalytic Inquiry Book Series

Joseph D. Lichtenberg
Series Editor

Like its counterpart, *Psychoanalytic Inquiry: A Topical Journal for Mental Health Professionals*, the Psychoanalytic Inquiry Book Series presents a diversity of subjects within a diversity of approaches to those subjects. Under the editorship of Joseph Lichtenberg, in collaboration with Melvin Bornstein and the editorial board of *Psychoanalytic Inquiry*, the volumes in this series strike a balance between research, theory, and clinical application. We are honored to have published the works of various innovators in psychoanalysis, including Frank Lachmann, James Fosshage, Robert Stolorow, Donna Orange, Louis Sander, Léon Wurmser, James Grotstein, Joseph Jones, Doris Brothers, Fredric Busch, and Joseph Lichtenberg, among others.

The series includes books and monographs on mainline psychoanalytic topics, such as sexuality, narcissism, trauma, homosexuality, jealousy, envy, and varied aspects of analytic process and technique. In our efforts to broaden the field of analytic interest, the series has incorporated and embraced innovative discoveries in infant research, self psychology, intersubjectivity, motivational systems, affects as process, responses to cancer, borderline states, contextualism, postmodernism, attachment research and theory, medication, and mentalization. As further investigations in psychoanalysis come to fruition, we seek to present them in readable, easily comprehensible writing.

After more than 25 years, the core vision of this series remains the investigation, analysis and discussion of developments on the cutting edge of the psychoanalytic field, inspired by a boundless spirit of inquiry. A full list of all the titles available in the *Psychoanalytic Inquiry* Book Series is available at www.routledge.com/Psychoanalytic-Inquiry-Book-Series/book-series/LEAPIBS.

History Flows through Us

Germany, the Holocaust, and the Importance of Empathy

Edited by Roger Frie

Routledge
Taylor & Francis Group
LONDON AND NEW YORK

First published 2018
by Routledge
2 Park Square, Milton Park, Abingdon, Oxon OX14 4RN

and by Routledge
711 Third Avenue, New York, NY 10017

Routledge is an imprint of the Taylor & Francis Group, an informa business

British Library Cataloguing in Publication Data
A catalogue record for this book is available from the British Library

Library of Congress Cataloging in Publication Data
Names: Frie, Roger, 1965– author.
Title: History flows through us : Germany, the Holocaust, and the importance of empathy / edited by Roger Frie.
Description: Abingdon, Oxon ; New York, NY : Routledge, 2018. |
Series: Psychoanalytic inquiry ; 55 | Includes bibliographical references and index.
Identifiers: LCCN 2017020108 | ISBN 9781138289376 (hardback : alk. paper) | ISBN 9781138289383 (pbk. : alk. paper) | ISBN 9781351972260 (epub) | ISBN 9781351972253 (mobipocket/kindle)
Subjects: LCSH: Psychohistory. | Psychoanalysis and history. | Holocaust, Jewish (1939–1945)–Psychological aspects.
Classification: LCC D16.16 .H568 2018 | DDC 940.53/18019–dc23
LC record available at https://lccn.loc.gov/2017020108

ISBN: 978-1-138-28937-6 (hbk)
ISBN: 978-1-138-28938-3 (pbk)
ISBN: 978-1-315-26717-3 (ebk)

Typeset in Times New Roman
By Out of House Publishing

Contents

Contributor biographies

Jörg Bose, MD, is Director Emeritus, Training and Supervising Analyst and a faculty member of the William Alanson White Institute of Psychiatry, Psychoanalysis and Psychology in New York. He is a Clinical Associate Professor of Psychiatry at Columbia University and has taught, lectured, and published on issues of self and narcissism, trauma, shame, depression, and the relationship between psychoanalysis and the arts. He is an avid pastel painter of landscapes and maintains a private practice in Manhattan.

Geoffrey Cocks is Professor Emeritus of History at Albion College. His areas of expertise include modern Germany, the Second World War, psychohistory, psychoanalysis, cinema, and the history of psychotherapy, health, and illness. He is editor of *The Curve of Life: Correspondence of Heinz Kohut, 1923–1981* (1994) and the author of *Psychotherapy in the Third Reich: The Göring Institute* (1985, 1997), *The Wolf at the Door: Stanley Kubrick, History, and the Holocaust* (2004), *The State of Health: Illness in Nazi Germany* (2012), and "Hors de Combat: Mobilization and Immobilization in Total War," in *The Cambridge History of the Second World War* (2015).

Alon Confino is Pen Tishkach Chair of Holocaust Studies at the Departments of History and of Judaic and Near Eastern Studies at UMass Amherst. His main interests include modern German and European history, nationhood and memory, the Holocaust and genocide, Israel and Palestine, and historical method. Among his many books are *Germany as a Culture of Remembrance: Promises and Limits of Writing History* (2006), *Foundational Pasts: The Holocaust as Historical Understanding* (2011), and *A World without Jews: The Nazi Imagination from Persecution to Genocide* (2014), which won a 2011 Guggenheim Fellowship. He is now at work on a book project on the 1948 war in Palestine and Israel.

Ute Daniel is Professor for Modern History at the Technical University of Braunschweig. She received her Ph.D. in History from Bielefeld University in 1980 for her dissertation on German working-class women in the First World War in Germany (published in German in 1989 and in English in

1997). She completed her *Habilitation* at Siegen University in 1994 with a *Habilitationsschrift* on the history of court theatre in the eighteenth and nineteenth centuries. She has been at the Technical University of Braunschweig since 1997, and her current topics of research are the history of war reporting and media history. Among her many publications is *Kompendium Kulturgeschichte: Theorien, Praxis, Schlüsselwörter* (2001).

Roger Frie is Professor of Education at Simon Fraser University and Affiliate Professor of Psychiatry at the University of British Columbia in Vancouver, Canada, and Psychoanalytic Faculty and Supervisor at the William Alanson White Institute of Psychiatry, Psychoanalysis and Psychology in New York. He trained in history and philosophy in London and Cambridge and is now a practicing psychologist and psychoanalyst. He has published many books at the intersection of psychoanalysis, philosophy, and history on topics relating to human interaction, memory and responsibility. His most recent book is *Not in My Family: German Memory and Responsibility after the Holocaust* (2017). He is Co-Editor of *Psychoanalysis, Self and Context* and Editorial Board Member of *Contemporary Psychoanalysis* and *Psychoanalytic Psychology*.

M. Gerard Fromm, Ph.D., is Senior Consultant to the Erikson Institute of the Austen Riggs Center and Assistant Clinical Professor, Yale Child Study Center. He is on the faculty of the Massachusetts Institute for Psychoanalysis and has taught at, and consulted to, a number of psychoanalytic institutes across the USA. He is President of the International Dialogue Initiative, an interdisciplinary group that studies the psychodynamics of societal conflict, Past President of the International Society for the Psychoanalytic Study of Organizations, and has directed or served on the staff of Group Relations Conferences. His books include the edited volumes *Lost in Transmission: Studies of Trauma across Generations* (2012) and *A Spirit That Impels: Play, Creativity and Psychoanalysis* (2013) and a volume of clinical papers, *Taking the Transference, Reaching toward Dreams: Clinical Studies in the Intermediate Area* (2012).

Alexandra Garbarini is Professor of History at Williams College in Williamstown, Massachusetts. She is the author of *Numbered Days: Diary Writing and the Holocaust* (2006), and the co-author with Emil Kerenji, Jan Lambertz, and Avinoam Patt of *Jewish Responses to Persecution*, Volume 2, *1939–1940* (2011). Her current research focuses on European Jewish and non-Jewish testimonial, literary, and photographic representations of mass violence in the era of the two world wars.

Emily Kuriloff, PsyD, is Director of Clinical Education, Training and Supervising Analyst and a faculty member of the William Alanson White Institute of Psychiatry, Psychoanalysis and Psychology. She is in private practice in New York City, and is also at the Institute for Psychoanalytic

Education. Her book *Contemporary Psychoanalysis and the Legacy of the Third Reich* (2014) explores how the trauma of the Shoah transformed the development of psychoanalysis at its apex and beyond.

Donna M. Orange, Ph.D., Psy.D., was educated in philosophy, clinical psychology, and psychoanalysis. She teaches at NYU Postdoc (New York), at the Institute for the Psychoanalytic Study of Subjectivity (New York), and in private study groups. She also offers clinical consultation/supervision in these institutes and beyond. Her recent books include *Thinking for Clinicians: Philosophical Resources for Contemporary Psychoanalysis and the Humanistic Psychotherapies* (2010), *The Suffering Stranger: Hermeneutics for Everyday Clinical Practice* (2011), *Nourishing the Inner Life of Clinicians and Humanitarians: The Ethical Turn in Psychoanalysis* (2015), and *Climate Crisis, Psychoanalysis, and Radical Ethics* (2016).

Robert Prince, Ph.D., ABPP, is Clinical Associate Professor, New York University Postdoctoral Program in Psychotherapy & Psychoanalysis, where he is also past co-chair of the Interpersonal Track. He is Past President of Psychologist-Psychoanalyst Clinicians and an Associate Editor of *The American Journal of Psychoanalysis*. He is the author of over 35 other articles and chapters. His books include *The Legacy of the Holocaust* (1985) and *The Death of Psychoanalysis* (1999).

Dorothee Wierling is Professor Emeritus in Modern History at the University of Hamburg, and former Deputy Director of the Research Institute for Contemporary History in Hamburg. Her research interests focus on modern German social history, history of experience, and oral history. She is the author of *Eine Familie im Krieg, Leben, Sterben und Schreiben 1914–1918* (2013), among many other publications. She has published studies on domestic servants, the First World War, and the history of East Germany, and has just finished a manuscript on the history of the coffee trade in twentieth-century Hamburg.

Acknowledgments

This book was developed over a number of years with the shared effort of colleagues and friends in the fields of history and psychoanalysis. Working with the contributors to this volume has been a gratifying experience and I thank each of them for their participation. Above all, this book is indebted to Thomas Kohut, whose presence is evident throughout. The idea for this collection of essays emerged out of my dialogue with Tom about Germany, the Holocaust, and the importance of empathy. Tom's interdisciplinary approach illustrates how psychoanalysis can be used to increase our understanding of one of modern history's darkest chapters. Each of the contributors reflects on a different aspect of this history.

My own interest in the connection between history and psychoanalysis dates back to my university studies. As an undergraduate student at the University of London I read history and politics and became fascinated with psychoanalysis. While some of my professors looked askance at the attempt to bridge the two disciplines, I benefited from the guidance of the historian Frank Snowden, who supported my pursuit of interdisciplinary work. Along the way Peter Gay provided some kind-hearted and helpful advice. I went on to specialize in philosophy, psychoanalysis, and psychology, but my initial fascination with the interaction of history and psychoanalysis remained.

My first academic position was in a History of Science Department, where I taught the history and theory of psychoanalysis. I began to train as a psychoanalyst and psychologist soon thereafter. To my surprise, I found that psychoanalysis was often taught and practiced in a kind of historical vacuum. There was little acknowledgment of the role that history and culture played in its development. As a result, the values and norms implicit in psychoanalytic theory and practice frequently went unquestioned. Over time my study of history and my work as a practicing psychoanalyst helped me to appreciate the degree to which "history flows through us." I firmly believe we are better able to respond to the emotional, social, and political challenges we face if we grasp the degree to which we are all shaped by history.

My interactions with Tom and his scholarship helped me to think about my own historical formation and how German families seek to keep the

Holocaust at bay through the transfer of memory from one generation to the next. Given the parallels between our interests, it seemed to me important to create a cross-disciplinary platform for the study of German memory and the Holocaust. The contributors to this book all share this interdisciplinary outlook. Together their essays expand our awareness of historical trauma and memory, and help us to think about new ways of responding to ongoing prejudices in our midst. My hope is that this collection of essays will form a useful companion to Kohut's book *A German Generation: An Experiential History of the Twentieth Century* (2012) and to my own recent book *Not in My Family: German Memory and Responsibility after the Holocaust* (2017).

I would like to thank Alexandra Garbarini, who provided valuable historical advice in addition to contributing one of the book's chapters. Joe Lichtenberg was enthusiastic about this project from the start and kindly recommended publishing it in the psychoanalytic book series he edits. I am grateful to Kate Hawes, Senior Publisher at Routledge. This is my fourth interdisciplinary book with Routledge, and I thank Kate for her continued support of cross-disciplinary scholarship. Editorial Assistant Charles Bath was helpful throughout the writing process. I also express my thanks to Katharina Walter and the *Museen für Kulturgeschichte der Landeshauptstadt Hannover* for permission to reproduce the photographs that appear on the book's cover and in the introduction. Finally, I could not have completed this book without the continued and loving presence of my family members. I thank my parents, Hans and Heide Frie, for their encouragement and support of my work, particularly my research into our family history. Writing and editing books can be a solitary pursuit that creates many demands on one's family. To my two teenage children, Elena and Andreas, and to my incredibly supportive and kind partner, Emily, I express my deepest thanks.

Historical trauma and lived experience

An introduction

Roger Frie

The spring day in Northern Germany was overcast and cool. The weather was changeable, but the political mood was increasingly resolute and the consequences of Germany's embrace of National Socialism were becoming more ominous. On May 21, 1936 the citizens of the city of Hanover gathered en masse to celebrate a long-awaited event: the opening of the Masch Lake. The newly created city lake was a massive public works project that became a cornerstone of the Nazi regime's propaganda campaign for full employment. To mark the occasion the authorities organized a parade through central Hanover. Marching Nazis were joined by a further 6,000 athletes. Together they formed a procession that was cheered by onlookers (see photo 1). Their destination was an unveiling ceremony at the lake, where they would hear local dignitaries and Nazi leaders speak. Several hundred thousand people assembled that day, and the crowd was a mixture of civilians and uniformed Nazis, standing side-by-side.[1] Only three years after its assumption of power, the Nazi regime had become integrated into nearly every aspect of civil society.

The massive parade was one of countless such events that took place throughout Germany. Images of Nazis marching in uniform have become part of our visual vocabulary, a way to identify a time and place in history that is filled with foreboding about the monstrous crimes of the Holocaust and the savagery of the Second World War. The powerful symbols of hate and belligerence – swastika-emblazoned flags, uniformed men in high leather boots and steel helmets, straight-armed Nazi salutes – are all linked to the atrocities committed by the German state and its people. Despite the passage of time, these images remain a disturbing reference point for one of the darkest chapters in modern history.

We also need to view this photograph beyond the prism of Nazi symbolism. What is the setting for this carefully orchestrated event? The city street shown in the image is typical of the 1930s, nineteenth-century and modernist buildings stand abreast. Overhead, the signs of the shops and restaurants reflect the daily routine of Hanover's citizens, while streetcar tracks in the foreground hint at the evening commute to come. Just behind the soldiers a mother and child engage in conversation. Onlookers of various ages stand at attention, some with their right arms raised in salute. Seen from this perspective, what

Photo 1: Nazi parade through central Hanover with onlookers, part of the ceremony for the opening of the Masch Lake, May 21, 1936.
Source: © HAZ-Hauschild-Archiv, Historisches Museum Hannover.

is truly frightening is the fact that the sight of uniformed marching men had become an accepted and familiar part of life in the Third Reich.

At the time it was taken, this photograph was not about the horrors to come. The marching parade seen in this image is a point of civic pride. A long-promised city lake was finally complete, a place to row boats and meander among newly planted oak trees, all within walking distance of Hanover's city center. What had begun during the Weimar Republic was completed under Hitler, an illustration for many Germans of the transition from the fledgling and seemingly ineffectual democratic republic to a determined totalitarian regime. In 1936 the men in uniform were not marching off to war, they were marching as proud representatives of their newly defined nation. For thousands of onlookers who gathered that day, the public celebration marked a resurgence of Germany from defeat and humiliation in the First World War, a return to what many saw as its rightful place, first among nations (see photo 2).

What were the marching Nazis and the parade's many onlookers that day feeling and imagining? Did the thousands of enthusiastic and excited Hanoverians standing by the lakeside think about the criminal actions taking place in their city? Did they look away or participate in the acts of persecution?

Photo 2: Crowd listening to a Nazi leader speak at the ceremony for the opening of the Masch Lake in Hanover, May 21, 1936.

Source: © HAZ-Hauschild-Archiv, Historisches Museum Hannover.

How many had the courage to stand up to the regime or were willing to help those who were suffering?

Outside the frame of these photographs, a very different experience was unfolding for anyone who did not fit into the Nazis' racist worldview. German Jews had been deemed "subhuman" and were living in constant fear. Hanover's Jewish community traced its roots back to the thirteenth century, but by the middle of 1936 its members were being actively persecuted, spat upon, beaten, arrested, and imprisoned. At the time the Nazi regime was still pursuing a strategy of persecution and dispossession, but this would soon change.

The Kristallnacht pogrom on the night of November 9 and continuing into the morning of November 10, 1938 led to the destruction of nearly 300 synagogues, thousands of Jewish-owned commercial properties and private residences, and the desecration of Jewish cemeteries throughout Germany and Austria. The destruction was greatest in Berlin and Vienna, home to the largest Jewish communities, where Nazis pursued and humiliated citizens in their homes and in public. Beyond the massive destruction of property, the violence unleashed during those November days targeted Jewish male bodies, subjecting them to widespread beatings and the first mass incarceration of

Jewish men in concentration camps. Some one hundred men were killed that night and hundreds more died in the coming weeks in Buchenwald, Dachau, and Sachsenhausen.

After the pogrom anti-Jewish legislation was accelerated, and deportations to concentration camps increased in frequency. The mass shootings of entire Jewish communities in territory conquered by the Wehrmacht in the East became a part of the "Final Solution of the Jewish Question," the planned and systematic mass murder of Europe's Jewish population. When the war in Europe finally ended on May 8, 1945, Germany's racial state had murdered six million European Jews, half a million Roma and Sinti, and 200,000 victims of the "Euthanasia" program, and had imprisoned and killed those accused of being homosexuals and political opponents of all stripes.

Memory across generations

For German descendants, the children and grandchildren of the so-called first generation that perpetrated the Holocaust, the Nazi past can evoke a deep sense of guilt and shame, feelings that are often associated with half-spoken family histories. When I look at the image of the marching Nazis, it is not only through the eyes of a historian or psychoanalyst. Rather, I see it as a grandson of Germans who were members of the first generation. I was bequeathed this history by way of family, language, and community. I am the son of second-generation Germans who immigrated to Canada. As a result I grew up in North America while most of my family continued to reside in Germany. My maternal and paternal grandparents lived in Hanover and my parents were born there in 1935, in the midst of the Third Reich. I see the photographs of the Masch Lake ceremony and inevitably wonder whether my family members participated that day. I scrutinize the onlookers to see whether I can recognize my relatives. And I ask myself how it was that all those people could be cheering when their Jewish neighbors were being persecuted, beaten, publically humiliated, and imprisoned in concentration camps. In the years to follow the massive proliferation of concentration camps, ghettos, and sites of detainment throughout Germany and Nazi-occupied Europe would be on a staggering scale.[2] What role did my own family play in this dark history?

Postwar Germany has done much to atone for the terrible crimes committed during the Third Reich. Public memory assumes guilt and responsibility for the horrors of the Holocaust. Contemporary Germany not only recognizes its perpetrator history but lives self-consciously with its Nazi past, determined to act more humanely in the future. Few former perpetrator nations have engaged in this level of collective self-reflection. Private memory in Germany is more ambiguous. Families often know little about what their relatives did during the Third Reich. Reactions to the Nazi past can vary greatly. In many families the history of the Nazi era remains hidden because it is experienced as shameful. Others see this history as lacking in relevance or believe the perpetrators were adequately punished. They prefer to look to the future rather than be concerned with a past that is not of their making. Some don't concern themselves with history at all, seeing it merely as a conceit of the educated and political classes.

I learned about the Holocaust early in life from my parents. It was important to them that I hear about it at home, yet my grandparents' role in the Nazi era remained gray and murky. My parents grew up without an oral narrative about their parents' participation in the Third Reich. In the Germany of their childhood questions were not asked and answers not offered. The silence with which my parents grew up was passed down to me. In my family, as in so many others, the Nazi past was covered up by an intergenerational guilt and shame.

As a child I knew that my paternal grandfather died in the war. What I did not know is that my maternal grandfather joined the Nazi Party. This was the party membership that no one talked about. I discovered it only after seeing an unfamiliar photograph, though I may have sensed it long before then (Frie, 2017). Archival research into my family's past revealed that in the spring of 1936, shortly before the Masch Lake's celebratory opening, my maternal grandfather wrote to Berlin asking to become a member of the Nazi Party. Such an application would have involved proving that his family met the Nazis' strict racial criteria of "Aryan heritage." One year later on May 1, 1937 my grandfather was granted his wish. The man whom I knew and loved as a child was a card-carrying member of the Nazi party. This knowledge fills me with shame. Looking back, I imagine this membership was a point of pride for my grandparents. Did they cheer the marching Nazis, vote for Hitler, and support his policies of hatred? Historians have shown that Nazi Party membership could be motivated by many factors. Whatever the reason for my grandfather's joining, one thing is certain, membership in the party was not about looking away.

The unspoken story of my grandfather is not unusual. German families have private histories of the Third Reich that remained untold, a reflection of a postwar German culture that sought to separate public from private memory. After the war, blame was apportioned to the leaders of National Socialism who were tried by the International Military Tribunal at Nuremberg and in the subsequent trials conducted by the Allies separately in the late 1940s. As a result the majority of the German population could remain silent about their role in the horrors of the Holocaust, reinforcing the view that guilt was not collective. In the decades that followed, acts of perpetration were believed to be limited to the Nazi elite and the members of the SS, the murderous branch of the Nazi regime. With the Frankfurt Auschwitz Trials, which began in late 1963, the wider ramifications of the Holocaust began to filter into public awareness. Yet it was not until much later, beginning in the 1990s, that studies of Wehrmacht soldiers demonstrated the full extent of the crimes that ordinary Germans were capable of, even though the historian Raul Hilberg had provided ample evidence of this in his book *The Destruction of the European Jews* (Hilberg, 1961). The fact that it took so many decades for the participation of ordinary Germans in the actions of the Nazi regime to be publicly acknowledged points to the shifting nature of historical memory. Every society constructs collective memories and narratives that focus on some elements of the past while neglecting others. In this sense collective memory and the stories we tell about the past cannot be separated from social and political developments or from the interests of each succeeding generation.

The separation of hate-filled killers from ordinary Germans was also reflected in the language used to describe the first generation of Germans after the Second World War. "Perpetrators" were distinguished from "bystanders," literally those who ran alongside or stood by. Placing the terms perpetrator and bystander side by side reinforced the impression that the two could be neatly distinguished from one another. Today it is widely acknowledged that the crimes of the perpetrators could not have been committed without the support of the bystanders. As a result many observers now prefer the term "enabler" to "bystander." It was, after all, the support of ordinary Germans for the policies of National Socialism that enabled the Holocaust to occur. Crimes against humanity were willingly carried out by the military. There was no substantive German opposition to the Nazi regime, and it was defeated only from without.

The history of the Nazi regime, indeed the history of the Holocaust, is the history of German family members who participated, stood by, or watched. In Hanover that spring day it was those who cheered the marching Nazis, those who pushed through the ranks of onlookers to salute them, those who ultimately chose to join up themselves because so many others already had. People like my grandfather, a hard-working artisan and caring father of three children. To my knowledge none of my family members were directly active in the crimes against European Jews. But they belonged to the vast majority of Germans who remained silent as these crimes were carried out. Their complicity haunts me.

Shaped by history

Today Hanover's Masch Lake is a green oasis in the middle of a busy urban center. Its Nazi beginning is a part of Germany's collective history, an increasingly distant past. Yet the sculptures commissioned by the Nazi regime still surround the lake and are seen by thousands. They present the viewer with unmistakable evidence of what was. Our knowledge of history is shaped by what we see and hear, and by the narratives of the past that are passed down to us by our families and communities. We rely on these stories to link the past with the present. The historical narrative we tell about the Third Reich is important because it informs how we respond to the catastrophe and influences what future generations will know and remember.

The Holocaust casts a long shadow, its lived history is transmitted in received memories and narratives from one generation to the next. As the daughter of Holocaust survivors, author Eva Hoffman has shed light on the power of traumatic history to shape future generations even though they have no direct experience of the trauma themselves. The lives of the "second generation" are circumscribed beyond their choosing, a function of the histories they inherit from their survivor parents. As Hoffman states, "A consciousness of war, in its most extreme and cruel manifestations, seemed to come with the first stirrings of consciousness itself. And yet I had no direct experience of extremity or collective violence. The paradoxes of indirect knowledge haunt many of us who came after" (Hoffmann, 2004, p. 25).

The historian Dan Diner (1986) has suggested that in the wake of the Holocaust German and Jewish lives have become paradoxically intertwined. Traumatic histories have been implicitly communicated in codes of silence and in family narratives, or more directly through the emotional experience of one's elders. As a result, each group is forced to struggle with family secrets and dissociations about the past, giving rise to fearful thoughts and fantasies about what could have happened. Postwar Germans are confronted by family histories of perpetration and support for the crimes of National Socialism. Descendants of Holocaust survivors are haunted by legacies of enormous loss and by memories of unimaginable cruelty and suffering that were endured before they were born.

Despite these affinities, it would be wrong to draw simplistic comparisons. Contemporary generations of Germans and descendants of Holocaust survivors are forced to address the legacy of the Third Reich from radically different, historically determined perspectives. This is what the historian Dominick LaCapra had in mind when he made the following statement:

> The Holocaust presents the historian with transference in the most traumatic form conceivable but in a form that will vary with the difference in subject-position of the analyst. Whether the historian or analyst is a survivor, a relative of survivors, a former Nazi, a former collaborator, a relative of former Nazis or collaborators, a younger Jew or German distanced from more immediate contact with survival, participation, or collaboration, or a relative "outsider" to these problems will make a difference even in the meaning of statements that may be formally identical. Certain statements or entire orientations may seem appropriate for someone in a given subject-position but not in others.
>
> (LaCapra, 1998, pp. 45–46)

In other words, our response to the Holocaust is inherently related to who we are, to our particular location in history and culture as individuals.

In a given sense we are positioned in history and culture before we are born, a fact that can be difficult to bear, especially in relation to the terrors unleashed by the Third Reich. The sheer scope and nature of the crimes easily overwhelm us, leading to different kinds of response. Some may seek distance from the Holocaust through a process of dissociation. Others may over-identify with its traumas or even use it for political ends. Many contemporary Germans increasingly express a wish to focus on the future, rather than on a long-ago history of perpetration. The links to the generation of perpetrators and survivors are becoming ever more tenuous. But, no matter how hard we may try, we cannot stand outside of history. We are bequeathed our past through the families, communities, and traditions to which we belong. According to the philosopher Alisdair MacIntyre, "I am born with a past … What I am, therefore, is in key part what I inherit, a specific past that is present to some degree in my present. I find myself part of a history and that is generally to say, whether I like it or not, whether I recognize it or not, I am one of the bearers of a tradition" (MacIntyre, 1981, p. 206).

How do we make sense of a traumatic past that is not of our own making? How do we understand the support that everyday people lent a regime determined to commit genocide? How do we comprehend the perpetration of unthinkable violence or the act of looking away in the face of prejudice and extreme cruelty? These are issues that continue to occupy us because they speak to larger questions about human nature and our continued capacity for hatred and violence.

In order to respond to history's traumas we need to enter into dialogue with voices from the past that shape our understanding in the present. Being engaged in this kind of historical and psychological inquiry is not easy. Asking potentially difficult and painful questions is about taking a stand. I believe that by acknowledging the connections that link us to the past we are able to avoid facile forms of remembering that are really about forgetting. This has important consequences for how we perceive the German generation of perpetrators and enablers. They no longer appear nameless, abstract figures (see Senfft, 2016). For German descendants like myself, recognizing the Nazi past in our own families lends the terrible history of the Holocaust a chilling reality that cannot be reduced or shunted aside. It forces us to reflect on the emotional meaning of what occurred and reinforces the obligation to remember.

Understanding the past

When I look back at my grandparents today I wonder what could have motivated them to lend their support to the Nazi regime. What was it like to live when they did? How did they reach their decisions? Above all, why did my grandfather decide to join the Nazi Party? My grandfather, born in 1906, watched his own father set off to fight for the German Kaiser in 1914 at the start of the First World War. Four years later he experienced his injured father's return from the trenches of the Western Front, where millions of young men lost their lives. Following the Armistice, Germans struggled to comprehend their defeat amid political violence and economic crises that culminated in the massive inflation of 1923. My grandfather came of age during this period of social turmoil. Political pressure from the communists on the left and the nationalists on the right presented serious challenges for the new democratic government. Many Germans at the time questioned the legitimacy of the Weimar Republic, perceiving it as the creation of Western powers in a country that lacked a tradition of democratic rule. Historians suggest that this tumult and uncertainty made people like my grandparents particularly susceptible to National Socialism. But how does a disheartened generation of young Germans end up supporting a dictatorial and heinous regime?

These are the kinds of questions that motivate Thomas Kohut's (2012) important study *A German Generation: An Experiential History of the Twentieth Century*. A historian and psychoanalyst by training, Kohut draws on extensive interviews that were carried out with some 62 middle-class Germans, all of whom had been born before the First World War. They would become members of the German generation that carried out and supported the policies of the Holocaust. Kohut brings the lived experience of this group of Germans to bear by telling their stories. As the children of the soldiers who fought in the First World War, they were born into a world that had been fundamentally altered by the Great War. This was also the world into which Kohut's own Viennese father, the psychoanalyst Heinz Kohut, was born in 1913.

In bringing history and psychoanalysis into conversation with each other, Kohut builds on his earlier book, *Wilhelm II and the Germans: A Study in Leadership* (Kohut, 1991). In his study of the German Kaiser, Kohut provides an account of the man most identified with Germany's role in the First World War, events that sent his own grandfather, and my great-grandfather, off to war. The First World War ushered in a new age and forever changed the nature of modern warfare. But, despite the tremendous loss of life and traumatic legacies, fighting in the service of the German Kaiser or the Hapsburg monarch was manifestly different than fighting in the service of Hitler and the Nazi war machine. In the First World War there was no outright segregation of Jews, no state-sanctioned campaign of genocide. Once the Nazis had assumed power, they celebrated First World War veterans like my great-grandfather, but they persecuted and then murdered veterans who were of Jewish heritage. Their loyal service to the crown could not save them from the racial hatred bent on murder.

The German generation described by Kohut in his book were enthusiastic Nazi supporters and thus complicit in the crimes that killed his own family members. Kohut's father escaped his native city of Vienna in 1939, but four of his father's five uncles and aunts, as well as cousins, were murdered. In light of this tragic history Kohut acknowledges the challenges but also the importance of researching these Germans. Their sense of morality and capacity for empathy was fundamentally altered during the course of the Third Reich. Their intense need for belonging informed a way of knowing and seeing that allowed the Holocaust to unfold, unhindered. They avoided registering what they saw around them because to do so might have caused them to feel uneasy and could have led them to feel empathy for the persecuted neighbors in their midst. As Kohut suggests, the Germans engaged in a stance of simultaneous seeing and not seeing, with deadly consequences: "The act of 'looking away' goes to the heart of the anti-Semitism of the interviewees. It was an act that eliminated the possibility of empathy, severing the bond of shared humanity connecting them to persecuted Jews. It was an act of dehumanization, an eradication of Jewish people from consciousness, that mirrored and facilitated their physical annihilation" (Kohut, 2012, p. 137).

Empathy enables us to grasp the experience of another human being, and for Kohut it is an essential part of the work of history and psychoanalysis. Empathy helps us to understand the historical experiences of the German generation that suffered so many losses, yet was unwilling to experience empathy for those to be excluded from the Nazi Volksgemeinschaft. Kohut does not just explain the failure of empathy in this German generation as a key factor that allowed the Holocaust to occur, but also insists on the need to develop an empathetic understanding of the German generation itself. This is quite likely the most challenging part of Kohut's analysis. After all, how do we empathize with the generation whose direct and indirect actions led to millions of deaths? But empathy should not be confused with sympathy. For Kohut, the purpose of empathy is to "reduce the intellectual and emotional distance separating us from them, in part by thinking our way inside their unique historical circumstances, in part by recognizing that on some level they were as we are and that we have within us the capacity to be as they were" (Kohut, 2012, p. 17). In this sense, Kohut uses history as a way to grasp our continued potential for hate, despite the many horrors of the past. As he points out, "all human beings have the need to belong to the group and to exclude others from it, a need that centrally motived the genocide, in my view. And all human beings have the capacity to dehumanize others by closing off empathy for them, a capacity that enabled the genocide to be carried out" (Kohut, 2012, p. 240).

Kohut's interdisciplinary outlook enables him to develop important insights into the nature of human prejudice. Given my own interdisciplinary background in philosophy, psychoanalysis, and psychology, I found myself particularly drawn to his approach. The fields of history and psychoanalysis are often at odds with one another, despite attempts to integrate them (see Gay, 1985). Whereas psychoanalysts struggle to account for the historical contexts in which psychological experience is formed, historians tend to neglect the psychological forces that inform the collective actions they study. Kohut's work creates a synergy between the two disciplines and narrows the gap between them.

But, all academic parallels aside, my interest in Kohut's work was also fundamentally personal. His account of the generation of my grandparents helped me to confront what they and their fellow Germans might have been thinking and feeling or how they could have supported the Nazi regime and stood by in the face of unspeakable crimes. It was while I was writing about the unspoken history of my family (Frie, 2017) that I entered into a correspondence with Kohut. He generously shared his insights as I developed my examination of how German families seek to keep the history of the Holocaust at bay. In the context of our interactions I soon realized the extent to which my interest in his work was shared by other historians and psychoanalysts. This created an opportunity to build a cross-disciplinary dialogue, using Kohut's scholarship as a bridge.

To facilitate this dialogue I invited like-minded historians and psychoanalysts to reflect on the themes that have occupied Kohut: German history, the Holocaust, psychoanalysis, and the importance of empathy. The response I received was immediate and overwhelmingly positive. I asked each contributor to develop his or her own perspective on the topic and to speak to a broad audience. The resulting volume is a testament to the vitality of Kohut's work at the intersection of the two professions. The chapters that follow all embody his stated aim of exploring "how the psyche and history mutually shape one another, or, put differently, how history flows through human beings" (Kohut, 2003, p. 226).

Plan of the book

The book is divided into four thematic sections. The first section considers how we remember the past and focuses on our shifting conceptions of history and memory. The opening chapter, "From psychohistory to memory studies: Or, how some Germans became Jews and some Jews Nazis," is written by the historian of culture and the Holocaust Alon Confino. He suggests that how we understand the past, especially in relation to trauma, shifts with time and varies in relation to the methods employed by historians and psychoanalysts. The recent shift toward memory studies has brought history closer to psychoanalysis. For Confino historical writing involves the process of storytelling, but these stories can convey different meanings about what took place. He provides contrasting illustrations of Holocaust stories in present-day Germany and Israel to reflect these shifts of historical memory. The second chapter, "'Memory' and its discontents," builds on the themes of the first. The German historian Dorothee Wierling offers a critical assessment of memory as a concept for examining historical experience. She challenges popular notions of "cultural memory" and points instead to the importance of narrative, or storytelling, to explain how individuals embedded in social worlds create a meaningful past. The social process of narrative always involves the storyteller and listener, and together they shape what is heard, a process that is equally apparent in both history and psychoanalysis.

The second section of the book examines our responses to traumatic history, prejudice, and genocide. The psychoanalyst and philosopher Donna Orange examines the notion of experience in her chapter on "Experiential history: Understanding backwards." She suggests that historians and psychoanalysts seek understanding of experience, while philosophers ask what the process of understanding experience involves. Orange reflects on the idea of an experiential history, one that crosses disciplinary boundaries, in order to show how it can help us understand the dark periods of history as well as the need for social justice in the present and future. The historian of the Holocaust Alexandra Garbarini develops a related approach in her chapter "'Unprecedented': Concepts and narratives about mass violence and the Holocaust." Garbarini examines the use of the concept of "unprecedented" to capture traumatic experiences that defy expression in everyday language. She suggests that characterizing European Jews' extreme suffering in the Holocaust as "unprecedented" became a means of connecting the catastrophe to earlier incidences of mass violence in an effort to create engagement and empathy for the survivors. Out of empathy, it was hoped, would follow recognition of the victims' suffering and their political subjecthood. In the following chapter, "Transmitting hate: On the process of hating and being hated," psychoanalyst Jörg Bose explores the notion of hatred and uses therapeutic vignettes and the phenomenon of German anti-Semitism to illustrate how cultural conditions breed and perpetuate hatred. Bose raises important questions about the motivational forces that drive ethnic hatred and about the kind of steps that are necessary to end hatred's tragic cycle.

The third section of the book considers how we are confronted by history's collective crimes, despite our attempts to distance ourselves from these traumas. In his chapter, "The Stowaway: Reality, the Holocaust and the historical unconscious," the psychoanalyst Robert Prince suggests that being open to knowing about history's collective crimes depends on our individual emotional readiness and on the point in time and the culture in which we live. He uses the research he conducted on the psychological effects of the Holocaust on the children of survivors in the early 1970s to illustrate the slow and often painful evolution of awareness about historical trauma. His discussion illustrates the challenges involved in understanding and defining the experiences of this diverse group. In the following chapter, "National nightmare: The legacy of perpetrator trauma," psychoanalyst Gerard Fromm considers similar questions from the perspective of the descendants of the German generation that perpetrated the Holocaust. These descendants can experience powerful feelings of guilt, shame, and horror for the crimes committed by their parents or grandparents. Fromm draws on the proceedings of a conference he organized with Thomas Kohut called "The Legacy of Perpetrator Trauma in Groups and Families" to examine the transmission of this trauma, the forms it takes, and some of the group dynamics that play out in relation to it. In her chapter "Not as one would like to imagine: Psychoanalysis during and after the Third Reich," psychoanalyst Emily Kuriloff examines how Germany's perpetrator history impacted the field of psychoanalysis. She discusses the struggle of German psychoanalysts to confront their profession's actions during the Third Reich and the effects that this dark history has had on German and Jewish psychoanalysts into the present.

The final section of the book addresses the intersection of history and psychoanalysis in Thomas Kohut's own contributions. The section begins with a chapter written by the German historian Ute Daniel, entitled "Psyche and history: Kaiser Wilhelm II and his role in German politics reconsidered." The German Kaiser was a central figure in the outbreak of the First World War, and the reverberations of his actions set in motion tragic historical events that eventually resulted in the Nazi Party's assumption of power in 1933. Building on Kohut's book on Wilhelm II, Daniel suggests that the development of a psychoanalytic perspective enables us to appreciate the complex history of the time and the entanglement of psychological, social, and political factors. The following chapter is written by Geoffrey Cocks, a historian known for his work on psychotherapy and health during the Third Reich. He examines the interconnections between Thomas Kohut and his father, Heinz Kohut. His chapter, entitled "Fathers and sons: The Kohut odyssey," weaves together their individual histories through the use of correspondence and analysis of their scholarship. Cocks shows how Kohut brings psychoanalytic insights into history and thereby helps us to appreciate the kindred nature of the two professions. The concluding chapter in the book is entitled "Psychoanalysis and history at the crossroads: A dialogue with Thomas Kohut." Given the collegial nature of the essays that comprise this volume, I felt it was important to bring Kohut's own voice to bear. The chapter begins with a discussion of how Kohut bridges the fields of history and psychoanalysis and ends with an extended dialogue between us. In response to my questions Kohut expands on the themes of German history, the Holocaust, and the importance of empathy, and reflects on the interaction between history and psychoanalysis.

Notes

1 The image on the cover of this book shows the ceremony for the opening of the Masch Lake. For information on the history of the Masch Lake in Hanover, see Röhrbein (1986).

2 The most recent count provided by the editors of *The United States Holocaust Memorial Museum Encyclopedia of Camps and Ghettos, 1933–1945* totals some 42,000 camps, ghettos, and sites of detainment in Nazi-occupied Europe. I thank Alexandra Garbarini for providing me with this information.

References

Diner, D. (1986). Negative Symbiose: Deutsche und Juden nach Auschwitz [Negative Symbiosis: Germans and Jews after Auschwitz]. *Babylon, 1*, 9–20.

Frie, R. (2017). *Not in my family: German memory and responsibility after the Holocaust*. New York, NY: Oxford University Press.

Gay, P. (1985). *Freud for historians*. New York, NY: Oxford University Press.

Hilberg, R. (1961). *The destruction of the European Jews*. New York, NY: Quadrangle Books.

Hoffman, E. (2004). *After such knowledge: Memory, history, and the legacy of the Holocaust*. New York, NY: Public Affairs.

Kohut, T. A. (1991). *Wilhelm II and the Germans: A study in leadership*. New York, NY: Oxford University Press.

Kohut, T. A. (2003). Psychoanalysis as psychohistory or why psychotherapists cannot afford to ignore culture. In J. A. Winer & J. Williams Anderson (eds.), *The Annual of Psychoanalysis, Psychoanalysis and History*, *31*, 225–236.

Kohut, T. A. (2012). *A German generation: An experiential history of the twentieth century*. New Haven, CT: Yale University Press.

LaCapra, D. (1998). *History and memory after Auschwitz*. Ithaca, NY: Cornell University Press.

MacIntyre, A. (1981). *After virtue: A study in moral theory*. Notre Dame, IN: University of Notre Dame Press.

Röhrbein, W. R. (ed.) (1986). *Der Maschsee in Hannover. Seine Entstehung und Geschichte* [*The Masch Lake in Hanover: Its origin and history*]. Hanover, Germany: Schlütersche Verlagsgesellschaft.

Senfft, A. (2016). *Der lange Schatten der Täter: Nachkommen stellen sich ihrer NS-Familiengeschichte* [*The long shadow of the perpetrators: Descendants face their Nazi family histories*]. Munich, Germany: Piper.

Part I

Remembering the past

Chapter 1

From psychohistory to memory studies

Or, how some Germans became Jews and some Jews Nazis

Alon Confino

In the 1970s and 1980s historians debated the merit of the relations between history and psychoanalysis. The term of the day was psychohistory. In 1986 Thomas Kohut (1986), a historian and a psychoanalyst by training, published an insightful essay on the topic in the *American Historical Review* entitled "Psychohistory as History." He underlined, among other factors, the close affinity between (some of) the practices of the historian and those of the psychoanalyst, both of whom seek to elucidate the subjective experience of their subject using an approach based on empathy, namely trying to imagine and reconstruct how and why the world made sense to their object of therapy or study. These principles received further emphasis in the mid-1980s with the rise of cultural history; historians these days would recognize them as essential to historical investigation. And yet, the discussion over psychohistory among historians rather disappeared at exactly that period. The term itself has today an air of a long-gone era. I read Kohut's essay as a mid-1980s piece that is both convincing on a certain affinity between history and psychoanalysis, and is also a testament to the way historians have found little use in a continued discussion on their theoretical and interpretative relations. Why, I have asked myself, has this been the case?

I would like in the first part of this essay to reflect on this question. My claim is that history and psychoanalysis had not simply been drawn unbridgeably far apart in the mid-1980s: instead, conversely, historians have adopted in the last generation key psychoanalytic terms such as memory, emotion, and empathy as fundamental topics within the broader field of cultural history, while at the same time they saw no use for psychoanalytic explanations to elucidate the historical investigation of these topics. In the second part of the essay I discuss how historians treat historical memory, first by articulating some of the possible merits in the notion of memory, which has become in the last generation one of the most influential terms in historical explanation and interpretation, and then by telling two Holocaust memory stories.

Between psychoanalysis and cultural history

The relations between history and psychoanalysis seemed traditionally distant and close at one and the same time. The two disciplines ask different questions and focus on different objects of study. Psychoanalysis focuses on the individual, while history attempts to draw general patterns and establish causes for collective motivations and actions. Historians have traditionally eyed with suspicion attempts to impose general psychoanalytic theories on the particularities of historical situations, as well as attempts to explain action in terms of unconscious motivations instead of conscious aims. Karl Mannheim, the eminent sociologist of knowledge, put it in 1937 in words that it is still worthwhile to think about today:

> We cannot jump straight from the general observation of individuals and their psychic mechanisms to the analysis of society. The psychology of society is not a million times that of an individual ... What for our purpose is needed is an historically-differentiated psychology by which the changes in attitudes, motivations and symbol-transmutations in different periods among different classes and under different social situations will be made plain.
>
> (Mannheim, 1937, p. 129; cited in M. Confino, 1967)

But the attraction of using psychoanalysis to decipher human motivations was also great. In the 1970s and 1980s there had been a growing discussion among historians, building on an earlier body of work, on the merits of psychohistory, as it was called. Interestingly, scholars of the Third Reich and the Holocaust were especially attracted to this topic, sensing that the extermination of the Jews demands certain insights that go beyond the expressed conscious motivations of the perpetrators. Saul Friedlander (1978) attempted a general argument in *History and psychoanalysis: An inquiry into the possibilities and limits of psychohistory* before attempting to use trauma, transference, and working through to understand the particular history of the Holocaust (Friedlander, 1992). Peter Loewenberg (1987), a historian engaged in clinical practice as a psychoanalyst, provided a psychohistorical interpretation of Kristallnacht and by extension, of the Holocaust.

Kohut's "Psychohistory as history" provided a refined analysis of the issues at hand. A major point of contention in the debate has been how, if at all, to apply psychohistorical method and theory to understand the past. Kohut insightfully argued that this is the wrong problem to pose: "the application of the psychohistorical method to the past is problematical. It is also unnecessary" (Kohut, 1986, p. 337). Instead, he articulated a set of shared concerns and concepts: "The historian and the psychoanalyst approach their human subjects in essentially the same way and share a common method of understanding ... In both disciplines the investigator feels or, perhaps better, thinks his way inside the experience of the other" (Kohut, 1986, p. 344). Distinguishing between sympathy (feeling sorry or experiencing compassion for someone) and empathy, Kohut observes that via the notion of empathy

> the investigator puts himself in the place of the other and imagines why – given the time, place, circumstance, and experience of the other – it makes sense that he felt, thought, and acted as he did. In contrast, then, to the psychohistorical method, which relies on theory to provide its understanding and explanation, both the historical and the clinical psychoanalytic approach rely on empathy to understand and explain the particular meaning of human subjects. This fundamental methodological unity makes clear that, in studying the past's psychological dimension, the historian can remain a historian; he can continue to use traditional historical methods and, in doing so, function in a way that is fundamentally compatible with the way in which the psychoanalyst functions as a clinician.
>
> (Kohut, 1986, pp. 344, 347)

This astute evaluation contains both the reasons for historians' adopting what Kohut calls "the past psychological dimension" and for their relinquishing of psychohistory. Kohut's evaluation goes hand in hand with the aims and approaches of cultural history in the mid-1980s. It is interesting that the connection between cultural history and psychohistory is not made in Kohut's essay, but perhaps this was unavoidable because the essay was written in the early 1980s just before the cusp of cultural history began to emerge in full force. The study of culture has postulated in the last generation that collective representations cannot be reduced to social and political origins. This approach moved away from explanation in terms of functionalist and structuralist models and toward, as the editors of the important French journal *Annales* put it in a 1989 historiographical statement, "analysis in terms of strategies, which allow memory, learning, uncertainty, and negotiation to be reintroduced to the heart of social interaction" (The Editors of the *Annales*, 1995, p. 487). Exploring "the world as representation," to use the title of an essay by Roger Chartier (1995), was ultimately a way to "cast a fresh eye on the social itself" by emphasizing the subjective experience of contemporaries, focusing not only on what happened in the past, but also on what people *thought* was happening, and how their memory of the past influenced their actions and identity through time. The historian and the psychoanalyst, then, came quite close together in this regard.

Moreover, the procedures of the historian have changed in such a way as to remind one, in some broad respects, of those of the clinical psychoanalyst. It has become a staple of historical work to own a historical past precisely by showing the limits of historical knowledge and the constructedness of historical representation.[1] The historian of the South of the USA Edward Ayers described this shift eloquently in a meditation on the different narrative forms in his book *The Promise of the New South*, published in 1992, and in C. Vann Woodward's *Origins of the New South*, published in 1951. Ayers, a student of Vann Woodward, views *Origins* as the finest Southern history. During the forty-one years that separated the publication of the two books historical writing markedly changed and became dominated by "a sense of contingency and possibility even within powerful structures ... when the authors let the reader in on the way the argument is being constructed ... when the appearance of coherence and a commanding argument may ultimately be less useful than a reckoning with the limits of our knowledge or understanding" (Ayers, 1997, pp. 40–41).

And yet, if all these changes brought history closer to psychohistory, they also, on a fundamental level, caused historians to lose interest in psychohistory, and to jettison the term and the controversy around it. I can raise some ideas as to why this happened. Historians are sorts of theoretical and methodological predators, they pick and choose from other disciplines what suits them to explain why things happened and how. I advance the claim that because cultural history shared, consciously and more often unconsciously, with psychohistory key concerns of method and topics of investigation, psychohistory itself – as a mode of explanation, of answering *why* things happened – provided little specific explanatory reward (Megill, 2007). The tradition of history of mentality, of anthropology, cultural studies, postcolonial and gender studies, and of everyday-life history proved to historians more useful to collect and interpret evidence (Hunt, 1989; During, 1993; A. Confino, 2008).

I would raise the question whether the rise of cultural history in the mid-1980s at all depended on psychohistory. I doubt it. Paying closer attention to memory and the subjective experience of people in the past would possibly have occurred independently of the discussion about psychohistory. Arguably, internal transformations within the historical discipline were more important. Take for example the shift from "society" to "memory" that occurred in historical studies in that period. It began in the early 1980s as a gradual and as yet not brisk shift, measured and not yet revolutionary (Nora, 1996, 1997, 1998, 2001; Anderson, 1991). By the 1990s, however, the notion of "society" – as it had been practiced by social historians throughout the twentieth century and particularly after 1945 – was swept away by the interpretative onslaught of memory and cultural studies. The notion of society, broadly speaking, was based on a linear concept of history developing along one temporal timeline and privileging social and economic topics interpreted in terms of their function and structure. The notion of memory, in contrast, is based on the idea that social groups have a multi-temporal concept of history, they look back and forward at the same time, they commingle past and present, they capture simultaneously different and opposing narratives – because identities always include contradictory elements and because social groups, similarly to individuals, remember the past in order to make sense of the present. To explore this, historians therefore privileged topics of representation interpreted in terms of experience, negotiation, agency, and shifting relationship. "Memory" now governs questions of historical interpretation, explanation, and method in such a way that it seems appropriate to speak of a paradigm shift in historical studies from "society" to "memory."

Paradoxically, then, historians have changed their explanatory toolbox by borrowing psychological terms such as emotions, sensibilities, empathy, and especially memory, but without following up by using psychoanalytic methods and theories (Forum "History of emotions," 2010; Assmann and Detmers, 2016). We need to note that historians obviously always considered memory and emotions as important to understand the past (A. Confino, 2011). But something different happened since the mid-1980s because these notions, I would argue, *changed the way historians understand the presence of the past and of emotions in the life of people in the past* by making it into an essential empirical, analytical, and theoretical tool with which to understand social, political, cultural, even economic phenomena that regularly had been seen as determined by a very different set of factors. In this, historians have become a little bit closer to psychoanalysts than they might wish to admit, while keeping their method of investigation, and collection and evaluation of evidence, at arm's length from psychoanalysis.[2]

History, memory, and storytelling

One notion that has brought historians and psychoanalysts closer is memory. On one level, the two disciplinary crafts endow memory with great meaning. But on a different level historians have their own way of exploring the subject. The notion of memory has become in the last generation a sort of totem, a revered notion for public identity and professional investigation. For scholars it has governed questions of interpretation, narration, and explanation (now perhaps less than 20 years ago).

The study of memory explores how a social group, be it a family, a class, or a nation, constructs a past through a process of invention and appropriation and what it means for the relationship of power within society. Of course, social groups cannot remember, for this is only a faculty of the individual. And certainly, people cannot remember events in which they did not take part. Yet you do not need to have stormed the Bastille in order to celebrate July 14 as a symbol of national identity. One's memory, like one's most intimate dreams, originates from the symbols, landscape, and past that are shared by a given society. Since the making and the reception of memories, personal and collective, are embedded in a specific cultural, social, and political context, we can explore how people construct a past in which they did not take part individually, but which they share with other members of their group as a formative sense of cultural knowledge, tradition, and singularity.

The meeting of history and memory has offered insightful opportunities for historians to reflect about and enhance their craft precisely because it challenges a clear-cut relationship where history and memory are fixed modes of apprehending the past. The history the historian creates is different from the tale created by memory – because history and memory have different claims for historical accuracy. Memory is an image of the past made by the present; it is always selective; its aim is not to get the past right but to get the past wrong in order to give meaning to identities in the present. It is not a vehicle to understand the past but a means to understand the present.

Of course, memory is not the only representation of the past that has limits. Also the discipline of history has inevitable limits to historical knowledge. It is also subjective. But historians have an obligation to represent the past accurately. They create narratives about the past using evidence and methods of verification as the primary material of their craft with the intention of telling true stories. The truth of their stories is never stable, for it is socially and culturally constructed, and their stories can never tell the whole truth about the past. But the foundation of all serious historical work is the search for truth and fairness in the representation of the past. History, when properly done, has a claim to accuracy.

When historians analyze the memories of people in the past, therefore, they do not accept these memories at face value. Instead they ask who wants whom to remember what, and why, and whether the memory was at all received or rejected. Obviously, different memories will be incompatible; that is what memories do, they are about identity, they lay claim for the legitimacy of one's narrative. This is not a problem for the historian, but rather an opportunity. Historians are not primarily in the business of accepting, rejecting, or adjudicating the accuracy of these memories. They are in the business of using methods and theories to articulate, in this case, the representations of the past in a given society. In this investigation, the further a memory of a given social group is from what really happened, the more revealing it is about the culture of the group.

For the historian, in other words, narratives of memory are evidence. With this evidence at hand, historians do what they do for a living: they evaluate different items of evidence in order to portray a complex picture of the past. This does not mean that historians have lost the concept of a "fact." Instead, it means that rules of evidence have become more sophisticated, and historians accept now as evidence everything that was produced in the past. At the same time, probing the status of evidence has resulted in a multifaceted understanding, namely that evidence is not a direct transmitter of knowledge about the past, but rather that all evidence is always apprehended through sediments of previous interpretations and representations. Evidence is, and has always been, merely a representation of the past, the raw material for the historian who ultimately produces stories that are also a representation – not a reflection – of the past.

Stories that represent the past: this reminds us that history commingles the firmness of rules of evidence, analysis, and method with the poetic beauty of storytelling. My aim in scrutinizing the relations of history and memory is to convey history's claim to accuracy and, at the same time, the fundamental elusiveness of the historical enterprise. For historians, the notion of fact was never hermetically objective, much as the notion of subjective experience was never radically subversive, and both – at any event – had to be placed within a story. The historical enterprise is elusive because the knowledge the historian can ascertain about the past is slippery and because, once the knowledge has been gathered, the historian works with words, which are always ambiguous, in order to produce a final product, which is a story that falls squarely in the realm of art, just as the best of history writing is touched by the grace and beauty of art. By thinking with memory, historians recognize the irreducible element of storytelling in historical writing, and the unstable character of the stories they tell.

How some Germans became Jews and some Jews Nazis

History and memory are not the same but they belong to the same genre: they tell stories about the past; their power and essence lie in storytelling. Kohut tells such stories in *A german generation: An experiential history of the twentieth century*, a book about how a group of Germans born just before the First World War remembered their personal and national life during the twentieth century. Kohut's innovation is the use of "composite interviews," namely distilling the multitude of stories into two biographies for each section of the book (the First World War, the Weimar Republic, the Third Reich, and post-1945). These Germans ultimately felt the national shame of the Holocaust, but they never brought themselves to feel personal guilt. In their memories they stuck to the story that they knew nothing and saw nothing, while Kohut shows convincingly that this was not the case: "In order to look away, one needs to know what it is that one does not wish to see" (Kohut, 2012, p. 167).

I would like to add to his account two different Holocaust stories that reflect the particularities and contrasts of historical memory, its bizarre and unexpected twists and turns. When, in 2005, the Federal Republic of Germany inaugurated, a bow shot from the Reichstag in Berlin, the Memorial for the Murdered Jews of Europe, it gave a seal of recognition that the extermination of the Jews has become part and parcel of German history and identity. It reflected a sentiment shared by many Germans that the crime against the Jews is an indisputable, inextricable, and intimate part of modern Germany. And in this, I would like to propose, some Germans became a little bit Jewish in their attitude to memory and in their identification with the victims.

Some scholars and public figures would question my depiction of the status of Holocaust memory in Germany. Some argue that German memory of the Third Reich is focused on victimhood at the expense of remembering the Jews (Bartov, 2000). Others point out that alongside public remorse there is widespread private indifference and even hostility to Holocaust remembrance. And still others view the Berlin Holocaust memorial not so much as a German acknowledgment of perpetrated genocide but as a vehicle used by Germans to free themselves from the stigma and shame of the Holocaust.

These arguments are insightful in their specificity, but they miss a larger meaning of Holocaust memory in today's Germany. The tacit expectation that all Germans should internalize the Holocaust is a theological redemptive idea, not a historical argument. There will always be different people with different ideas about the Holocaust. There will be more battles over Holocaust memory since it is a foundational event that tests the limits of our humanity; there will never be a point where Germans will reach a final memory destination. The main question is how memory battles and minimizing of the Holocaust fit within a universe of German and transnational memory.

In this respect, in Germany all representations of the Second World War – especially by those who would like to minimize the extermination, who focus on German victimhood, who profess to have had enough – are constructed against the background and within the predominance of the presence of the past of the extermination of the Jews. Indeed, I would argue, this has been the case right from 1945. Differently put, the query I pose is not what do Germans remember, but why do Germans speak at all since 1945 with so much passion, resentment, and conflicted emotions about memory? The insistence on memory is an incitement to make sense of that event that cannot be displaced, the extermination of the Jews.

Germans remember the Holocaust whether they minimize it in a tale of victimhood, atone for it in a tale of penitence, or recount it in the language of the historian. Their memory work is a continuous process, producing different, opposing, variegated representations, which are often quite impressive in their democratic culture. Germans are, in a sense, destined to remember, and remember, and remember, to tell the tale in different ways, from generation to generation, which is epitomized in the repeated injunction to remember.

This way of describing opens up a space for an appreciation of German memory that is not without its ironies and paradoxes. Throughout history the people of memory par excellence have been the Jews. "Memory of the past," wrote Yosef Haim Yerushalmi in his classic *Zakhor: Jewish history and Jewish memory*, "was always a central component of Jewish experience" (Yerushalmi, 1989, p. 1). Already in the Bible the injunction to remember was a religious imperative. In exile the importance of memory became paramount for ensuring survival in a state of global dispersion. The Passover Haggada, a document composed in the Middle Ages telling the story of Exodus, became the "foundation of exilic memory" (see Raz-Krakotzkin, 2007, p. 533). It is recited annually to our days as a story of Jewish redemption: "In every generation each individual is bound to regard herself as if she had gone personally forth from Egypt." Every generation of Jews thought of its own contemporary Pharaoh, and after 1933 Hitler represented the ruler who set out to destroy the Jews. This culture of memory was a fundamental reason for the outpouring of individual Jewish writing during the Holocaust. No other genocide is so well documented by its victims. The Jews wrote possessed by their belief in the power of the word, of testimony, and of memory. At some point, testimony became more important than life itself: the last line in the diary of Chaim Kaplan, an educator and chronicler of the Warsaw Ghetto, on August 4, 1942 was "If my life ends – what will become of my diary" (Kaplan, 1999, p. 400).

This culture of memory about the Holocaust is shared now not only by Jews, but also by Germans. Indeed, it seems worthwhile to wonder whether the current dominance of memory does not owe much to Jewish culture. (I note in parenthesis that key scholars of memory were Jewish: Sigmund Freud, Emile Durkheim, Aby Warburg, Maurice Halbwachs, Marc Bloch, and Pierre Nora.) More concretely, it is not only that the content of German memory of the Holocaust changed since 1945. There was also a change in the substance of German identity: namely, that by placing remembrance at the center of their identity, by internalizing Jewish perceptions of the past, by identifying with the victims, Germans became a little bit Jewish. That was quite a reversal from 1945.

But Jewish perceptions of the past – like all memories, as we know – are malleable, multifaceted, and prone to change. No one has a copyright on memory, least of all on Holocaust memory that has become in the last generation a symbolic manual the world over for representing evil. It could be appropriated for the most different aims.

In 2005 Israel pulled out of the Gaza Strip, withdrew its army to the 1967 borders, and evacuated the Jews who had settled there in previous decades. The Gaza Strip was in 2005 a home for about 8,000 settlers, who lived in 16 settlements, and 1.4 million Palestinians. It is a piece of land 27 miles long and 7 miles across at its widest point. Over the years, Israel had taken control of some 15% of the Gaza Strip (54 square kilometers out of a total of 365) as land allocated for the use of the settlers; this area was not accessible to the Palestinian population. The Palestinian areas had been among the poorest and most densely populated in the world.

While most Israelis supported the disengagement plan, the settlers fervently opposed it on religious, national, and historical grounds. They evoked symbols of the Holocaust in a move that partly reflected a public relations strategy to attract attention but also expressed a deep-seated belief in the historical analogy. The symbol of the opposition was an orange star, worn on the clothing. Settlers tattooed their Israeli identity number on their forearm and dressed in a striped concentration camp uniform. Graffiti were scrawled labeling Ariel Sharon, the prime minister behind the disengagement plan, the heir of Pharaoh, Titus (who destroyed the Temple in 70 AC), and Hitler.

Settlers created mini-dramas, barricading themselves in their houses and calling soldiers "Nazis."

One of the initiators of the plan to use Holocaust symbols, Roni Bakshi from the settlement of Neveh Dekalim, explained it as follows in December 2004: "I would not dare to do this if I did not have the bad feeling that the plan here is to expel Jews." (Urquhart, 2004). Moshe Freiman, a son of a Holocaust survivor who is buried in a settlement, said he would wear the star on his shirt: "We, the second generation of Holocaust survivors, always complained to those who were there – why did they not rise up, why did they not cry out and do something? Today, justifiably, this is said about us – why are we not doing anything against this plan?" (Urquhart, 2004). And 75-year-old Ruth Matar observed that, "As an eight-year-old girl, the Nazi stormtroopers came and kicked down the door of my home in Austria and beat my mother because she wanted to go back into the house to get warm jackets for the children. Well there is no difference now, except it's Jewish police coming into a home and dragging unwilling people out." (De Quetteville, 2005).

This use of Holocaust symbols caused an outpouring of anger in Israel from across the political and cultural spectrum, including by members of the settler movement, political figures, journalists, and various Holocaust organizations of survivors and their offspring. Yad Vashem condemned "using in political debates terms and expressions from the Holocaust." But the Israeli historian of the Holocaust Hanna Yablonka (2005) was correct when she identified in this event deeper trends of Holocaust memory in Israeli culture. She lamented the everyday ideological use of Holocaust memory as well as the widespread ignorance about the Holocaust among young Israelis who are taught the "lesson" of the Holocaust but not its history. According to this lesson, "it is always the Jewish people that is in the right and is the accuser. The people of the world are obligated to stand before it abashed and ashamed." In light of this, wrote Yablonka (2005), in the debate over the "results of the Six Day War, it is very convenient to invoke an event in which we were only right and the world was only guilty."

Indeed, the symbolic manual of the Holocaust could work for any cause. In well-choreographed scenes, children were instructed to leave their homes with their hands raised, with each child wearing an orange Star of David with the word "Jude" visibly written on it. The analogy to a specific, famous photograph from the Holocaust was clear. This was quite a radical transformation of Holocaust symbols: Jews who for years had lived by denying their Palestinian neighbors basic human and national rights blamed other Jews for being Nazis. This, too, is quite a reversal from 1945.

The point is to see just how far some representations of the Holocaust in the two societies could go from the starting point of 1945. There are no boundaries to human imagination in the use of the past. We know the starting point of the memory process – the event as it happened in history – but we have no way of knowing how the story will be told and for what purpose.[3]

Stories that don't always tell what we thought they tell

I would like to end with an additional dimension to the exploration about Germans, Jews, and memory from my own work. In recent years I explored these relations from the following perspective: while there is a massive literature on German memories of the Holocaust, I investigated the German memories that made the Holocaust, the perceptions of time and of history that made the persecution and extermination of the Jews possible, imaginable, and justifiable.

I found out that the Nazis themselves appreciated the symbolic Jewish power derived from the Hebrew Bible, from history and memory. The Holocaust, I argued in *A world without Jews: The Nazi imagination from persecution to genocide* (A. Confino, 2014), was a memory project. By eradicating the Jews, the Nazis told themselves a story of origins about who they were and where they were headed, as they attempted to rewrite the history and memory of Jewish, German, and European-Christian history and memory. The annihilation of one memory deemed evil and the creation of another deemed redemptive were complementary, not contradictory.

The notion of historical origins gave meaning not only to the Holocaust as it happened in 1933–1945 but, significantly, also to the Holocaust in memory after 1945, underlying a fundamental link between the Third Reich and post-1945 memory of the Holocaust. If the Holocaust was for the Nazis a necessary, positive point of origin to construct their racial civilization, in the postwar world it became a negative memory of origin. The Nazis viewed the Holocaust as a historical rupture and a point of historical beginning, while we too view the Holocaust in this way, with a different moral and human understanding than the Nazis, of course. Across the divide of 1945, I would like to suggest, the metaphor of origins gave meaning to the Holocaust. The extermination as a foundational metaphor of origins, a sort of genesis, has thus stood at the center of how Germans, Jews, and others understood the Holocaust during the event and thereafter.

I can see now several filiations between the concerns of this exploration and of Kohut in his 1986 essay. There is, first, the insistence on empathetic understanding of Germans and the Nazis, and capturing their view of the world, however objectionable it may have been. The point of departure of my investigation was in a sense the basic question a psychoanalyst asks her patient: what is your story, tell me? I asked what story the Nazis told themselves to justify and legitimize the persecution and extermination of the Jews. Surely, such a transgressive act demanded a very good story to go along with it because Nazis and other Germans, like other human beings (apart from rare exceptions), still wished to perceive themselves as moral human beings, while killing. It was this story I was after in my book.

A further point of convergence of sorts between my method in *A world without Jews* and psychoanalysis was that I sought the meaning of the Nazis' obsession with Jews not only in explicit racial ideological expressions – what Germans said they were doing, the kind of evidence historians can access easily – but also in inexplicit, but possibly more fundamental, motivations expressed in social actions and cultural representations that commingled old and new symbols. Behind this approach there is a certain idea of historical causality and evidence. Beliefs cannot always be articulated, not even in private letters and diaries, while motivations are often hidden, subterranean, contradictory. We often tell ourselves stories that we would like to believe about ourselves, but that in fact obscure more than they reveal. Racial ideology, whose importance to the Third Reich is uncontested, is often too explicit and cerebral to capture the range of German fantasies about the Jews.

The book thus begins with scenes of the burning of the Hebrew Bible on Kristallnacht, the Night of Broken Glass on November 9, 1938, when 1,400 synagogues were burned in the German Reich. Public burning of the Hebrew Bible was widespread that day, as I found out by closely reading the documents. The Nazis themselves, who were never short of words when it came to spewing hatred of Jews and Judaism, did not elaborate on this transgressive act. And yet, here it was: burning a book that was holy and foundational to European-Christian civilization. I asked a simple question: why did the Nazis, set on constructing a *racial* civilization, burn the Bible and synagogues, which are *holy, religious* symbols? How was this act connected to the story the Nazis told themselves about Germans, Jews, and time? It is in this sense that understanding the burning of the Bible, and by extension the Nazis' anti-Jewish actions, demands exploring the relation between what is, on the one hand, explicit and conscious, and, on the other hand, implicit or unconscious.

Reading Kohut's essay of late and writing this essay has revealed to me how elements of my own approach are owed to the conversation between history and psychoanalysis, even if indirectly. And it reminds me that as historians our narratives don't always mean what we thought they meant, and they don't always tell only the stories we thought they tell.

Notes

1 We can think of works such as Ginzburg (1980) and Zemon Davis (1983).
2 I realize that this is a generalization. I cannot enter here into a full-fledged discussion of the relations of history and psychoanalysis in the last generation. For a brilliant book that uses psychoanalysis to understand history, see Roper (2004).
3 Some would argue against using the Holocaust and the Palestinians in the same argument, observing that it either reeks of a shallow desire to shock or disguises political motivations. But for the historian of culture this is not really an option. The prime target of the historian of culture is the subjective experience of contemporaries, and for Germans, Israelis, and Palestinians these topics are connected. The question is not whether to explore them, but how to do it insightfully. On the relations between the Holocaust and the Nakba, see Bashir and Goldberg (2014) and A. Confino (2016).

References

Anderson, B. (1991). *Imagined communities. Reflections on the origins and spread of nationalism*. London, UK: Verso.

Assmann, A., & Detmers, I. (eds.) (2016). *Empathy and its limits*. London, UK: Palgrave Macmillan.

Ayers, E. L. (1997). Narrative form in origins of the New South. In J. Roper (ed.), *C. Vann Woodward: A Southern historian and his critics* (pp. 37–46). Athens, GA: University of Georgia Press.

Bartov, O. (2000). Germany as victim. *New German Critique*, *80*, 29–40.

Bashir, B., & Goldberg, A. (2014). Deliberating the Holocaust and the Nakba: Disruptive empathy and binationalism in Israel/Palestine. *Journal of Genocide Research*, *16*, 77–99.

Chartier, R. (1995). The world as representation. In J. Revel & L. Hunt (eds.), *Histories: French constructions of the past, postwar French thought* (Vol. 1, pp. 544–558). New York, NY: The New Press.

Confino, A. (2008). Memory and the history of mentalities. In A. Erll & A. Nünning (eds.), *Cultural memory studies: An international and interdisciplinary handbook* (pp. 77–84). New York, NY: Walter de Gruyter.

Confino, A. (2011). History and memory. In A. Schneider & D. Woolf (eds.), *The Oxford history of historical writing* (Vol. 5, pp. 36–51). Oxford, UK: Oxford University Press.

Confino, A. (2014). *A world without Jews: The Nazi imagination from persecution to genocide*. New Haven, CT: Yale University Press.

Confino, A. (2016). Review of Bashir, B., & Goldberg, A. (eds.), The Holocaust and the Nakba. Memory, national identity and Jewish–Arab partnership. Jerusalem 2015. *H/SOZ/KULT*, 22.04.2016, www.hsozkult.de/publicationreview/id/rezbuecher-25731.

Confino, M. (1967). Histoire et psychologie: à propos de la noblesse russe au XVIII siècle. *Annales*, *22*, 1163–1205.

De Quetteville, H. (2005). Settlers evoke images of Holocaust in Gaza. *The Age*. www.theage.com.au/articles/2005/08/15/1123958007019.html.

During, S. (ed.) (1993). *The cultural studies reader*. New York, NY: Routledge.

Forum "History of emotions" (2010). *German History, 28*(1), 67–80.

Friedlander, S. (1978). *History and psychoanalysis: An inquiry into the possibilities and limits of psychohistory*. New York, NY: Holmes & Meier.

Friedlander, S. (1992). Trauma, transference and 'working through.' *History and Memory*, *4*, 39–59.

Ginzburg, C. (1980). *The cheese and the worms: The cosmos of a sixteenth-century miller*. Baltimore, MD: Johns Hopkins University Press.

Hunt, L. (ed.). (1989). *The new cultural history*. Berkeley, CA: University of California Press.

Kaplan, C. (1999). *Scroll of agony: The Warsaw diary of Chaim A. Kaplan*. A. Katsch (ed.) (trans.). Bloomington, IN: Indiana University Press.

Kohut, T. (1986). Psychohistory as history. *The American Historical Review*, *91*, 336–354.

Kohut, T. (2012). *A German generation: An experiential history of the twentieth century*. New Haven, CT: Yale University Press.

Loewenberg, P. (1987). The Kristallnacht as a public degradation in ritual. *Leo Baeck Institute Yearbook*, *32*, 308–323.

Mannheim, K. (1937). The psychological aspect. In C. A. W. Manning (ed.), *Peaceful change: An international problem* (pp. 105–129). London, UK: Macmillan.
Megill, A. (2007). *Historical knowledge, historical error. A contemporary guide to practice*. Chicago, IL: University of Chicago Press.
Nora, P. (1996). *Realms of memory, Vol. 1: Conflicts and divisions.* P. Nora & L. D. Kritzman (eds.), A. Goldhammer (trans.). New York, NY: Columbia University Press.
Nora, P. (1997). *Realms of memory, Vol. 2: Traditions.* P. Nora & L. D. Kritzman (eds.), A. Goldhammer (Trans.). New York, NY: Columbia University Press.
Nora, P. (1998). *Realms of memory, Vol. 3: Symbols.* P. Nora and L. D. Kritzman (eds.), A. Goldhammer (Trans.). New York, NY: Columbia University Press.
Nora, P. (ed.) (2001). *Rethinking France – Les lieux de mémoire* (Vol. 1). Chicago, IL: Chicago University Press.
Raz-Krakotzkin, A. (2007). Jewish memory between exile and history. *Jewish Quarterly Review, 97*, 530–543.
Roper, L. (2004). *Witch craze. Terror and fantasy in baroque Germany*. New Haven, CT: Yale University Press.
The Editors of the *Annales* (1995). Let's try the experiment. In J. Revel & L. Hunt (eds.), *Histories: French constructions of the past, postwar French thought* (Vol. 1, pp. 484–491). New York, NY: The New Press.
Urquhart, C. (2004). Settlers fight back with symbol of the Holocaust. *The Guardian,* December 22, www.guardian.co.uk/world/2004/dec/22/israel.
Yablonka, H. (2005). Verging on Holocaust denial. *Haaretz*, July 23.
Yerushalmi, Y. H. (1989). *Zakhor: Jewish history and Jewish memory*. New York, NY: Schocken Books.
Zemon Davis, N. (1983). *The return of Martin Guerre.* Cambridge, MA: Harvard University Press.

Chapter 2

"Memory" and its discontents

Dorothee Wierling

For some time now, I have been dealing with the problem of "memory" as a concept that has lost its potential to produce new questions and interesting answers for my work as historian – to the same degree that it became a universal instrument for various disciplines in the humanities, it lost precision, poignancy, and force. I know that other historians have similar concerns, among them Thomas Kohut, to whom this chapter is dedicated.[1]

As a social historian of the twentieth century, most of my research was and is based at least partly on oral history as source and method. I have made use of oral sources in order to come up with plausible suggestions about history as subjective experience and interpretations; in other words, as the production of meaning by various historical subjects. The focus of my interest is the representation of the past by concrete individuals in the framework of their social and cultural belonging. Subjective experience of and personal "knowledge" about history matter, because they not only shape biographies in retrospect, but also form the basis for social and political practices as well as expectations for the future and intergenerational exchange. Given my research interests linked with "memory," the fact that the concept has become ever more separated from real human beings and their mentalities, and has therefore lost significance for my own work without offering much compensation, prompts the following remarks.

My discontent – and not only mine – is felt regularly when texts about the issue of memory begin with cursory reference to Maurice Halbwachs (1992), Jan Assmann (2008), Aleida Assmann (1999), and Pierre Nora (1989) as merely legitimating reference to "cultural" and "communicative" memory, to its "social cadres" and "lieux de mémoire." All these concepts seem to have degenerated to trite plastic words, whose intellectual value is reduced already by the use of these conceptual suggestions as canonical texts, which cannot be criticized but may only be interpreted. While I have enormous respect for all the above-mentioned authors and am grateful for their immense contribution to our understanding of memory, unfortunately, their concepts have long since developed a superficial life of their own, while the existing critical debate on the theoretical and practical implications of the concept of memory is mostly ignored.[2] What follows, therefore, is intended not so much as an argument against the authors in question, who have provided us with central insights into the social production of interpretations of the past, but more as a discussion that takes the empirical question of how individuals, embedded in their social worlds, create a meaningful past as its starting point – and asks for the concepts we need in order to find plausible answers.

Conceptions of memory

The problem I deal with begins already with basic questions of translation. In German the term "memory" has two equivalents: *Gedächtnis* and *Erinnerung*. The latter could also be translated as remembrance or recollection, which is, however, seldom used in the context of memory studies. While in German, too, the two terms are sometimes used as synonyms, and one might refer to somebody's good or bad *Gedächtnis*, or an *Erinnerung* could also be a reminder or a public act of memorialization, in general *Gedächtnis* would refer more to the repository, archive, or neuronal network that is the structured "matter" of what could be remembered and expressed, while *Erinnerung* would more often be used for the very act of searching and recovering the past – and thereby point to the individual act of remembering.[3]

These manifold ways of using the term in everyday language are further complicated in the context of scholarly use. Here, history, sociology, and cultural studies seem to be locked quite uncomfortably between a mere metaphorical use of "memory," where individuals or concrete social groups are missing, on the one hand, and the seemingly scientific description of chemically based processes in the human brain, which lead to remembering or forgetting, on the other. In the case of memory as a metaphor, its place is outside of human agency and instead identified with the state, society, a culture, a movement or other social entities and institutions. Here concepts such as urban or media memory have their origin, although this language leaves open to what degree these spaces are seen as "having" a memory or merely enabling and organizing human memories – and who these humans would be.[4]

On the other hand, neurologists often suggest that it is possible to directly observe "memory" happening: one can watch the hippocampus light up in bright colors under the impact of new images; neurons releasing transmitters and thereby retrieving images of the past; and neuronal connections forming and creating an ever-denser web, spreading over different regions of the brain.[5] But what are the psychological, social, and cultural conditions under which these activities are initiated and unfold their subjective effects? Why are some images of the past ready to be invoked, but others refuse to come up? Why do memories change over the course of a life and how are these changes embedded socially and historically? These are questions neurologists will seldom ask and cannot answer, while the humanities have a hard time relating their own questions to the unquestionable findings of the natural science of life. Psychoanalysis seems one of the few disciplines with the potential to consider and link these two approaches in a productive way.[6]

One of the most important conceptual contributions to the problem is the distinction between cultural and communicative memory as developed by Jan Assmann (2008). He insists on a clear line between the two, when he defines the communicative memory, based on personal experiences, as limited in regard to both content and time span, covering no more than three generations or less than a hundred years. Accordingly, the "communicative" memory moves toward the future and is described by Assmann (2008) as spontaneous, relatively amorphous, mostly communicated face to face, and under constant revision. Against this is juxtaposed the "cultural" memory, which has its fixed place in archives and cultural artifacts. Its scope is in principle unlimited, since it is carefully formed and preserved.

My own field, oral history, is commonly identified with the communicative memory, an ascription which I find highly problematic. On the one hand, some of the attributes of communicative memory do indeed apply to a typical oral history interview. This happens, however, under the conditions of technical conservation and subsequent interpretation by the historian, two procedures which aim to make the interview part of a scholarly text and thereby change the character of the interview from a supposedly spontaneous conversation to an aspect of cultural memory in a given society – and even of historiography, a sphere which Maurice Halbwachs (1980) and Pierre Nora (1989) were anxious to separate sharply from the realm of memory. In reflecting this process, we might argue that the oral history interview represents less the shift from one mode into the other, but rather the conflation of the two.

Already during the interview itself, the close links between aspects of the cultural memory, for instance acceptable public interpretations of the past and the individual narrative, are obvious. This is different from the social framing of individual memories, as it is broadly accepted by most theoreticians of memory, following Maurice Halbwachs. Instead, it is about the conscious or unconscious, but always purposeful, attempt of the narrators to inscribe themselves with their personal recollections into (or outside of) dominant and historical discourses in order to establish collective belonging. This mechanism can be shown, for example, with biographical interviews conducted shortly after the implosion of the German Democratic Republic (GDR), when interviewees would refer to old GDR discourses such as antifascism as well as to West German discourses about the GDR as a problematic past, and try to integrate those discourses into their own experiences, or rather the other way round: trying to make their personal experiences fit into these discourses, often in a most contradictory and informative manner (see Wierling, 2002).

But we can think also about the reverse mechanism, that is the shifts in public discourses about the past through the inclusion of personal memories communicated first in private circles, as was the case with the so-called "children of war" in Germany around the year 2000. This shift can be reconstructed in detail from the first meetings of West German male friends with an educated middle-class background, among them several historians who had lost their fathers during the Second World War, conversations which soon resulted in a publication (Radebold, Reulecke, & Schulz, 2007). The group was then joined by psychoanalysts as experts and discovered by political actors who happened to belong to the same generational group. This made access to the public sphere easy and introduced the group experience to the media, with it thus becoming part of the cultural memory of West Germany (see Seegers & Reulecke, 2009; Wierling, 2010). We can conclude not only that communicative and cultural memory are hardly separable phenomena, but also that, under the conditions of democracy and a strong media presence, they constantly interact and mutually shape each other. The result is a continuous negotiation of historical meanings and "memories" which can be at the same time alive and fluid, as well as archived and fixed.

We owe to Maurice Halbwachs the basic insight into the social construction of memory and remembrance. There is today virtually no theory of memory which does not refer to him – mostly by accepting (and even overstating) his dictum that "we, in reality, are never alone" when we remember (1980, p.23). The titles of his book on "the social cadres of memory" and the posthumously published monograph on "collective memory" suggest that the individual can be understood only in the frames of his or her social existence – in particular during the act of remembering.[7] There is another quote from Halbwachs (1992, p. 41), however, which is mostly ignored or seen as irrelevant for his understanding of memory: that "while sleeping [that is, while dreaming, DW] man to a large extent flees the control of society." Here Halbwachs acknowledges the existence of a sphere where the individual is indeed "alone" in the sense of being shielded against the agencies of social control which dominate his/her daily life.

Jan Assmann, whose reading of Halbwachs I follow, does not identify the latter's concept of collective memory with his own concept of cultural memory, but rather sees the former in the sphere of communicative memory; but we often find all of this confused in introductions to empirical studies. Halbwachs has become a trademark, and his assumption of the social construction of memory is often invoked by scholars merely to argue for the relevance of their own work by claiming that their results stand for a larger collective, a whole society, or the "identity" of a political movement.

It is not my goal to deny or belittle the social construction of memory and experience, although our methodological tools to describe the social impact and its mechanisms are limited. Instead I would like to question more systematically two aspects of this discussion. One is the ease with which "collective memories" are taken for granted, as in the case of Pierre Nora, where the so-called collectively acknowledged "sites of memory" he claims to exist are often identified with an overarching national memory. Very often, however, this "national memory" is exclusively based on interpretations of the past held by national elites, usually the educated classes, which tend to be relatively blind in regard to the seemingly minor (or at least less outspoken) role history plays in the lives (or minds) of the less educated.

The German case is particularly complicated, given that the whole complex of dealing with the German atrocities during National Socialism and the Second World War seems to play a relatively weak role in the lives of working-class youth, families on welfare, young migrants, and consumer-oriented young urban elites. These groups do not always feel that they need "history" in order to lead a meaningful life, nor do they care a lot about the discourses of "Vergangenheitsbewältigung" (coming to terms with the Nazi past), which are dominated by members of specific generational and more educated social groups.[8] In a similar fashion, the historical narratives which political and social movements create are mostly based on the lives of prominent activists of these groups, which they offer the wider public as "their" collective memory, leaving no room for alternative memories, even concerning their own story, let alone the memories of the movements' rank and file. My critique at this point cannot be more than an assertion, because there is a lack of systematic research into the many "memories" co-existing in larger collectives such as political movements or the reception of "grand narratives" by ordinary group members, although Alon Confino (1997) has noted this problem.

Scholars mostly refer to "collective memory" in the singular. Halbwachs has made it quite clear, however, that each individual belongs to different, often overlapping, but also independent and even competing, collectives, all of which have a claim on his/her memory – so that individuality could be based on the unique mixture of social frames as the conditions under which each person constructs his or her memories. To a certain degree, then, I can rely on Halbwachs himself to defend himself against the simplifying appropriation of his ideas by many of his followers, all the more so because, as Lutz Niethammer (2005) has convincingly shown, his theory of memory was by no means as coherent as the use made of his writings, in particular the posthumous book on "collective memory," suggests. What I am attracted to is indeed the sleeping, dreaming individual, and I assume – following psychoanalytic thought – that humans are able to express themselves not only in dreams, but also in involuntary memories, which take the individual by surprise, bypassing and overwhelming the wary ego. To the degree that psychoanalytic assumptions claim that these memories represent the unconscious and that the unconscious is a sphere of the a-social, we as oral historians can conclude for our own work that such memories are possible and that, accordingly, the potential insight from an oral history interview goes far beyond the social frame of "collective" memories.

Social history and the limits of memory

Concluding that the prominent theoretical concepts of "memory," in particular those developed by sociologists and historians, have been overused, dogmatized, and simplified, so that they have lost most of their intellectual value for empirical research, leaves us with another, unresolved problem: how to deal with these problematic concepts and assumptions not just in theoretical discussions, but in our own empirical work.

As a social historian I try to understand how real people perceive the events happening to them, how they, by integrating their perceptions into earlier ones, create a multilayered experience, and how they produce, on this basis, biographical and historical meaning – or rather a system of meanings which serves to identify their interests and needs, and shapes their personal understanding of what a good life would be. Only on the surface is memory directed toward the past; instead, remembering helps to assure individuals of their present and to imagine a future. Obviously, all this happens within social, cultural, and political frameworks not totally under their control – frameworks which must be explored by the historian in order to draw conclusions and create knowledge beyond the individual case. But, in order to grasp these mental and cultural processes, historians need material in which they find the substance of "memory" expressed in a way that can be understood, interpreted, and communicated to others in a plausible and transparent manner.

The most important mode in which personal memories are expressed during an oral history interview is that of storytelling. But the words spoken in an interview and the event that the words refer to are separated (or rather, mediated) by a chain of reductive processes whereby *the event itself* moves more and more into the background. First, it is perceived only insofar as it befell and had a direct impact on the narrator, such as sitting in the basement of one's own house during the bombing of Hamburg in the summer of 1943 and fleeing through the burning streets of the city: personal recognition and emotional response turn the external *event* into an internal reality, an *Erlebnis*, for which the common English translation offers "experience" – let us call it *experience I*. Already during this immediate act of appropriation the relevant aspects are separated from the non-relevant, and this is even more the case in the following integration of the event into the memory of previous ones, in order to create a coherent chain of experiences in the sense of the German *Erfahrung* (also translated as experience), that is *experience II* – a long-term process of learning, or the production of meaning. During all these steps the social environment plays an important role, such as the family and neighbors who were with the narrator in the basement, but also the first pictures in newspapers and the various occasions of public commemoration. In this way an event turns into a memory which then itself becomes the point of reference for new experiences, thereby undergoing possible changes of meaning. All these "single" memories form a specific, multilayered interpretation which is under continuous, lifelong revision: thus, the economic reconstruction after the war, professional careers, and first journeys abroad changed the "taste" of the war memories for many West Germans and East Germans in a significant way.[9]

The role of narrative

Not everything is retrievable at any particular time, due to personal patterns of relevance, anxieties, shame, or the traumatic character of some experiences.[10] Telling one's life story, be it to a chance acquaintance, a new lover, a psychoanalyst, or an oral historian, means making choices, which, again, are made mostly unconsciously, but never arbitrarily: on the one hand, narrators develop biographical constructions that support a consistent and acceptable story of themselves; on the other, the specific situation in which the story is communicated, the listening other, the timeframe, the obviously intended purpose of the conversation, and the actual mental state of the narrator, can form specific patterns of relevance, which determine the version of the story.[11] As listeners, we cannot know what people remember beyond what they talk about. Even if we have reason to hope that their narrative is based on parts of their memories, we can never be totally sure about it. But *the narrative* is all we have to work with. In order to stay aware of these limits of knowledge, I suggest that one should entirely give up talking about "memory" in favor of "narrative." That would seem more honest and abandons the illusion of being able to know about aspects of my interviewees' inner worlds, from which instead I am excluded, in a manner perhaps similar to the way in which the psychoanalyst depends on the patient's narrative of his/her dream while the dream itself is no more than an ephemeral, puzzling set of images lost again in the morning to the depths of the unconscious.[12] In contrast to the narratives of the patient on the couch, however, the oral history interview is recorded as audio or video, and thus has the advantage of a certain fixity which allows the interviewer as interpreter to apply ever new readings to the text and reach an ever more complex understanding of the ways in which the narrators express their memories, while their text remains as a powerful intervention.

This is significant not only for historians. Alfred Lorenzer (1986) defined the narrative as the central research material also for psychoanalysis and, in analyzing literary texts, demonstrated how the repeated reading of these texts was equivalent to the repeated communication between psychoanalyst and patient, in which ever new aspects and meanings come to the surface and the interpretation of the narrative is continuously enriched.[13] And it is to the degree that the text eventually reveals its many co-existing meanings that it turns out to be open, even if fixed on video or audio tape and in writing.

Looking at interviews as narratives (instead of memories) furthermore allows connection and comparison of the oral history interview with other texts that qualify as narrative, such as fictional, journalistic, and historiographic texts – each with their own claim to truth. Scholarly narratives whose statements have to be verifiable and plausible stand in obvious contrast to other narratives, for instance to those texts which claim to be built on memories. But these differences are not necessarily the sharp ones between history and memory as such on which Halbwachs and Nora have insisted. The so-called narrative constraints (*Erzählzwänge*) which the sociologist Fritz Schütze has discovered, namely communicative necessities which are unavoidable once a story unfolds, apply not only to the biographical interview, but also to an academic narrative (Schütze, 1983).[14] Subsuming all of these genres under the category of narrative enables us to better discover the hidden links between them, their similarities in using narrative strategies, and not least the mutual references they make to each other.

There is another advantage that comes with making narratives (instead of memory) the object of our scholarly analysis: the possibility of a multidisciplinary exchange. Each language-based discipline has developed its own questions and tools to interpret texts, all of which can be related to genres of narrative. Besides history and the already-mentioned psychoanalysis, these disciplines include philosophy, ethnology, the qualitative social sciences, literature, and the newly developed transdisciplinary field of narratology.[15]

It is not my intention here to describe the contributions of all these disciplines to the productivity of narrative as a category – because of a lack both of space and of expertise. But I began to realize the significance of other disciplines when I met a young East German ethnologist in the late 1980s, and was deeply impressed by her way of transcribing the interviews she had conducted with women activists in the early 1950s: namely beginning a new line for every part of a sentence, thus creating the appearance of a poem, slowing down the act of reading and enabling an immediate in-depth approach to the text (see Clemens, 1990). Reading an interview as if it were a poem means acknowledging the combination of obvious and hidden meanings, of fact-based and symbolic images, of words leading into the past and words used to create meaning, of text and subtexts. The narratives of our interviewees open up a path into their personal (albeit socially constructed) subjective cosmos of a meaningful past. Other disciplines focus on other aspects: psychoanalysis looks for relational patterns, of which we are most often unconscious; ethnologists seek the function of narratives as a social ritual; literary scholars inform us about the function of various genres; sociology analyzes narrative constructions referring to social patterns which are based on class, gender, or generation. The potential of an interdisciplinary approach to the concept of narrative has not yet been exhausted.

As always, however, interdisciplinarity also functions as an eye opener for the specifics of one's own discipline, in this case my position as a historian and the reasons why I made this and no other choice. It was, among other experiences, the close cooperation with psychoanalysts in a project on survivors' narratives about the bombing of Hamburg in July 1943 that made some of these differences and choices become clearer to me again (see Kohut, 2013; Wierling, 2013). One aspect was related to the different ways of asking questions, both as interviewers and as scholars; another concerned the different types of answers we were seeking. In our discussions based on the interview transcripts the psychoanalysts tended to begin by addressing the narrators' emotions in order to discuss signs of trauma, while the historians first looked at the stories told and then asked what their meaning might be, putting aside the question of trauma which for them was too difficult to answer on the basis of the narratives. In interdisciplinary conversations we exchanged our various readings of interviews, a practice which enabled us, but also asked all of us, to argue for our interpretations by accepting the interventionist power of the text as evidence.

While for historians this appears as the advantage of their approach, we do face methodological problems that other disciplines do not have to bother with, such as the use of narratives as evidence for the actual past they are referring to.[16] Oral historians hope that their interviewees help them to get access to and provide hints or signs of past experiences, or even sometimes past events themselves. The degree to which this is possible, or can be made plausible, is not clear.

Nor does the choice of "narrative" as the object of analysis solve the problem of determining the power of social frameworks or explaining the resilience of the individual against this power by insisting on his/her personal experiences. However, the focus on narratives offers the opportunity to analyze a given text in search of signs and suggestions, which point to the conflicting forces of the social and the self (to put it casually) and enable the historian to at least describe the obvious connections between the two levels.

In 2003, the Hamburg-based Körber-Stiftung, a foundation to support political education, asked me to publicly interview a group of ethnic Germans from Russia about their historical experiences in front of a Hamburg audience and thereby create more empathy and solidarity with these immigrants (see Wierling, 2004). The oldest interviewee, born in 1918, belonged to the cohort of so-called Russian Germans who suffered most from Stalinist repression and thus represented the collective victimhood of this group most obviously. In the 1930s his father, a protestant minister, had been shot by the state security; his older brother was later imprisoned; and he himself was deported to a forced labor camp at the beginning of the German invasion of the Soviet Union. My interviewee, who had trained as an engineer, had survived the camp and had even been able to acquire more professional expertise that would help him to a major career in the postwar era. Since the 1980s, he had been employed as a leading engineer in the Kazakhstan Ministry for Construction. But when the currency crisis of the late 1990s broke out, he decided to migrate to Germany with his family to offer his sons better opportunities. He told me in our private conversation before the public interview that his motivations were chiefly economic and that he was rather disappointed with the way Germany differed from his expectations. His sons were already preparing to go back to Kazakhstan. When I asked him later, on stage, why he had decided to leave, he began to repeat the explanation he had given me, but was interrupted by the president of the "Association of Germans from Russia," which dominated the audience, who got up and handed him a short note written in Cyrillic script. My interviewee then immediately interrupted his sentence and started all over again: It was the continuous repression of Germans by the Russians, he now assured us, which was behind his decision.

The scene is a wonderful illustration of what the US-American cultural theorist Anthony Appiah (1992, p. 160) calls the "social script" which narrators try to follow when they tell their life story. Their narrative shall testify their social, political or cultural belonging, in this case the collective suffering of Russian Germans that is their entry ticket into Germany. But the social script is not so much the "collective" memory Halbwachs refers to, but rather a socially acceptable narrative, which has often been collectively created in so-called narrative communities.[17] When my interviewee was caught in the unacceptable narrative of his professional career in the Soviet Union, he just used the wrong script for the occasion. For the German public, the victims' narrative was the appropriate one. My interviewee's narrative about his career belonged to another script, which Russian Germans would also use – but only amongst themselves, and in Russian.

The controlling social authority, here personified by the association's president, is typically present inside the narrator him/herself – but it does not necessarily control all the memories of the narrator. My interviewee earned a public rebuke for involuntarily revealing the complexity of his individual experience in a public space. His insistence on personal agency was reprimanded as a violation of the rules of the narrative game. In this way, the use of "narrative" instead of "memory" as our analytical tool also reveals the interactive character of the social construction of such accounts. While the concept of "memory" refers vaguely to somehow identifiable materializations on the one hand, or to hidden phenomena in the innermost corners of the psyche on the other, a narrative can be listened to, conserved, read and – in the case of video interviews – watched. And it is obviously directed to a listener, watcher, or reader. The real or at least imagined audience reacts with silence or sounds, confirming one narrative, ignoring another or disapproving of yet another one.

The oral history interview is a communication in which a specific narrative about the past is enabled and shaped in a comprehensible way that is part of the source itself. This is true even if one does not assume that the interview's validity reaches beyond the specific interview situation itself. Even if the communication fails, if the trust, understanding, or curiosity necessary to get the story moving are missing, this is documented in the transcript in an instructive and enlightening way. The reader of a transcript, often identical with the interviewer, becomes aware of his/her unconscious evasions, emotions, and agendas. The similarities to the psychoanalytic setting, in which patients share their experiences through narrative and analysts get involved in acts of transference, are obvious. In the oral history interview, the historian becomes part of the source itself and, rather than merely relying on the narrator's memory, has to analyze the text's meaning by engaging in a communicative process that is based on exchanged words, gazes, and gestures. But there are also limits to our endeavor to fully understand the creation of historical meaning, a process which is partly hidden from us and never completed – we can only hope to get as far and as deep as possible. Using the concept of narrative instead of memory should help us to stay more modest and honest in regard to the limits of our achievements as historians.

Obviously, a narrative is not the only expression of memories. People fill their lives and environments with things and images, which make memories visible and touchable: photographs, which show themselves or loved ones forever young and houses forever new; things which show their individual marks of wear and tear, like used shoes; or objects which explicitly represent the past, such as cups rescued from a house destroyed in a fire. And our aging body, with its wrinkles and scars, is a reminder of time passing, a magazine of memories, while the consciously public or unconsciously private repetition of rituals represents a medium of memories in gestures.[18] I will not refer to any of these phenomena as narratives, however. Rather, they should be used in the sense of uses or practices which give us (limited) access to the past as reminders, through re-enactment and its observation. After all, the very reason for giving up "memory" is its inflationary use which has made it ever more empty and meaningless. As a result, the choice of narrative as a category to understand the past was motivated by a strong wish for precision, which is based on the dictum that memories cannot exist outside of human beings. But we can learn about them only to the degree they are expressed, preferably in words and signs that we can hope to understand.

Notes

1 In his groundbreaking recent book *A German generation. An experiential history of the twentieth century*, Kohut (2012) experiments – successfully – with the creation of composite narratives that are based on several interviews. This chapter draws on a talk I gave at the Centre Marc Bloch in Berlin in May 2015 ("Vom Überdruss am 'Gedächtnis.' Ein Rettungsversuch"), when I was asked to critically assess the concept of memory for a conference on "Gedächtnis und Erinnerung in Frankreich und Deutschland: interdisziplinärer Dialog zwischen Geschichtswissenschaft und Soziologie." It was inspired also by conversations with Gadi Algazi. I became aware of Algazi's (2014) text "Forget memory: Some critical remarks on memory, forgetting and history" only after I had finished writing this essay.

2 See for instance Kansteiner (2002). For a critical appraisal of Halbwachs, see Krapoth and Laborde (2005).

3 It goes without saying that these are rather crude definitions and descriptions of a very complicated procedure. They serve at this point merely to make a distinction between different aspects of the complex memory process.
4 See for instance Crinson (2005) and Neiger, Meyers, and Sandberg (2011).
5 The imaging method has made these processes obvious, when those brain regions are involved in the act of retrieving the past (van Dijck, 2005).
6 As indicated by numerous publications on their mutual interest. Attachment theory seems to be one of the links between them. See Green (2003).
7 See note 9. Halbwachs' *On collective memory* (1992) is based on excerpts of both *Les cadres de mémoire* (1925) and *La topographie légendaire des évangiles en Terre sainte* (1941).
8 The complex relationship between the ways in which the Nazi past is dealt with, on the one hand, and social categories such as generation, class, gender, and West vs. East German upbringing, on the other, is rather under-researched. As to generation, it has been argued convincingly that the West German so-called *Achtundsechziger* or 1968ers (whose social background was mostly educated bourgeois and petty bourgeois) define themselves as *the* generation which critically confronted their parents' role in the Third Reich (Jureit, 2005). In East Germany, this kind of politicized generational conflict was basically absent (Wierling, 1999). To the best of my knowledge, there has been no systematic analysis of the relationships among youth, class, and attitudes toward the Nazi past. Studies of historical education in different types of school (attendance of which is partly linked to class) allow one to make preliminary suggestions (Zülsdorf-Kersting, 2007).
9 These examples refer to an interdisciplinary study carried out by historians and psychoanalysts about the impact of the bombing of Hamburg in 1943 (Lamparter, Wiegand-Grefe, and Wierling, 2013).
10 Trauma in the narrow sense of the term means the basic impossibility of integrating certain perceptions (i.e. from the violent first half of the twentieth century) into a meaningful narrative at all.
11 This is not to say that the narrative depends, in its essence, on these factors. There seems to be a subjective center which remains unaffected even by dramatic changes in the historical context, such as the fall of the Berlin Wall in 1989. See Wierling (1992). On narratives as social constructions depending on constructions of the self as well as reactions to specific conditions in the act of telling a story, see also Freeman (2010), Andrews (2014), and Brockmeier (2015).
12 Thus, Walter Benjamin identifies the moment of awaking as the recognition of the dream in the moment of being separated from it, a constellation he calls the "now of knowability." (Benjamin, 1999, p. 463f. (N 3a 3)). For the interpretation of this note see Weber (2008).
13 See in particular Lorenzer (1986, pp. 14f., 84f.).
14 See White (1973).
15 Achim Saupe and Felix Wiedemann offer a good (online) introduction for historians to the theories of narrative offered by different disciplines: "Narration und Narratologie. Erzähltheorien in der Geschichtswissenschaft," http://docupedia.de/zg/Narration (2015).
16 Leopold von Ranke, the nineteenth-century Prussian historian, has long been described as a naïve believer in positivistic historiography on account of his statement that the historian just wants to know "how things actually were." Today, historians tend to see his dictum in a more complex light. Thus Lutz Raphael (2003, pp. 67f) states that "Sein Streben, zu 'zeigen, wie es eigentlich gewesen ist' wurde dabei unter Mißachtung der für Ranke und seiner Schüler so prägenden

idealistisch-historistischen Geschichtsphilosophie in der Regel als Ausdruck eines trivialpositivistischen Objektivitätsideals interpretiert."

17 The term "narrative community" (*Erzählgemeinschaft*) goes back to the ethnologist Albrecht Lehmann (2007). See also Kohut (2012, p. 11).

18 See Bennett and Joyce (2010) and Lorenz (2000).

References

Algazi, G. (2014). Forget memory: Some critical remarks on memory, forgetting and history. In S. Scholz, G. Schwedler, & K.-M. Sprenger (eds.), *Damnatio in Memoria: Deformation und Gegenkonstruktionen von Geschichte* (pp. 25–34). Vienna, Austria: Böhlau.

Andrews, M. (2014). *Narrative imagination and everyday life*. New York, NY: Oxford University Press.

Appiah, K. A. (1992). Identity, authenticity, survival: Multicultural societies and social reproduction. In C. Taylor & A. Gutman (eds.), *Multiculturalism: Examining the politics of recognition* (pp. 149–163). Princeton, NJ: Princeton University Press.

Assmann, A. (1999). *Erinnerungsräume. Formen und Wandel des kulturellen Gedächtnisses*. Munich, Germany: Beck.

Assmann, J. (2008). Communicative and cultural memory. In A. Erll & A. Nünning (eds.), *Cultural memory studies: An international interdisciplinary handbook* (pp. 109–118). New York, NY: Walter de Gruyter.

Benjamin, W. (1999). *The arcades project*. In R. Tiedemann (ed.). Cambridge, MA: Harvard University Press.

Bennett, T., & Joyce, P. (2010). *Material powers: Cultural studies, history and the material turn*. London, UK: Routledge.

Brockmeier, J. (2015). *Beyond the archive. Memory, narrative and the autobiographical process*. New York, NY: Oxford University Press.

Clemens, P. (1990). Die »Letzten«. ... Die Betriebsfrauenausschüsse der 50er Jahre in lebensgeschichtlicher Sicht. *Feministische Studien*, *1*, 20–34.

Confino, A. (1997). Collective memory and cultural history: Problems of method. *American History Review*, *102*, 1386–1403.

Crinson, M. (ed.) (2005). Urban memory. History and amnesia in the modern city. London, UK: Routledge.

Freeman, M. (2010). Telling stories: Memory and narrative. In S. Radstone & B. Schwarz (eds.), *Memory: Histories, theories, debates* (pp. 263–280). New York, NY: Fordham University Press.

Green, V. (ed.) (2003). *Emotional development in psychoanalysis, attachment theory and neuroscience: Creating connections*. London, UK: Brunner-Routledge.

Halbwachs, M. (1980). *Collective memory*. New York, NY: Harper & Collins.

Halbwachs, M. (1992). *On collective memory*, Chicago, IL: Chicago University Press.

Jureit, U. (2005). Generationen als Erinnerungsgemeinschaften. Das "Denkmal für die ermordeten Juden Europas" als Generationsprojekt. In U. Jureit & M. Wildt (eds.), *Generationen. Zur Relevanz eines wissenschaftlichen Grundbegriffs* (pp. 244–265). Hamburg, Germany: Hamburger Edition.

Kansteiner, W. (2002). Finding meaning in memory: A methodological critique of collective memory studies. *History and Theory*, *41*,179–197.

Kohut, T. (2012). *A German generation. An experiential history of the twentieth century*. New Haven, CT: Yale University Press.
Kohut, T. (2013). Psychoanalyse und Geschichtswissenschaft. Theorie, Praxis und Kritik. In U. Lamparter, S. Wiegand-Grefe, & D. Wierling (eds.), *Zeitzeugen des Hamburger Feuersturms 1943 und ihre Familien* (pp. 58–66). Göttingen, Germany: Vandenhoeck & Ruprecht.
Krapoth, H., & Laborde, D. (eds.) (2005). *Erinnerung und Gesellschaft. Mémoire et Société: Hommage à Maurice Halbwachs (1877–1945)*. Wiesbaden, Germany: Verlag für Sozialwissenschaften.
Lamparter, U., Wiegand-Grefe, S., & Wierling, D. (eds.) (2013). *Zeitzeugen des Hamburger Feuersturms 1943 und ihre Familien*. Göttingen, Germany: Vandenhoeck & Ruprecht.
Lehmann, A. (2007). *Reden über Erfahrung. Kulturwissenschaftliche Bewusstseinsanalyse des Erzählens*. Berlin, Germany: Reimer.
Lorenz, M. (2000). *Leibhaftige Vergangenheit: Einführung in die Körpergeschichte*. Tübingen, Germany: Diskord.
Lorenzer, A. (1986). Tiefenhermeneutische Kulturanalyse. In H. D. König, A. Lorenzer, H. Lüdde, S. Naghol, U. Prokop, G. Schmid-Noerr, & A. Eggert (eds.), *Kultur-Analysen: Psychoanalytische Studien zur Kultur* (pp. 11–98). Frankfurt am Main, Germany: Fischer.
Neiger, M., Meyers, O., & Sandberg, E. (eds.) (2011). *On media memory: Collective memory in a new media age*. London, UK: Palgrave.
Niethammer, L. (2005). Frontstellung und Unabschließbarkeit der Gedächtnistheorie von Maurice Halbwachs. In H. Krapoth & D. Laborde (eds.), *Erinnerung und Gesellschaft. Mémoire et Société: Hommage à Maurice Halbwachs (1877–1945)* (pp. 105–123). Wiesbaden, Germany: Verlag für Sozialwissenschaften.
Nora, P. (1989). Between memory and history: Les lieux de mémoire. *Representations, 26, Special Issue: Memory and Counter-Memory*, 7–24.
Radebold, H., Reulecke, J., & Schulz, H. (2007). *Söhne ohne Väter. Erinnerungen der Kriegsgeneration*. Berlin, Germany: Christoph Links.
Raphael, L. (2003). *Geschichtswissenschaft im Zeitalter der Extreme. Theorien, Methoden, Tendenzen von 1900 bis zur Gegenwart*. Munich, Germany: C. H. Beck.
Schütze, F. (1983). Biographieforschung und narratives Interview. *Neue Praxis, 13*, 283–293.
Seegers, L., & Reulecke, J. (eds.) (2009). *Die Generation der Kriegskinder. Historische Hintergründe und Deutungen*. Gießen, Germany: Psychosozial.
van Dijck, J. (2005). *The transparent body: A cultural analysis of medical imaging*. Seattle, WA: University of Washington Press.
Weber, S. (2008). *Benjamin's abilities*. Cambridge, MA: Harvard University Press.
White, H. (1973). *Metahistory: The historical imagination in nineteenth-century Europe*. Baltimore, MD: The Johns Hopkins University Press.
Wierling, D. (1992). Gewendete Biographien? In B. Rauschenbach (ed.), *Erinnern, Wiederholen, Durcharbeiten* (pp. 217–227). Berlin, Germany: Aufbau.
Wierling, D. (1999). Nationalsozialismus und Krieg in den Lebensgeschichten der ersten Nachkriegsgeneration der DDR. In E. Domansky & H. Welzer (eds.), *Eine offene Geschichte. Zur kommunikativen Tradierung der nationalsozialistischen Vergangenheit* (pp. 35–56). Tübingen, Germany: Diskord.

Wierling, D. (2002). *Geboren im Jahr Eins. Der Geburtsjahrgang 1949 in der DDR, Versuch einer Kollektivbiographie*. Berlin, Germany: Links.
Wierling, D. (2004). *Heimat finden. Lebenswege von Deutschen, die aus Russland kommen*. Hamburg, Germany: Körber.
Wierling, D. (2010). Generations as narrative communities. Some private sources of official cultures of remembrance in postwar Germany. In F. Biess & R. Moeller (eds.), *Histories of the aftermath: The legacies of the Second World War in Europe* (pp. 102–120). New York, NY: Berghahn.
Wierling, D. (2013). Das Feuersturmprojekt. Eine interdisziplinäre Erfahrung aus der Perspektive der Geschichtswissenschaft. In U. Lamparter, S. Wiegand-Grefe, & D. Wierling (eds.), *Zeitzeugen des Hamburger Feuersturms 1943 und ihre Familien* (pp. 45–57). Göttingen, Germany: Vandenhoeck & Ruprecht.
Zülsdorf-Kersting, M. (2007). *Sechzig Jahre danach: Jugendliche und Holocaust. Eine Studie zur geschichtskulturellen Sozialisation*. Berlin, Germany: Lit-Verlag.

Part II

Responding to the past

Chapter 3

Experiential history

Understanding backwards

Donna M. Orange

Historians and psychoanalysts, each in their own ways, seek truth and understanding in the past, while we philosophers ask them what it could mean to do this. Already involved in a multidisciplinary task, we find ourselves faced with historical burdens, etymological hints, and psychoanalytic enigmas and intensities interrogating any assumptions we bring to our search for more adequate concepts. This study takes up the idea of experiential history, one crossing disciplinary boundaries, to ask what it may contribute both to understanding the "dark times," as well as to social justice now and ethical response in the future.

Experiential history

Signaling a subtle surprise, announcing an enigmatic shift in approach to the historian's work, even sneaking a philosophical question into our imaginations, Thomas A. Kohut (2012) entitled his masterwork *A German generation: An experiential history of the twentieth century*. Fascinated since childhood with history, but without realizing that this attraction probably led me into psychoanalysis, I had thought we studied history to find facts, to find out what really happened. Seeing Kohut's title, following his narrative and reflections, I remembered that my love of history had included devouring historical fiction, both childhood and adult. Something had led me to wonder what those long-ago people had felt, how they had lived, loved, raged, and died in their own times and places. So the expression "experiential history" intrigued me. Was this a subdiscipline of professional historians unknown to those of us who had not been reading their professional literature? If so, I am so far unable to find them. Apart from a series of British war videos, I find little reference to this expression apart from citations of Kohut's book.

What, we may ask, would be the natural history of this expression in Western thinking, and how is Kohut using it? Taking the second question first, Kohut tells us that the 62 interviews, and the use he makes of them, do not serve as witness to historical events. Rather,

> The interviewees, in all their subjectivity, are the subject of this book … this book is a case study [of the generation that grew up in the Bunds, became mid-level Nazis, and lived to tell their memories]. A particular historical phenomenon is studied historically and in depth not only for its own sake but also with a view to making generalizations that transcend it … An in-depth study of the lives of these sixty-two people, then, enables us to identify and to understand aspects of their experience and response to experience that they shared with generational peers.
>
> (Kohut, 2012, p. 14)

Identifying the case study as a legitimate approach to studying history, to searching for historical truth beyond mere facts, dates, and lists of events or perpetrators, even beyond memorials, trials, and attempts at restorative justice, Kohut borrows from psychoanalysis the narrative, the personal story, the subjective truth, as means to historical understanding. But what is this category called experience that he hopes, like the psychoanalyst he has also been trained to be, to find? And if we can develop a few of its meanings more clearly, then why should it matter to the historian, and, by extension, to all of us? Let us begin with the idea of experience, then return to experiential history.

Experience itself

Experience, as a concept, turns out to have a long story of its own in the Western history of ideas. (Asian and African equivalents are, I am sorry to say, not well known to me.) Recent deconstructionists had good reasons for their rejection of this concept. They objected in particular to claims to absolute authority and concreteness, as in "Experience teaches …" or "That's not my experience." (Jay, 2005). Martin Jay, nevertheless, explores its history, especially in its more pluralistic and fluid forms. Beginning with the word's relationships to several European languages, he notes that its root (*periculum*, danger) in Latin connects experience with peril. Ex-perience suggests something about emergence – perhaps sadder and wiser – from extreme circumstances, about having learned from an escape. The experienced person has lost innocence, perhaps, in French (*experience*), in Italian (*esperienza*), and in English. German, famously, gives us two words for experience: *das Erlebnis*, lived (*das Leben*, life) experience or personally lived event; and *die Erfahrung*, accumulated learning, even practical wisdom.[1] (Book learning, *Bildung*, differing from experience, also gets great reverence.) In *Erfahrung* we hear both *fahren* (to travel) and *Gefahr* (danger), where the word resonates with the peril we hear in the Romance languages. Both danger and travel may remind us of Odysseus. All these linguistic hints lead us to contrast experience with abstract theorizing, but make us hesitate to absolutize or reify.

Instead, as Jay acknowledges, we might take a clue from Ludwig Wittgenstein's language games (Wittgenstein, 2003), asking how the word is used in various contexts, looking for significances lent by the textures (Figal, 2010) of particular discourses. Tempting as it may be to ask whether Wittgenstein would claim that we mistakenly take our pictures for experience, as Augustine took his picture for the origin of linguistic meaning, we must stay on track and just remember his dictum that the meaning of a word is its use in a context. Then we may be able, perhaps, to claim that experience covers a range of meanings, including its many contexts and their resonating relations with each other. To explore these meanings in their full texture would require a very large book, but let us scan just a few, to get some sense of what Kohut may be picking up when he speaks of "experiential history."

Experience in psychoanalysis

First, once again, we have the psychoanalytic case study. Pioneered by Freud and his earliest followers – if only we could say "collaborators" – this approach to theory construction, also beloved by phenomenologists (Atwood, 2012; Merleau-Ponty & Landes, 2012) forms a contrast, even an opposite approach to the hypothesis-testing, rigidly controlled, statistically analyzed scientific research prevalent in the past century, especially in academic psychology. Though Freud used the "*einzige Krankengeschichte*" (single illness history) heavily in the building of his theories, still, well trained in scientific method and logic, he emphasized repeatedly the limitations of this approach. It is, he wrote in introducing the Dora story,

> obvious that a single case history, even if it were complete and open to no doubt, cannot provide an answer to *all* the questions arising out of the problem of hysteria. It cannot give an insight into all the types of this disorder, into all the forms of internal structure of the neurosis, into all the possible kinds of relation between the mental and the somatic which are to be found in hysteria. It is not fair to expect from a single case more than it can offer. And anyone who has hitherto been unwilling to believe that a psychosexual etiology holds good generally and without exception for hysteria is scarcely likely to be convinced of the fact by taking stock of a single case history. He would do better to suspend his judgement until his own work has earned him the right to a conviction.
>
> (Freud, 1953b, p. 12)

Notwithstanding Freud's warning to himself and to his readers, the single case history became the gold standard for psychoanalytic writing. It seemed to offer a window through the analyst's experience and interpretation of the patient into the patient's unconscious motivations for illness manifested in symptoms. As dreams were the "royal road," the *Via Regia*, to the unconscious, the case study became the royal road to experience from which the analyst could build theory. But once again, what was this experience? Freud, since his work with Breuer in the 1890s, and even more since his *Interpretation of Dreams*, written in 1897 and issued in 1900 (Freud, 1953a), had exposed a crack in the western unitary mind, claiming that conscious "experience" showed gaps appearing in dreams, symptoms, slips, and jokes. Reality lay elsewhere, in the dark. The dark realm, full of forbidden wishes, conflicts, and terrors, involved complicated efforts to conceal itself, called defenses. Often these defenses, the denials and evasions of reasonable people, seemed themselves to be experience, until the analyst unmasked them according to the hermeneutics of suspicion (Orange, 2011; Ricoeur, 1970). So experience, at least that of the patient, became a shape-shifting morass, handed over to the authority of the analyst, the expert. He or she could write a case study, theorizing "on the basis of clinical experience," occasionally remembering Freud's warnings.

Not until Ferenczi, in the late 1920s and early 1930s, listening to his patients' protests, began to suspect that clinical experience emerged from at least two psychological worlds did the one-person case study's authority come into question. As Ferenczi[2] came back from oblivion in the 1980s, just when intersubjectivists (Atwood & Stolorow, 1984; Stolorow, Brandchaft, & Atwood, 1987) began to imagine a field-emergent psychological experience and a relational psychoanalysis (Aron, 1996; Benjamin, 1988; Mitchell, 1988), new forms of writing history emerged in psychoanalysis. Once two (or more) people showed up in "experience," experience itself could not claim unambiguous authority. Now these stories, often called "clinical narratives," even occasionally told from two perspectives (Brickman, 2007; Jacobs, 2007) or from the patient's side (Dimen, 2011), illustrate ever more clearly that we have no access to pure experience, phenomenologists like Husserl and the late William James to the contrary, and fact-seekers to the contrary as well.

Analysts, historians, patients, all of us, we read and elaborate our *Erfahrung*, our endangered and accumulated lives, in relational spatiality and *nachträglich*, backwards and forwards temporally. *Nachträglichkeit*, in particular, Freud's own idea originally, has commanded contemporary attention in many psychoanalytic schools, redefining our sense of sedimented and experiential meanings. As we live forward, our experience develops backwards. I read my own history, and that of my worlds, through ever greater acquaintance with familial violence and secrecy, with slavery and colonialism. Likewise, Kohut and his subjects' experiential history develops *nachträglich*.

Without really defining experience, Kohut's book shows that he has deeply digested the lure and the pitfalls of the psychoanalytic case study. Just as Freud and later psychoanalysts have, he wants to learn from others what goes so profoundly awry that one people can deliberately and methodically destroy another people with whom they have lived for centuries as neighbors. Even more, he wants to know how it becomes possible that people who seem ordinary in their family and daily lives and aspirations can participate in a massacre, or do nothing to stop it. So he, like a good psychoanalyst, listens carefully to those who were there and can still speak.

But Kohut has left many assumptions of early psychoanalysis behind. Knowing that his own feelings, his own generation, his own legacy as a son of one who fled, position him non-neutrally, he takes seriously what he brings to the table. "I do not particularly like the interviewees," he tells us (Kohut, 2012, p. 16). He continues as follows:

> Although neither of my parents identified themselves as Jewish, both, according to Nazi racial criteria, would probably have been victims of the Final Solution had they been living in territory controlled by Germany during World War II. Although from a German American family, my mother appears racially to have been a quarter Jewish, on her mother's side. And my father was racially wholly Jewish. Indeed, my father escaped the Holocaust only by fleeing Austria in 1939, and four of his five uncles and aunts, as well as cousins, perished in the genocide. In addition to what the interviewees had been in the past … I found their smugness and sense of superiority annoying.
>
> (Kohut, 2012, p. 16)

Kohut worried that his dislike for them may have limited the empathy needed for understanding, for carrying out the task of experiential history he had set himself. Not only do we trust his account more because of his honesty; we also hear his capacity to formulate questions that others without his positioning might not ask. So perspective not only limits, as it surely does; it also brings to the historian or to the psychoanalyst the opportunity to test hypotheses, knowing they are only hypotheses. Limited perspective, held lightly, fallibilistically, and humbly in a pragmatist spirit (Peirce, 1932, pp. 13–14) can open horizons, as it does for Kohut. If we already know what generalizations we hope to draw from our case study, if we want to validate rather than simply to explore, even if we undertake the study yearning to support our hunches and hypotheses, Kohut's sincere fallibilism can keep us ready to learn something we did not expect. Experience, with its dangers and its unseen future, can still teach us.

Experience in the history of ideas

The word experience, however, has accumulated textural meanings. Here are a few: humanistic, early hermeneutic, anticipating the phenomenological, and pragmatic. To begin at the dawn of modernity, Michel de Montaigne (1958) considered a human life as what Giorgio Agamben (1993, p. 23) called "an achieved totality of experience." Without defining the word, but clearly opposing the emergent scientific rationalism of his day, his essays portray experience as the path to maturity. In Martin Jay's words,

> More like an unruly life than a logical demonstration, [Montaigne's] "Of Experience" meanders digressively, combining anecdotes and *aperçus* with arguments and quotations, reprising themes and coming at them from different angles. Its own temporality, rhythmically uneven and irreducible to a unified narrative, duplicates the unsystematic ruminations on time itself to be found in Montaigne's work as a whole ... [It] performatively instantiates what it substantively argues.
>
> (Jay, 2005, p. 25)

Already, then, experience, embodied and sensual, messy, aesthetic, and unrepeatable, as Hans-Georg Gadamer (1972, 2004) would later claim, forms a source of learning independent of the scientific demand for method and replicability.

Jumping forward to the Romantic period, we find philosopher, theologian, and ethicist Friedrich Schleiermacher, founder of modern hermeneutics. Immanuel Kant (1793, 1998) had insisted that religion depended on moral and practical reason – it was not theoretical but originated in the experience of moral obligation. Schleiermacher, as William James (1902) and Rudolf Otto (Otto, 1958; Otto & Dicker, 1931) would do later, mounted a full-throated defense of religious experience as a primary source of truth. Kant had claimed that experience limited in every realm what reason could reach; Schleiermacher treated religious experience (*Erlebnis*), "the feeling of absolute dependence," (Schleiermacher, 1976) as more than a limit, as that which defines and measures religion and theology. Although this kind of experience may seem distant from the "experiential history" we are trying to examine here, we may note that its claim to authority through direct personal intuition, bypassing the claims of logic and reason (and theology), may also be important. Later phenomenological claims of access to the "things themselves," placing the previous structures of reason under the *epoché*, echo this Romantic-era appeal to the claim of experience.

Schleiermacher's biographer Wilhelm Dilthey (1870), perhaps the first to realize that personal history (or experiential history) shaped theory-building, not only gave us the distinction between the *Naturwissenschaften* (natural sciences) and the *Geisteswissenschaften* (humanities), arguing that the latter provided fully respectable access to truth, and deserved their own place; but also explained the difference between *Erlebnis* (lived experience),[3] the core of his *Lebensphilosophie*, and *Erfahrung*, accumulated, often social, experience that could live only from *Erlebnis*. For Dilthey, *Erlebnis* meant a kind of direct, immediate, description: "this suffering is unbearable," for example;

that contained reference both to the context that holds it and to what transcends it. Although Gadamer would later prefer, after extensive examination, *Erfahrung* as dialogical experience, he incorporated much of the immediacy of Dilthey's beloved *Erlebnis*.

From North America came both the Transcendentalists (Emerson, 2001) and pragmatists, their partial heirs. Emerson had written, two years after his five-year-old son's death, a mournful essay entitled "On Experience":

> I grieve that grief can teach me nothing, nor carry me one step into real nature ... The dearest events are summer-rain, and we the Para coats that shed every drop. Nothing is left us now but death. We look to that with a grim satisfaction, saying, there at least is reality that will not dodge us.
> (Emerson, 2001, p. 200).

For Emerson, experience teaches, or it does not. *What* it teaches, or does not, he also seems to call experience. The problem, he thought, was our incapacity to learn, or, perhaps worse, the likelihood that we would die before making use of what we might learn.

Among the pragmatists, like the transcendentalists well educated in European philosophy and Romantic currents, logician Charles Sanders Peirce contributed something more than the pragmatic definition of meaning:

> Consider what effects, which might conceivably have practical bearings, we conceive the object of our conception to have. Then the whole of our conception of those effects is the whole of our conception of the object.
> (Peirce, 1992, p. 132)

Peirce thus relied on a view of experience as what meaning predicts. Meaning, then, as well as experience, has a cumulative sense, more like *Erfahrung*.

William James, on the contrary, emphasized the variety and plurality of lived experiences, even writing of a pluralistic universe (James, 1977). Resisting the neo-Hegelianism developed in dialogue with the pragmatists by Josiah Royce (1916, 1919), James not only affirmed the value of plurality in religious experience, but also insisted, having learned from cultures beyond the West, that experience itself was variegated and could not be subsumed as the hidden forms of the absolute oneness so dear to idealistic thinkers and monists.

For John Dewey, closer to these Hegelians, experience, both lived and cumulative, formed the ground of all learning (Dewey, 1958, 1963). Nevertheless, schooled by Peirce and James, he had learned to regard experience as an ultimate test, and applied this appeal to experience everywhere, most notably in politics and in educational methods, his greatest area of influence. From Emerson through Dewey, these thinkers took their European intellectual heritage down to earth.

Experience becoming experiential history

From this unforgivably distilled summary, we ask again, what can "experiential history" mean? Clearly, Kohut, born with a mixed intellectual and cultural heritage, writing a history of mid-twentieth-century Europe from a closeness and distance from it, enriched by all the traditions we have sketched and many more, brings an inclusive complexity to his use of "experiential history." Doing history, thinking, feeling, and undergoing history, living as an historian has been his life, as for many others. He knows his work, his craft. My question remains: why "experiential"? Perhaps he wants to exclude, or at least bracket, at least for this project, other ways of doing history.

What would "experiential history" require bracketing, or excluding? First, it means dropping a single-perspective view of truth. It means that more than one story can be told, that these plural stories, as James or Gadamer might have thought, bring us closer to understanding truth, if not Truth, about the narrators themselves, and about the times in which they lived. Kohut's attempt to find out from the Nazis themselves, ordinary Nazis whose names no one knows, what they were thinking and feeling, how they became these people, and how they talked to themselves afterwards about their participation, takes *Erlebnis* (or rather, *die Erlebnisse* in the plural), and transforms them into *Erfahrung*, accumulated or collective experience, something from which we can continue to learn.

Such an emphasis on the plurality of experiences has, since Nietzsche, often been mistaken for a claim that there is no truth independent of what we choose to think about it. Instead, we can read Nietzsche's protest, as well as that of his more thoughtful readers, as a dissent from authoritarian views of religion and morality, which are dependent on one-perspective (God's-eye) notions of truth. To write "experiential history," it seems to me, gives no quarter to the truth deniers, but rather provides a richer, if even more painful, account of history, that challenges us in dangerous moments. Getting closer to those who have committed, or assented to, or supported unspeakable crimes contests our own sense of innocence. It reminds us that experience concerns peril, that *Erfahrung* records the sense that we are morally *gefährdet* (endangered).

Shouted down once again by demagogues who want to eliminate those different from the ruling white male class from among us; unable, out of fear, to welcome the stranger, to shelter the refugee; continuously blind to inherited privilege created by historical crimes of settler colonialism and chattel slavery; and thus paralyzed in the face of scientific demands for radical change in our way of life to cope with climate crisis and to protect the world's most vulnerable people, we are once again endangered as were Europeans, and all of us, in the 1930s. Studying the so-called "facts," in isolation from their experiential history, keeps this knowledge abstract and theoretical, sectioned away from our feelings, passions, and convictions. (I have made this argument more extensively elsewhere (Orange, 2017).)

"Experiential history" might disturb and disrupt us. Following the aging Germans' account of their adolescent experiences (*Erlebnisse*), Kohut writes that "The common experience of these [social and historical] circumstances led them to develop a shared generational consciousness [*Erfahrung*] and a shared sense of past, present, and anticipated future" (Kohut, 2012, pp. 10–11). This "shared sense" came to include an elitist and exclusionary sense of Germanness that permitted them to commit and support crimes against humanity in its service. Experiential history means unraveling the cumulative history, now so repulsively recounted, to see what subjective lived experiences tangled together to create such disaster. What Thomas Kohut has done to create experiential history out of heaps of "facts" challenges us to do likewise, to lay bare the sense of privilege that allows us to demonize or to ignore the other.

Seeing this experiential history, we may ask, how is our own time different? Instead of the Jews, Roma, Sinti, homosexuals, and disabled people destroyed by Kohut's "German generation" in their collective superiority and inability to see these others as human, we have other fragile populations who seem not to merit consideration as individuals of equal dignity and worth to our own. Darker skin color, unfamiliar language, unfamiliar religion, unfamiliar sexuality, all place people in categories and quotas, as dangerous migrants, not as fellow human beings, as sisters and brothers. Am I my other's keeper?

But who are these people? Apart from the high-profile crucifixions, we have the sex-slavery and rapes and bombed-out children and parents and elders. We have young men from Eritrea who make drawings of excruciating procedures of torture which, allegedly, hundreds are suffering and trying to escape. We have whole regions in severe famine from rapid climate change their own areas have not created. We white North Americans and Europeans, believing that the lands where we live belong to us, set ourselves above these millions of refugees, building walls and fences. Our experiential history, accumulated from rags-to-riches Horatio Alger stories, creates a narrative saying that good and worthy people do not suffer in these ways. They make it. Experiential history teaches us, as it taught Germans in the 1930s, to despise the weak and to embrace an ideal of strength and masculinity. Avoiding our own vulnerability, we despise others who mirror it back to us. Empathy, as Kohut's book painfully teaches, then extends only to people just like us.

Could experiential history have a different outcome? Can the inherited past avoid the curse of repetition? The lived experiences constituting it would need to include, perhaps, something like what Donald Winnicott (1965) called the capacity for concern. This early developmental relational achievement would then also require an environment that regarded all people as valuable, and questioned all forms of bias. Building on children's common obsession with fairness, it could prepare a person to question any preferential treatment, especially that from which the subject profits. In the school years, both teaching about civic courage and modeling inclusiveness could continue to develop these possibilities, even in the face of historical burdens from slavery and discrimination. Teachers could tell stories of the French town of Chambon, or of the underground railroad, to let children know that an ethical response to suffering and injustice is actually possible. To those who say this kind of education already exists, I say yes, but it is exceptional. It will require tremendous communal determination, together with relentless self-questioning, to generate a different experiential history.

And yet, truly formidable obstacles stand in the way. Just as injustice thrives on elitism and demagoguery, that is, on the appeal to the desire to belong and to identify with the rich, famous, and powerful, so does an effective turn toward justice require a critical mass. The kind of ethical education described above would need to spread, and to be enriched by the study of what Kohut, toward the end of his book (Kohut, 2012, pp. 237ff), calls "historical experience," the fruit of experiential history. We share our human nature, he writes, with the Nazi generation who carried out and enabled the massacre. We have the same need for group belonging, for exclusiveness, the same capacity to dehumanize those different from us. "We should not count on cultural context to distance us from the Nazis. What separates us from them who carried out the worst horror in modern European history is nothing intrinsic to them or us. What separates us from them is 'the grace' of historical experience" (Kohut, 2012, pp. 240–241). In other words, if we learn from historical experience, we need not repeat it.

What Kohut calls the "authority" of historical experience means that we cannot escape our history. Whether we are twentieth-century Germans or twenty-first-century whites of European descent, our experiential history determines our possibilities for future undergoing and making of history. We can continue down the current path of racism, indifference, and climate destruction. Or we can draw on the best of our heritage and values to embrace the other of every color, religion, and language, while healing our devastated earth. Which of those possibilities we take up depends, it seems, on whether we study, mourn, and begin to atone for the history into which we are born, so that we can reject the automatic repetition of dehumanizing, and embrace an inclusive humanity.

Notes

1 Aristotle, though in the end he claimed for theoria, the fruit of contemplation, the rank of highest knowing, also wrote that "the unproved assertions and opinions of experienced, old and sagacious people deserve as much attention as those they support by proofs, for they grasp principles through experience" *Ethics*, 1143b, 10–15.

2 Ferenczi, too, at first questioned the ethics of "using" patients to advance psychoanalytic science (Ferenczi & Dupont, 1988).

3 Although many similar terms show up in Schleiermacher's texts, *Erlebnis* itself did not commonly appear, according to Gadamer (2004), until Dilthey's biography of Schleiermacher.

References

Agamben, G. (1993). *Infancy and history: The destruction of experience*. London, UK: Verso.

Aron, L. (1996). *A meeting of minds: Mutuality in psychoanalysis*. Hillsdale, NJ: Analytic Press.

Atwood, G. E. (2012). *The abyss of madness*. New York, NY: Routledge.

Atwood, G. E., & Stolorow, R. D. (1984). *Structures of subjectivity: Explorations in psychoanalytic phenomenology*. Hillsdale, NJ: Analytic Press.

Benjamin, J. (1988). *The bonds of love: Psychoanalysis, feminism, and the problem of domination*. New York, NY: Pantheon Books.

Brickman, B. (2007). Analytic transformation of tragic trauma and loss: The recovery of an analysis following the analyst's life-threatening head injury. *International Journal of Psychoanalytic Self Psychology*, *2*, 383–404.

Dewey, J. (1958). *Experience and nature*. New York, NY: Dover Publications.

Dewey, J. (1963). *Experience and education*. New York, NY: Collier Books.

Dilthey, W. (1870). *Leben Schleiermachers*. Berlin, Germany: G. Reimer.

Dimen, M. (2011). Lapsus linguae, or a slip of the tongue?: A sexual violation in an analytic treatment and its personal and theoretical aftermath. *Contemporary Psychoanalysis*, *47*, 35–79.

Emerson, R. W. (2001). *Emerson's prose and poetry: Authoritative texts, contexts, criticism*. In J. Porte & S. Morris (eds). New York, NY: W. W. Norton.

Ferenczi, S., & Dupont, J. (1988). *The clinical diary of Sándor Ferenczi*. Cambridge, MA: Harvard University Press.

Figal, G. (2010). *Objectivity: The hermeneutical and philosophy*. Trans. T. D. George. Albany, NY: State University of New York Press.

Freud, S. (1953a). *The interpretation of dreams. The standard edition of the complete psychological works of Sigmund Freud, volume IV (1900)*. London, UK: Hogarth Press.

Freud, S. (1953b). *A case of hysteria, three essays on sexuality and other works. The standard edition of the complete psychological works of Sigmund Freud, volume VII (1901–1905)*. London, UK: Hogarth Press.

Gadamer, H.-G. (1972). *Wahrheit und Methode. Grundzüge einer philosophischen Hermeneutik* (3rd, rev. edn.). Tübingen, Germany: Mohr.

Gadamer, H.-G. (2004). *Truth and method* (2nd, rev. edn.). Trans. J. Winsheimer and D. G. Marshall. New York, NY: Continuum.

Jacobs, L. (2007). From the couch: Trauma and recovery after analytic impingement. *International Journal of Psychoanalytic Self Psychology*, *2*, 405–422.

James, W. (1902). *The varieties of religious experience; A study in human nature*. New York, NW: Longmans, Green, and Co.

James, W. (1977). *A pluralistic universe*. Cambridge, MA: Harvard University Press.

Jay, M. (2005). *Songs of experience: Modern American and European variations on a universal theme*. Berkeley, CA: University of California Press.

Kant, I. (1793). *Die Religion innerhalb der Grenzen der bloßen Vernunft*. Königsberg, Prussia: Nicolovius.

Kant, I. (1998). *Religion within the boundaries of mere reason and other writings*. Trans. A. W. Wood & G. Di Giovanni. Cambridge, UK: Cambridge University Press.

Kohut, T. A. (2012). *A German generation: An experiential history of the twentieth century*. New Haven, CT: Yale University Press.

Merleau-Ponty, M., & Landes, D. A. (2012). *Phenomenology of perception*. Abingdon, UK: Routledge.
Mitchell, S. A. (1988). *Relational concepts in psychoanalysis: An integration*. Cambridge, MA: Harvard University Press.
Montaigne, M. de (1958). *Complete essays*. Stanford, CA: Stanford University Press.
Orange, D. M. (2011). *The suffering stranger: Hermeneutics for everyday clinical practice*. New York, NY: Routledge.
Orange, D. M. (2017). *Climate crisis, psychoanalysis, and radical ethics*. London, UK: Routledge.
Otto, R. (1958). *The idea of the holy; An inquiry into the non-rational factor in the idea of the divine and its relation to the rational*. New York, NY: Oxford University Press.
Otto, R., & Dicker, E. B. (1931). *The philosophy of religion, based on Kant and Fries*. London, UK: Williams & Norgate Ltd.
Peirce, C. P. (1932). A fragment. In C. Hartshorne & P. Weiss (eds.), *Collected papers of Charles Saunders Peirce* (Vol. 1). Cambridge, MA: Belknap.
Peirce, C. P. (1992). *The essential Peirce* (Vol. 1). Bloomington, IN: Indiana University Press.
Ricoeur, P. (1970). *Freud and Philosophy: An essay in interpretation*. New Haven, CT: Yale University Press.
Royce, J. (1916). *The hope of the great community*. New York, NY: Macmillan.
Royce, J. (1919). *Lectures on modern idealism*. New Haven, CT: Yale University Press.
Schleiermacher, F. (1976). *The Christian faith*. Philadelphia, PA: Fortress Press.
Stolorow, R. D., Brandchaft, B., & Atwood, G. E. (1987). *Psychoanalytic treatment: An intersubjective approach*. Hillsdale, NJ: Analytic Press.
Winnicott, D. W. (1965). *The maturational processes and the facilitating environment*. London, UK: Hogarth Press.
Wittgenstein, L. (2003). *Philosophical investigations: The German text, with a revised English translation by G. E. M. Anscombe* (3rd edn.). Malden, MA: Blackwell.

Chapter 4

"Unprecedented"

Concepts and narratives about mass violence and the Holocaust

Alexandra Garbarini

The unprecedented, the unimaginable, the unspeakable, the indescribable: these words – each on its own and all of them taken together – express rupture, catastrophe, and *ex nihilo*. As anyone familiar with writing about the Holocaust knows, they are central words and concepts in Holocaust representations. Among historians, literary scholars, and theorists, these words tend to be used interchangeably, practically as synonyms (Tresize, 2001, pp. 39–40; Jurgenson, 2009, p. 9). On the one hand, the "unprecedented" is but part of this list, is yet another way of articulating the inarticulable, of signaling: here, there is an excess – of violence, of suffering, of helplessness, of loss – that exceeds the limits of representation (Friedlander, 1992, pp. 1–6). Such vocabulary is a means of expressing trauma, of the extent to which trauma defined individuals' experiences and the collective Jewish experience. Furthermore, it carries a moral/ethical injunction inside an aesthetic/literary claim, as scholars have repeatedly pointed out in their discussions of Theodor Adorno's proscription against writing poetry after Auschwitz or Jean-François Lyotard's comparison of the Holocaust to an earthquake that destroys all instruments of measurement. Literary critic Michael André Bernstein (1998, p. 6) once described this sense of rupture with its epistemological and ethical significance as a "received idea" of our epoch. The Holocaust is unimaginable and unspeakable, and yet it is the event most in need of being imagined and spoken about.

On the other hand, the "unprecedented" as a concept does not blend with these other signifiers of rupture as seamlessly as might first appear. For while the unprecedented signifies a rupture, it is categorically distinct from the rest of the terms that mark out the limits of representation insofar as it makes a *historical* claim, a chronologically specific claim. The unprecedented is that which has no precedent; it is, to quote the *Oxford English Dictionary* (2014), "unparalleled; never previously done, known, or experienced." We might consider Yehuda Bauer's argument in *Rewriting the Holocaust* (Bauer, 2001, pp. 14–20, 53) about the unprecedentedness of the Holocaust to appreciate how, among other signifiers of rupture, the "unprecedented" interpolates a distinct element. Bauer is interested in shifting the terms of the debate about the Holocaust's uniqueness or comparability to other genocides. Characterizing the Holocaust as "unprecedented" is, for Bauer, a way of insisting on its explicability and even repeatability, and thus of recasting the Holocaust in historical terms. Thus, with the notion of the Holocaust as "unprecedented," Bauer endeavors to move away from prior characterizations of the Holocaust as a "unique" historical event, which effectively set it outside human history, outside the realm of what could be explained and understood, and thus also outside comparative analytical frameworks. Ultimately, Bauer may not have succeeded in shifting the terms of the uniqueness debate, if that was actually his intention. Nevertheless, his setting the concept of "unprecedented" apart from other notions of unrepresentability is helpful for our purposes. In Bauer we see how the "unprecedented" has been invoked to reflect not only on how the Holocaust has appeared in our cultural imagination but also on the event itself, on the elements that comprised the event itself. It pushes toward the recognition of the potential specificity of that concept.

Within the rhetoric of catastrophe, differences can and ought to be parsed among the terms that we repeatedly invoke. Parsing the differences need not return us to the still-electric scholarly conversations and debates about whether and how the Holocaust relates to other genocides in history, but opens up an analysis of the history of the concepts themselves.[1] This, then, is an exploratory piece that attempts just such an analysis. I develop here a line of inquiry about the centrality of rupture in understandings of the Holocaust and in particular about the concept of the "unprecedented."

The "unprecedented" as historical concept

Significantly, rupture and the "unprecedented" were as important to contemporaries' efforts to make sense of what was happening at the time the Holocaust was occurring as they have been to scholarly conversations about the Holocaust decades later. In other words, such concepts recur in texts produced both contemporaneously and retrospectively. Contemporaries to the Holocaust, including victims and victims' advocates, described the destruction of European Jewish life as an "unprecedented" occurrence. (They also resorted to the tropes of the "unimaginable" and "indescribable" in their writing about mass violence, but I will restrict myself here to an analysis of the "unprecedented.") How did it come to be that the Third Reich's persecution and mass murder of Jews was *perceived* to be "unprecedented"? In what ways were Europeans, in general, and European Jews, in particular, drawing upon and redeploying concepts and tropes about mass violence that were already circulating? That is to say, can we approach the "unprecedented" as a concept with its own history? As Alon Confino has provocatively suggested, historians' emphasis on rupture may "reflect too closely the expressed beliefs of contemporaries about rupture" (Confino, 2012, p. 80). Confino proposes instead that "[i]magining during the war what happened to the Jews as unprecedented was a cultural artifact and, as such, for the historian, a vehicle to make sense of how people made sense of the events around them" (Confino, 2012, p. 63). Even more recently, literary scholar Alan Rosen (2014) has pointed toward the potentially unintended consequences of such rhetoric and categories of thought, where "the value placed on 'rupture' over that of 'continuity'" has meant that "the more the events or episodes of the Holocaust are viewed as having created a rupture with the past, the greater their significance." One result has been the comparative neglect of topics that "point to continuity with previous life" (Rosen, 2014, p. 44). I argue here that, paradoxically, the very concept of "rupture" and specifically of the "unprecedented" opens an avenue of exploration in the direction of continuities.

Individuals in many contexts, of course, grapple with the search for words to describe and account for experiences that resist straightforward articulation (see, e.g., Brison, 2002). This difficulty of language and narration particularly pertains to trauma, but can relate to the whole range of human emotions, positive as well as negative. Drawing on the insights of psychological theory, scholars have previously analyzed how, for example, Jewish diarists wrote during the Holocaust about the unprecedented and unrepresentable nature of their experiences, and how diarists' consciousness of the exceptional nature of their experiences was an outgrowth of their trauma (Garbarini, 2006, pp. 129–161; Goldberg, 2017). One aspect of the difficulty diarists and other writers encountered in trying to write about their experiences related to the fact that the extent of the physical violence and emotional anguish could not be put into words. Another aspect of their difficulty stemmed from the sense of distance they felt from their imagined interlocutors. And finally scholars have analyzed how Jewish diarists' difficulty was the result of their trauma, which rendered the self incoherent, disconnecting them from a sense of being located in a present that was connected to the past and a future (Clendinnen, 1999, p. 31). It is most certainly true that the discourse about the unprecedented relates to trauma and to what eluded meaning. The very effort to write about their experiences could at times prove therapeutic or at other times provoke a deeper consciousness among Jewish diarists of the impossibility of articulating their experiences and assigning meaning to them.

Beyond trauma, however, the discourse of rupture and specifically of the "unprecedented" signifies more than an expression of individuals' feelings of extreme, unspeakable suffering. The concept of the "unprecedented" was more than a way for people to characterize their not being able to make sense, on a personal level, of their own or others' exposure to mass violence. This discourse was also an outgrowth of social processes, even social consensus. Knowledge and understanding are constituted socially; they are mediated through the intersection and interaction of individuals with various social groupings, institutions, and networks of communication (Rothberg, 2009,

p. 15). Here we turn to the work of Thomas Kohut, which proves deeply significant for thinking through the connections between the individual and collective, between psychology and history. As Kohut reminds us, "Without social affirmation, perception remains ungrounded, uncertified, and ultimately without meaning. Knowledge held in common is a condition of community, and a community conditions what its members know" (Kohut, 2012, pp. 140–141). In his discussion of "German knowledge of the 'Final Solution' before 1945," Kohut's analysis of what ordinary Germans saw and did not see, what they knew and did not know about the Final Solution, opens a crucial framework for analyzing what people said and felt they could not say about the fate of Jews during the war. Kohut sets aside the question *if* Germans knew or *what* Germans knew in order to shift the terms of the historiographical discussion from "knowledge" to "knowing," to explore "knowing" as a psychological process of cognition that is simultaneously individual and social, as well as being historically distinct in different times and places. As he puts it, "Obviously, determining what it means to 'know' is crucial in attempting to answer the question: What did the Germans know about the Holocaust before 1945?" (Kohut, 2012, p. 165). The process of gaining knowledge, he demonstrates, was as much a subjective as an objective process, and he shows how it was possible for a person simultaneously "to know" and "not to know" about the Final Solution, "[r]ecognizing that knowing takes place on many levels, from the completely conscious to the deeply unconscious, and that one can simultaneously not know and know something" (Kohut, 2012, p. 166). Furthermore, he analyzes the different ways in which the splitting of consciousness occurred and that it did not work the same way for every person.[2] He concludes that "knowing" was inextricably tied to empathy. "Not knowing" was a related process to not seeing, to looking away from that which "one does not wish to see" (Kohut, 2012, p. 166).

Kohut's analysis linking perception, knowledge, and empathy is crucial here. It makes sense of the function and meaning of the discourse of rupture and the "unprecedented" to which people had recourse who were writing about mass violence in the era of the two world wars – not exclusively about the Holocaust – and who sought to reach a wide readership. Deploying and redeploying the concept of the "unprecedented" appears to have worked on many levels of consciousness. On the one hand, to assert that an event was "unprecedented" in conjunction with the "unimaginable" worked as a means of articulating the incomprehensibility and unknowability of such experiences of mass violence, thereby forestalling the work of empathy. Another reading is possible, however, on the basis of Kohut's work. The characterization of mass violence in terms of the "unprecedented" signified political action. It reflected that these writers were modern individuals who were endeavoring to construct legible historical narratives and thereby to constitute the victims of mass violence as active political subjects. They sought to connect the present episode of mass violence to the past and future. Significantly, the past to which these narratives connected the calamitous present was the past of particular people (Jews, Armenians), whereas the present, with its "unprecedented" violence, and the future, which would emerge out of the carnage, were portrayed in broader terms, in terms of human history. Such a historical emplotment of current events implied that people in the outside world ought to take an interest in and grasp the scope and implications of the violence then under way. It was a means of calling out for engagement and empathy on the part of readers. Out of empathy, it was hoped, would follow recognition of victims' suffering and political subjecthood, as well as humanitarian relief for survivors. Drawing upon the concept of the "unprecedented" was a way of trying to expand what fit into accepted frameworks and norms, and even to alter those frameworks and norms in important ways.[3]

In this essay are assembled a handful of examples drawn from a larger pool of evidence, including published pamphlets, document volumes, and articles from a wide array of European and American newspapers, that allow us to trace how this conceptual vocabulary was employed and what it signified politically in the era from the First World War to the Second World War. In the early texts – which are exemplary but hardly exceptional – we find victim advocates emphasizing rupture and disbelief in the narratives they constructed about two prolonged episodes of mass violence from the First World War era: the deportations and mass murder of Armenians in the Ottoman Empire carried out during the First World War and the pogroms committed against Jews in Ukraine during the Russian Civil War. In particular, the authors of these texts made use of the trope of the "unprecedented" to convey the extent of the violence and the meaning of the violence then occurring. In the early 1940s we find in writings about the Nazi extermination of European Jews the redeployment of the discourse of the "unprecedented." The similarities are striking. We discover a degree of consistency, even consensus, in contemporaries' strategies for generating attention and knowledge about the plight of victims of mass violence in the hope that comprehension would lead to empathy and political engagement.

"A calamity that has no parallel in world history"

Two of the most prominent champions of the Armenians' plight during the First World War were James Bryce, a respected British Liberal politician and member of the House of Lords, former Ambassador to the United States, Oxford professor and author of numerous scholarly works on history, government, and jurisprudence, and Arnold Toynbee, then a freshly minted Oxford historian of ancient history who had taken a position after the start of the war in the British Foreign Office (Tusan, 2014, p. 66). In 1915, Toynbee published *Armenian Atrocities: The Murder of a Nation*, a hundred-page account of the massacres, deportations, and death toll as of that time of the Ottoman Armenians (Toynbee, 1915). *Armenian Atrocities* also included a lengthy preface by Bryce consisting of a revision and expansion of the speech he had delivered to the House of Lords on October 6, 1915. Toynbee referred to this volume as a "statement," a word choice suggesting that he had attempted to write not a work of history but rather a piece that was advancing a certain position, and explicitly so, in the hope of reaching a wide readership and inspiring political action. Toynbee's *Armenian Atrocities* preceded by a year the publication of Bryce and Toynbee's important and well-known document volume, *The Treatment of Armenians in the Ottoman Empire*, originally commissioned by the British government as a Parliamentary Blue Book.

In *Armenian Atrocities*, both Bryce and Toynbee framed the ensuing mass murder of Armenians as an unprecedented event in modern history. Bryce emphasized, in his overview of the round-ups, killings, and death marches of Armenians, the "exceedingly systematic" nature of the entire process. No Armenian was supposed to survive. He concluded, "It would seem that three-fourths or four-fifths of the whole nation has been wiped out, and there is no case in history, certainly not since the time of Tamerlane, in which any crime so hideous and upon so large a scale has been recorded" (in Toynbee, 1915, p. 11) Comparing the Young Turk regime's policies with those of its predecessor, the Sultan Abdul Hamid, Bryce insisted that while the intention might have been the same, nonetheless these two policies were not to be equated: "the policy of extermination has been carried out with far more thoroughness and with far more bloodthirsty completeness" (in Toynbee, 1915, p. 13). Toynbee elaborated on the points made by Bryce in his "statement" that followed Bryce's preface, and then at greater length in the historical summary he included in the document volume they published jointly in 1916 (Bryce & Toynbee, 1916). The latter volume reached a large readership, if the number of references to it in contemporary publications is sufficient evidence. Toynbee emphasized that the extermination was meant to be complete: "The scheme was nothing less than the extermination of the whole Christian population within the Ottoman frontiers" (Toynbee, 1915, p. 27). He emphasized that it was carried out in a systematic fashion: "The crime was concerted very systematically, for there is evidence of identical procedure from over fifty places. [...] a monotonous tale of horror, for the uniform directions from Constantinople were carried out with remarkable exactitude by the local authorities" (Toynbee, 1915, p. 28). Toynbee set out that while there were precedents upon which the Young Turks had drawn – including previous massacres of Armenians carried out in the mid-1890s and again in 1909, which combined were responsible for the deaths of more than 300,000 people – those precedents had been surpassed, even superseded. Indeed, drawing on the language of "problems" and "solutions" and indicating the euphemistic quality of such language by means of the careful insertion of quotation marks to set off those words, Toynbee insisted the Young Turks had "insured themselves against any measures of relief that might at the eleventh hour have deprived their 'Armenian problem' of its complete 'solution'" (Toynbee, 1915, p. 65).

The concept of the "unprecedented" was repeatedly deployed in public statements, journalistic accounts, and academic treatments of the extermination of Armenians. The Swiss humanitarian organization Comité central suisse de secours aux Arméniens (Swiss Central Relief Committee for Armenians) issued an appeal in May 1916 for contributions to support their relief efforts that was printed in Swiss newspapers. The appeal set out the significance of the catastrophe befalling Armenians in the following terms: "Months have passed since the Armenians in Turkey were struck by a calamity that has no parallel in world history [*une calamité qui n'a pas de pareille dans l'histoire du monde*]: the cold-blooded massacring of all able-bodied men, followed by, for the rest of the population in its entirety, a deportation on a route of several hundred kilometers accompanied by the most barbarous treatments. [...] If in a short time there is no change, those who remain in the south of Turkey will be annihilated" (*Comité central suisse de secours aux Arméniens*, 1916, n.p.; my translation). The preeminent French war correspondent Henry Barby published a multi-part series about the calamity targeting Armenians which appeared over several months in 1916 in the French daily *Le Journal*; he then republished the series in redacted form in 1917 as the book *Au pays de l'épouvante. L'Arménie martyre* (*In the Country of Terror. Martyred Armenia*), with a preface by the French president of the Chamber of Deputies, Paul Deschanel. Barby characterized the Armenians' situation as "the extermination of an entire race," and set it apart from the previous massacres to which they had been subjected by the Young Turks' predecessor, who had "ordered their extermination *en masse*" (Barby, 1917, pp. 3–4). The Armenians' current plight was, Barby insisted, "a martyrdom without precedent [*sans exemple*]" (Barby, 1917, p. 11). Barby's articles and book were cited and quoted in other newspapers and also in speeches at public gatherings to raise awareness and sympathy for the plight of the Armenians.

"Dante's Inferno pales ..."

In public statements that drew on the same conceptual and rhetorical wellspring as had writing about the Armenians, Jewish and non-Jewish groups condemned the violence and attempted to elicit sympathy and support for Ukrainian Jewish communities which, during the Russian Civil War, had become the targets of the various warring parties (Budnitskii, 2011; Ashtakevich, 2013). To cite but one example, the "Memorandum on the Extermination of the Jews of Ukraine" was presented by the Committee of Jewish Delegations (Comité des Délégations Juives) to the first assembly of the League of Nations in Geneva in 1920 (cited in French in Gliksberg, 2004, pp. 66–68; reprinted in English in Engel, 2016, pp. 136–140). Its authors called for "civilized peoples to make their voices heard" in condemning the violence. The memorandum insisted that "The terrible suffering that the entire population of this country [i.e., Ukraine] is enduring due to famine and epidemics cannot be compared to the inferno in which Ukrainian Jews have been submerged for the last year and a half. It has no parallel in history. [*Les terribles souffrances que toute la population de ce pays endure du fait de la famine et des épidémies ne peuvent se comparer à l'enfer dans lequel les juifs ukrainiens sont plongés depuis un an et demi. L'histoire n'en a jamais connue de pareil.*]" And, linking the unprecedented with the unrepresentable, the plea continues as follows: "[Even] the greatest poet would lack the imagination to depict the horror. Dante's Inferno pales next to the realities of daily life in Ukraine. [*L'imagination de plus grand poète ne saurait en dépeindre l'horreur. L'enfer de Dante pâlit à côté des réalités de la vie quotidienne en Ukraine.*]" In response to such a historically significant event, "to remain silent at the present time is tantamount to becoming complicit in these killings" (my translations of French version, cited in Gliksberg, 2004, pp. 66–68). Decades before Primo Levi would write "The Canto of Ulysses" about his urgent attempt to recall and recite Dante to a fellow inmate as they retrieved that day's soup ration in Auschwitz, the East European Jews clamoring for recognition of Ukrainian Jews' plight found in Dante the cultural referent they hoped would awaken European statesmen's consciences (Levi, 1993, pp. 109–115).

Dante and his efforts to represent hell were repeatedly invoked in representations of mass violence in the First World War era. Perhaps the most popular twentieth-century Armenian poet, Yeghishe Charentz, titled his long poetic treatment of the annihilation of the Armenian people, which he published in Tbilisi (then known as Tiflis) in 1916, "Dantean Legend" (Charentz, 2008, p. 5). Other Armenian survivors, in their writing about their experiences under the Young Turk regime during the First World War, made reference to Dante's representation of hell while also seeing Dante's Inferno as having been superseded by recent events. The Armenian survivor Aram Andonian, one of the few survivors of the deportation of April 24, 1915, which targeted key figures from the Constantinople Armenian political and cultural elite, wrote, in a volume he published in 1921, "Three years later, when I recollect those days of terror, it seems to me that I fall back into the inferno – not that inferno whose horrors religious writers have competed to render more and more terrifying and which Dante intoned, but something infinitely more horrific, whose horrors will never be able to be comprehended except by those who saw them at first hand, who will never be able to describe them because human language is incapable of doing so. [*Trois ans après quand je pense à ces jours de terreur, il me semble que je retombe en enfer, non point cet enfer dont les écrivains religieux cherchèrent à qui mieux mieux à rendre plus effrayantes les horreurs et que chanta Dante, mais quelque chose d'infiniment plus horrible, dont les épouvantes ne seront jamais comprises que par ceux qui l'ont vu, lesquels ne sauront jamais le décrire, car la langue humaine est incapable de le faire.*]" (Andonian, 1921, p. 61; my translation). The boldness of Dante's imaginative portrayal of hell captured something for these writers and became a touchstone for them. They, like Dante, were seeking to represent the unrepresentable, even though his depiction of hell did not do justice to the experiences they were describing. Nevertheless, their references to Dante testify to their active and self-conscious struggles with the problem of representation.

The "unprecedented" redeployed

Armenians' political claims remained unrecognized and unfulfilled, yet the memory of the extermination of Armenians did not fade, as the work of Wolf Gruner (2012) and Stefan Ihrig (2014, 2016) demonstrates for the German context in the 1920s and 1930s. Gruner's and Ihrig's work on Germany can be extended to show that ongoing awareness of what Armenians had suffered continued to touch other Europeans and Americans. This runs counter to the conventional wisdom that the Armenians were "quickly forgotten when the war was over" (Becker, 2008, p. 71). That these earlier episodes of mass violence were remembered in some form is also captured in contemporaries' articulations of rupture about the Nazis' mass murder of the Jews. Paradoxically, in such articulations of rupture, Jews and non-Jews drew a connection between what was then unfolding and the acts of mass violence from that previous era. To cite just one example, we find the redeployment of previous concepts and tropes in the *Black Book of Polish Jewry*, which was produced by the American Federation of Polish Jews in New York in 1943.

> The *Black Book of Polish Jewry* is the first full account of the tragedy of the Jews of Poland – a tragedy unique in its horror and scope. The pages of this book constitute a powerful accusation against the German nation. This book is an indictment thrown on the bench of the Court which will one day sit in judgment over the crimes committed by a nation of 80,000,000 people. This book asks in a loud voice for the punishment of the culprits and for satisfaction from the United States. [...] Here is Dante's Inferno, a nightmare of suffering and desperation; pain frozen on the faces of mothers and innocent children. The blood of these martyrs demands retaliation for the crimes committed by a nation which, by the will of Adolf Hitler, is the instrument of suffering and torture and death for millions of helpless victims. [...] If after this war, notwithstanding our unprecedented sacrifices and losses, our rights as citizens and our right to a national life are not realized and guaranteed, it will mean that still another crime has been committed against the Jewish people. May this *Black Book of Polish Jewry* serve to awaken the hearts and conscience of the nations of the world.
>
> (Apenszlak *et al.*, 1943, pp. xiii–xvi)

Reading this passage in light of the earlier passages about the plight of Armenians and Ukrainian Jews, it is hard not to be struck by the echoes it intones. Without a doubt, the editors of the *Black Book of Polish Jewry* were seeking to impress on their readers that Polish Jewry's tragedy was "unique" and "unprecedented." Such an appraisal of the meaning of the ensuing extermination of Polish Jewry, however, built upon what was considered socially normative, socially necessary even, by the editors and their readers. What was "sayable" was thus tied to what was knowable. For justice to be served, "the nations of the world" had to be convinced not to avert their gaze. To inspire others to see, to know, and to feel empathy: such was the hope of the editors.

In one final example, we have the opportunity to reflect not only on the importance of the discourse of rupture for rendering experiences of mass violence legible, but also ironically on the epistemological chasm produced by the absence of such descriptors. The French political prisoner Robert Antelme reflected on the power of the word "unimaginable" in the memoir *L'èspece humaine* he wrote in 1946–1947 about his ten months in German concentration camps. He evokes a series of conversations gone amiss between the newly liberated men in Dachau and the American soldiers who became their guards after liberation. "The guys," as Antelme refers to the former concentration camp inmates, rapidly come to realize that the stories about their experiences that they want to share with the soldiers can't be shared, are "untransmittable knowledge." The soldiers cannot understand "the guys'" experiences and as a result stop listening. However, Antelme remarks, the deployment of one single word could overcome that divide and forge a link between "the guys" and the soldiers: that word was "unimaginable." "*Unimaginable* [Antelme's emphasis]: a word that doesn't divide, doesn't restrict. The most convenient word. When you walk around with this word as your shield, this word for emptiness, your step becomes better assured, more resolute, your conscience pulls itself together" (Antelme, 1998, pp. 289–290). Thus, one way to reinsert experiences of mass killing and destruction into prevailing meaning-making systems was to insist on their being "unimaginable" and "unprecedented." Even if part of the way in which that semantic system worked was by not representing the event in its wholeness, it still made possible the attribution of meaning to the event in and through the use of these terms.

Conclusion

This passage of Antelme and those of the other writers attest to the problems that victims of mass violence and their advocates faced during the years of the Holocaust and its aftermath. The extermination of European Jews was unprecedented, but the use of that term to characterize what we would today call genocide was not. Indeed, witnesses to mass violence against Jews during the Second World War redeployed the familiar trope of the "unprecedented" to make sense of and communicate experiences that words seemed inadequate to capture and convey. The word "unimaginable," a related though conceptually distinct trope, also possessed this potential power and efficacy. The existence of such concepts suggests that the "unrepresentable" was actually a way of representing trauma, though the tension between representation and the unrepresentable was not therein resolved but maintained. Paradoxically, then, characterizing European Jews' extreme experiences of suffering as an "unprecedented" event in history was a way of connecting the present crisis to humanitarian crises in the past. Such characterizations reveal the existence of a social consensus about what language was appropriate to use and the way that language use changed over time.

In articulations of rupture we find a surprising opportunity to respond to the challenge to pay attention to continuities with life before the Holocaust. The long history of the concepts and tropes describing extermination and the capabilities of human beings to commit mass violence against other human beings is crucial to our rethinking what knowledge, ignorance, the believable, and the conceivable meant during the years of the Holocaust and in its aftermath.

Notes

1 At the International Network of Genocide Scholars (INoGS) conference in Jerusalem, Israel, in June 2016, the Holocaust's comparability or singularity vis-à-vis other genocides remained a pronounced and emotionally charged topic of discussion. The heated exchange provoked by Israel Charny made the news in Israel; see Ahren (2016).

2 Kohut (2012) differentiates between those interviewees who underwent a "vertical split of consciousness," in which "knowledge of the Final Solution before the end of the war was conscious but set off from the main sector of awareness, which remained blissfully ignorant," and those interviewees who developed a "horizontal split of consciousness," in which "those who knew enough to have known absolutely [...] discerned but then immediately repressed [knowledge of the Final Solution]" (Kohut, 2012, p. 140).

3 By contrast, it appears that the notion of the "unimaginable" constituted an encounter of the writer with accepted frameworks and norms, and the reinscribing of those social norms and taboos. On the issue of "unrepresentability" and how it relates to challenging or reinforcing social norms, see Dorota Glowacka (2018).

References

Ahren, R. (2016). Academics go to war over the study of mass killings. *Times of Israel*, June 26.

Andonian, A. (1921). *Documents officiels concernant les massacres arméniens*. Trans. M. S. David-Beg. Paris, France: H. Turabian.

Antelme, R. (1998). *The human race*. Trans. J. Haight & A. Mahler. Evanston, IL: The Marlboro Press/Northwestern University Press.

Apenszlak, J., Kenner, J., Lewin, I., Lewkin, I., & Polakiewicz, M. (eds.) (1943). *The black book of Polish Jewry: An account of the martyrdom of Polish Jewry under the Nazi occupation*. New York, NY: American Federation for Polish Jews.

Ashtakevich, I. (2013). *The pogroms in Ukraine in 1917–1920: An alternate universe* (doctoral dissertation). Brandeis University, Waltham, MA.

Barby, H. (1917). *Au pays de l'épouvante. L'Arménie martyre*. Paris, France: Albin Michel.

Bauer, Y. (2001). *Rethinking the Holocaust*. New Haven, CT: Yale University Press.

Becker, A. (2008). Suppressed memory of atrocity in World War I and its impact on World War II. In D. Bergen (ed.), *Lessons and legacies VIII: From generation to generation* (pp. 65–82). Evanston, IL: Northwestern University Press.

Bernstein, M. A. (1998). Homage to the extreme: The Shoah and the rhetoric of catastrophe." *Times Literary Supplement*, March 6, pp. 6–8. Retrieved from http://find.galegroup.com, Gale Document Number: EX1200490269.

Brison, S. J. (2002). *Aftermath: Violence and the remaking of a self*. Princeton, NJ: Princeton University Press.

Bryce, J., & Toynbee, A. (1916). *The treatment of Armenians in the Ottoman Empire, 1915–1916. Documents presented to Viscount Grey of Fallodon* (Secretary of State for Foreign Affairs). With a preface by Viscount Bryce. London, UK: Hodder and Stoughton.

Budnitskii, O. (2011). *Russian Jews between the Reds and the Whites, 1917–1920*. Trans. T. J. Portnice. Philadelphia, PA: University of Pennsylvania Press.

Charentz, Y. (2008). *13 Poems*. Trans. D. Kherdian and G. Basmadjian. Glendale, CA: Abril Publishing.

Clendinnen, I. (1999). *Reading the Holocaust*. Cambridge, UK: Cambridge University Press.

Comité central suisse de secours aux Arméniens (1916). Les massacres d'Arménie. *Genevois*, May 18, n.p. (Retrieved from newspaper clippings file at AGBU Nubar Library, Paris, France.)

Confino, A. (2012). *Foundational pasts: The Holocaust as historical understanding*. Cambridge, UK: Cambridge University Press.

Engel, D. (ed.) (2016). *The assassination of Symon Petlyura and the trial of Scholem Schwartzbard 1926–1927: A selection of documents*. Leipzig, Germany: Vandenhoeck & Ruprecht.

Friedlander, S. (1992). Introduction. In S. Friedlander (ed.), *Probing the limits of representation: Nazism and the "final solution"* (pp. 1–21). Cambridge, MA: Harvard University Press.

Garbarini, A. (2006). *Numbered days: Diaries and the Holocaust*. New Haven, CT: Yale University Press.

Gliksberg, A. (2004). *Kaddish pour les miens*. Paris, France: Mille et une nuits.

Glowacka, D. (2018). Gender and the Holocaust: Relational imagination in the cul-de-sacs of remembrance. In A. Garbarini & P. Jaskot (eds.), *Lessons and legacies XIII*. Evanston, IL: Northwestern University Press.

Goldberg, A. (2017). *Trauma in first person: Diary writing during the Holocaust*. Bloomington, IN: Indiana University Press.

Gruner, W. (2012). "Peregrinations into the void?" German Jews and their knowledge about the Armenian genocide during the Third Reich. *Central European History, 45*, 1–26. DOI: 10.1017/S0008938911000963.

Ihrig, S. (2014). *Atatürk in the Nazi imagination*. Cambridge, MA: Harvard University Press.

Ihrig, S. (2016). *Justifying genocide: Germany and the Armenians from Bismarck to Hitler*. Cambridge, MA: Harvard University Press.

Jurgenson, L. (2009). L'indicible: outil d'analyse ou objet esthéthique. *Protée, 37*(2), 9–19. DOI: 10.7202/038451ar.

Kohut, T. A. (2012). *A German generation: An experiential history of the twentieth century*. New Haven, CT: Yale University Press.

Levi, P. (1993). *Survival in Auschwitz*. Trans. S. Woolf. New York, NY: Touchstone Books/Simon and Schuster.

OED Online (2014). *Oxford English Dictionary*, 3rd edn. Oxford, UK: Oxford University Press. Retrieved from http://oed.com/view/Entry/216439?redirectedFrom=unprecedented.

Rosen, A. (2014). Tracking Jewish time in Auschwitz. *Yad Vashem Studies, 42*(2), 11–46.

Rothberg, M. (2000). *Traumatic realism: The demands of Holocaust representation*. Minneapolis, MN: University of Minnesota Press.

Rothberg, M. (2009). *Multidirectional memory: Remembering the Holocaust in the age of decolonization*. Stanford, CA: Stanford University Press.

Toynbee, A. J. (1915). *Armenian atrocities: The murder of a nation*. London, UK: Hodder & Stoughton.

Tresize, T. (2001). Unspeakable. *The Yale Journal of Criticism, 14*(1), 39–66. DOI: 10.1353/yale.2001.0016.

Tusan, M. (2014). "Crimes against humanity": Human rights, the British Empire, and the origins of the response to the Armenian genocide. *The American Historical Review, 119*(1), 47–77. DOI: https://doi.org/10.1093/ahr/119.1.47.

Chapter 5

Transmitting hate

On the process of hating and being hated[1]

Jörg Bose

A patient of mine who had emigrated from Eastern Europe many years ago found herself living in Jackson Heights, a neighborhood in Queens, New York that is famous for being home to many nationalities. A recent estimate suggested that there are at least 84 different native languages in Queens. This diversity is not something my patient could appreciate. Instead she was consumed with hatred and disgust for all who were divergent from her culturally and ethnically. Her hatred was often so intense that remaining impartial as her therapist was challenging.

Hatred has many faces, and ethnic hatred is perhaps the most ugly and tenacious, particularly because it has led to so many horrors, past and present. Ethnic hatred is multiple, like the heads of the Hydra, forever recurring and yet, unlike the myth, at no time can we hope for a Hercules to put an end to it. In thinking about hatred it is tempting to postulate, in an almost despairing way, that humans have an innate, instinctual disposition to be aggressive and to hate, an irrepressible urge that is barely restrained by the thin layer of civilization. However, an alternative and ultimately more hopeful perspective emerges when we think of hate as resulting from the fragility of human identity and the instability of the sense of self when the essential other is unavailable or hostile. The search for that essential recognition, often concealed in hating the other, may appear to have a driven quality, and yet, as a process of cognition it emerges from a most human, rather than animalistic, level. As an alternative to being empowered by hatred, recognizing weakness and vulnerability and accepting it provides a different kind of strength. It is certainly an emotional challenge to accept one's hate as a stance that is (on some level) deliberately chosen, rather than claiming to be the helpless victim of an aggressive instinct running rampant when the controls of civilization break down.

When considering psychoanalytic theories on the origin of hate and hatred, we are squarely confronted with the debate about whether hate is the result of the lid of civilization that covered an inner caldron of ever-ready aggression (Rothstein, 1980) having been blown off, or whether hate arises from a current interpersonal and cultural context (Lachmann, 2000). Heinz Kohut's

(1972) revolutionary formulation of rage as emerging from narcissistic injury in the form of a threat to the sense of self, or from a breakdown of identity, provides a more complex understanding of hating behavior than the traditional notion of instincts going rampant. Building on Kohut's ideas, Frank Lachmann (2000) emphasizes the identity-enhancing function of aggression and allows us to grasp the horrifying appeal of hatred and destructive aggression that result in violence. Lachmann elaborates the notion of reactive versus eruptive aggression, the former being clearly context-dependent while the latter is without an immediately knowable cause. Joseph Lichtenberg and Barbara Shapard (2000) similarly address the issue of the chronicity of hate by describing how a persistent aversive motivation develops in infants with an insecure attachment pattern and creates a drive-like disposition toward hatred. Lichtenberg and Shapard (2000, p. 377) follow Webster's definition of hatred as a "strong aversion or detestation coupled with ill will" and understand hate as having become rigid and target-fixated. In addressing the determined nature of hatred Lichtenberg and Shapard draw a parallel to romantic love when the hated other, like the loved one, is overinvested with meaning and often intensely pursued.

Drawing on these perspectives, I will explore the compulsive nature of ethnic hatred through an understanding of the experience of power that such hate provides. I examine how this psychological process relates to grandiose and hypomanic states of mind that can end in mania, and I consider the possibility that hatred is ultimately driven by an unconscious desire of the victimized to be recognized by the original perpetrator. In everyday life aversive responses from anger to rage are normal but usually short-lived. However, hatred regenerates itself by incessantly reiterating objectional themes and content. Ethnic hate becomes chronic when it employs relatively rigid, global judgments of others that are used mindlessly. This process defines the nature of prejudice. As labels and shorthand terms, such preconceived, prejudicial ideas are part of the usual set of preconscious tools with which we orient ourselves in everyday life. When they are connected to chronic resentment and rage, these preconceived notions can become inflated and incorrigibly absolutist. This is part of what Christopher Bollas (1992, p. 193) has termed "the fascist state of mind." In light of the vile consequences that this state of mind has created in past and current times, it is essential to understand more closely what it consists of and why it can lead to such unspeakably cruel human behavior.

Hatred in context and hatred as function

The complexity of hatred becomes evident in looking at the familial and cultural settings in which hatred emerges and serves a variety of expressive, supportive, and empowering functions. Hatred and hating behavior, with all its dreadful consequences, often stabilizes an unstable sense of self or identity, a phenomenon Lichtenberg, Lachmann, and Fosshage (1992) addressed with their concept of a "vitalizing selfobject experience."

The understanding that hate is related to context rather than instinct emerges persuasively in the arena of family settings with their display of patterns of hating and being hated. Often these experiences are dissociated while leaving behind a state of chronic resentment with a readiness to focus on a new target; or there is no dissociation and hate that is expressed openly in both directions at family members and at outsiders. To use an example, a combative young man from South America, of Arabic and Spanish ancestry, who suffered from depression, felt that from early on he had to fight as if for his life. This young man had a history of traumatic separations from his mother and his siblings. He believed that his mother thought of him as inferior because the color of his skin was darker than that of his siblings. It turned out that his grandmother perceived his mother as being darker skinned than her other children, and for that reason kept a separate whip for her daughter. This kind of family situation repeats in a small social context the prejudicial absurdity that pervades larger social contexts, when it postulates significant qualitative differences that are as realistically irrelevant as the different shades of skin color.

Encountering global, prejudicial judgments shapes the young person's emerging identity and sense of self. Being the target of such condemnatory hatred is nevertheless a form of recognition. Such situations can at times evoke a counter-response of hate and violence, a response which will be the more intense, the more the recipient of the condemnatory prejudice unconsciously agrees with the value system, by hating and condemning himself or herself as well.

Hating in response to being hated or mistreated means encountering relative helplessness and frustration. In the process the sense of self is rendered fragile, and hatred may provide the welcome, albeit delusional, experience of feeling powerful again. Such a sense of empowerment may even be greater if the hater inflates his or her sense of self by assuming a position of superiority in the contempt for the hated other. With such an inflated sense of self, self-idealizing grandiosity, when injured or threatened, may grab on to ethnic hatred as a welcome cudgel for the offender or the offense. Additionally, engaging in contempt may spur on the hater's fantasies of superiority even more.

The young man I was working with said that "New Yorkers tend to look at you with condescending eyes in the subway. They have an elitist attitude that reminds me of my mother. But if anybody gives me a 'staring down,' I am fed up with taking crap from people, I am not afraid of getting hurt. I feel the sense of empowerment when I am angry, sort of invincible." It is evident that this young man learned to use hate to stabilize his damaged self-esteem. By hating he achieved an inflated sense of empowerment and would right the imbalance that resulted from having been humiliated by a superior-acting and -feeling other. What is also remarkable in this case is the intergenerational perpetuation of prejudice, something Harry Stack Sullivan remarked on in his essay on "Anti-Semitism." As Sullivan states, "One knows what to expect, not because one has a correct view, but because there is a community of assumptions, usually the result of a rather methodical education. It is not necessary to set up a special teaching situation in order to inculcate in the young the most consistent and constantly manifested traits of the family culture complex" (Sullivan, 1964, p. 51). Sullivan noted that prejudicial condemnatory judgment is based on fantasy and cannot be realistically verified and that it "always includes characteristics of the (hating) person himself" (Sullivan, 1964, p. 76). This conceptualization points to the remarkably multi-targeted nature of prejudicial hatred, which, seen as an act of projection, is sometimes simultaneously directed at the other person and at dissociated aspects of the hater's self.

Hatred of the self or other as inferior and simultaneous hate of the superior and arrogant other was also particularly evident in a septuagenarian patient, a storeowner of southern European ancestry who had been diagnosed as suffering from manic depressive (bipolar) syndrome. This condition was largely contained by his medication, although he still experienced frequent mood changes. He was often quite arrogant when his life went smoothly, with a "not suffering fools gladly" attitude, giving his views as the ultimate opinion on the financial market, on politics, or on aesthetic and intellectual matters. He harbored many prejudicial stereotypes: Jewish people bothered him when they didn't have "Nordic" looks. He was extremely contemptuous of anything he considered to be a physical imperfection. He also hated Catholic priests and Catholic nuns, whom he thought should be "exterminated." When he was in such a state of hate he experienced manic excitement and, in the process, bathed himself in a sense of superiority. He liked to entertain the belief that there were superior people in the world, most likely blonde and blue-eyed, who were able to lead totally successful and perfect lives. It was as if Mount Olympus and its gods actually existed, although he was not always sure that he belonged to this idealized world. Thus any intrusions into this perfect universe by the realities of this world – be it a difficult customer, a drop in sales, or a building defaced by graffiti – would shatter his self-aggrandizement and return him to the dung heap and to depression. Alternatively he would turn to rage, fantasizing about how he would kill "all these weaklings" or how he would smash the display of his own store in a kind of "personal *Kristallnacht*." This was his way of handling what was to him an unbearable disappointment. As he put it, "devaluing the other was a relief, only in that way can I bear the pain." His self-hatred was most evident in his reaction to a foot injury. He experienced limping as a humiliation and only gradually became aware that he insulted himself with the same kind of condemnation that he would normally have for another person with a physical impairment. Such self-directed condemnation usually resulted in a deep depression.

The man had lost his adoring and nurturing father at an early age, which left him at the mercy of his mother, a woman hardened by the trials and tribulations of immigration, a successful businesswoman who had only scorn and ridicule for the awkward and bookish teenager whom she would often call "poor thing." Over time the man became able to dissociate less, and recognized that it was the experience with his arrogant and superior-acting mother that had made him feel inferior and so very envious and deeply resentful of people who were successful and who appeared to exclude him from their world of privilege. What was particularly noteworthy in this case was how hatred (in particular, ethnic hatred) appeared to bring about a hypomanic or even manic self-state. Whenever he encountered the usual setbacks of everyday life he turned to viciously attacking the Catholic Church, raging against its claims of infallibility, and fantasizing about exterminating its officials. When he hated, he no longer saw himself as an ordinary human being but as having become one of the gods. While he initially was not aware of his own arrogance, he was nevertheless morally outraged and enraged when he encountered the stance of superiority in the other.

This patient was actually a complexly developed, relatively sophisticated man, who consciously espoused liberal humanist values, and who was also able to be engaging and sensitive to others. These were qualities that helped him to gradually understand and accept his cruel hypomanic self-state. With his varying victimized and hating states he illustrates the phenomenon of self-state fluctuations that appeared clinically as frequent mood swings. Bollas (1992) appears to refer to such volatility when he states that "the fascist state of mind is ordinary, it can indeed support the Democratic mind." He suggests that the shift from healthier to the insane aspects of the self can come about more easily than we like to think, and not only just in isolated clinical conditions.

Ethnic hatred in groups and culture

The way that hatred comes about in the family group and the various functions it serves the individual may have similarities to so-called tribal and national groups in larger social contexts. When Yugoslavia and, with it, President Josip Broz Tito's attempt to create a nation out of diverse ethnic and religious groups collapsed, tribal and religious identities reemerged. The fervent desire of many citizens of Yugoslavia to define themselves individually as Serbs, Croats, and Slovenes, or as Roman Catholics, members of the Eastern Orthodox Church, or Muslims, not only broke up the country but also divided established communities, families, and marriages. In the process, neighbor turned on neighbor.

The recent resurfacing of racial tension and hatred of Muslims in the United States, kindled in the minds of vulnerable disaffected individuals by a political demagogue, painfully supports Bollas' observations that the fascist state of mind can easily come into being. The explosion of Islamist ethnic hatred toward Jews stoked by the Wahhabists' distorted interpretation of the Koran proves this point as well. Certain prejudicial notions are like dormant delusions, laying in wait, perhaps mothballed, but ready to be used again and played on, particularly by an eloquent fanatical leader.

The historical example of German anti-Semitism serves to demonstrate the complexity and deep embeddedness of prejudice and chronic hatred in a culture. It also illustrates its particular tenacity, in spite of the many serious efforts to address anti-Semitism in contemporary Germany. A 1987 survey by the Center for Research on Antisemitism (ZfA) in Berlin revealed that 33% of the German citizens who were polled maintained covert negative images of Jews, 12% were overtly anti-Semitic, and 7% were expressly anti-Semitic and tended to be actively discriminatory (Haller, 1992). In 2014, a survey carried out by the Anti-Defamation League found that 27% of Germans still harbor anti-Semitic views. It is of little comfort to know that the number is 37% in France and 69% in Greece, when in the Netherlands and in Sweden only 4% and 5%, respectively, appear to hold on to this prejudice. Anti-Semitism may still exist in Germany to an even higher degree if one accepts the argument that the passionate anti-Zionist position of the current German Left implies anti-Semitism.

Certainly anti-Semitism is not a German invention: its roots in Europe go far back to the Middle Ages before there was a modern German nation; and, of course, anti-Semitism has a much longer history, dating back to the destruction of the Jewish temple in Jerusalem. From St. Augustine in the fourth century to Martin Luther in the sixteenth century, Jews were excoriated as rebels against God and held in principle responsible for the crucifixion of Christ. According to Sara Lipton (2014), the shift toward a more actively persecutory attitude emerged around 1100 when the Christians saw themselves as more threatened, in part by the military successes of the Turks and by "an internal reform movement questioning the fundamentals of faith." Lipton points to a change in the images of Christ on the cross, no longer looking healthy and alive, the image of a divine God triumphant over death with his executioners depicted as Romans, but now portrayed as a pained victim. The focus on Christ's torment, and on the Jews as his tormentors, was used to stir compassion and to foster "a sense of Christian unity." Lipton also notes the power of visual images, as Jews were depicted as "hook-nosed caricatures of evil." These vile images were used in the sermons that agitated the crusaders who were on their way to the Holy Land to kill the Muslims and stopped in the German Rhineland to kill local Jewish populations. The Jews' Christian neighbors stood by as if paralyzed, perhaps shocked that words could lead to violence so easily, perhaps unwilling to become engaged and endanger themselves.

Hatred and grandiosity

The political use of ethnic hatred can serve in a society as a vehicle for scapegoating to deflect from the real problems. There also appears to be a deeper foundational relationship between ethnic hatred and grandiosity as a group phenomenon. It appears that German anti-Semitism grew out of a culture that has driven its people to pursue with a vengeance that which is conceived as ideal. The undeterrable pursuit of a connection with ideal experience in the form of assuming oneself to be perfect and superior to others or to be part of a group or country that is unrealistically overvalued and idealized can serve as a person's or a group's compensatory effort to make up for the shame of developmental or historical trauma and its resultant sense of insecurity and inadequacy. Such fantasies of specialness and exceptionalism, be it in regard to oneself or through belonging to an exalted other, function as a counterbalance to experiences of being overpowered by others, be such experiences personal or national in scope, that have left a sense of being humiliated and permanently devalued in their wake.

Such superiority and inferiority issues existing at a group level appear to be a significant part of the developmental history of Germany as a nation. For example, the historian Leon Poliakow (1971) describes how the Germans derived their national identity differently than did other European nations, not from the specificity of tribe or territory but from a linguistic notion of sharing the common Teutonic language, a phenomenon that was then idealized. The name of the German language (Theodiscus, Diutisk) first appeared in the eighth century and preceded by a hundred years the generic application of *tütsche* or *deutsche* (Poliakow, 1971, p. 73). The German humanists in the fifteenth and sixteenth centuries developed the first notions of German superiority on the basis of descriptions found in the work of the Roman historian Tacitus of the Germanic tribes as not having "contaminated" themselves through intermarriage. The "German man" was envisioned as noble, invincible, driven, and able to stop at nothing, the blond beast without a conscience (Poliakow, 1971, p. 66).[2] Thus "Germanomania" came into being, with the glorification of the German language and the glorification of German blood. So-called foreign blood was not only considered to bring impurity (as in the nationalist sentiment of the Marseillaise, for instance), but also deemed to be inferior in the sense of non-ideal. How did such delusional thinking come about?

Notions of superiority and inferiority in German culture and nationality have been addressed in the classical studies of the authoritarian personality by Erich Fromm (1936), Bertrand Schaffner (1948), and Theodor Adorno (Adorno *et al.*, 1950). Authoritarian and servile attitudes appear to be part of behavior patterns that have historically evolved from a social climate shaped in the quilt of a multiplicity of kingdoms and feudal mini-states that comprised what we identify as Germany today. The fact that Germany became a coherent nation state only very late in comparison with its European neighbors may very well be a contributor to a sense of national inferiority.

The traditional concept of the authoritarian personality was shaped by a culture that historically emphasized authoritarianism. It can be paired with our current understanding of the self as a more precarious system that manifests a narcissistic vulnerability in a person, group, or society when it is based on notions of exceptionalism. In such instances the sense of self, or of identity, is not anchored in reality but becomes fragile as it stretches itself to match the fantasy of being the incorporated ideal, or of belonging to an exalted group or endeavor. Even a relatively small injury becomes a kind of "lèse-majesté." Paradoxically, the greater the unrealistic claims of exceptionality, the greater will be the need for affirmation through merger and likeness, and the greater will be the vulnerability of that system. As the historical evolution of the German nation-state suggests, an insecure identity will use for its protection an ongoing rageful and targeted hatred. Different personal value systems or a different culture and religion will be experienced as threats because they may call into question claims of uniqueness. On the individual as well as on the societal level, people will react to such non-affirmatory threats with protective aggression or with avoidance and dissociation. The target of ethnic hatred, the other, who is simply different, challenges an identity that is so precariously and rigidly based on fundamentalist ideas and judgments which require that an ideal be matched absolutely. This requirement extends its demands to the members of the faith, who have to fear ostracism, as well as to outsiders, who have to fear for their lives. Such a rigid system requires for its maintenance the all-or-nothing stance of abolishing the different other, who has to either completely surrender or be killed. Hating the different other will then serve as an ongoing empowerment, continuously deflecting from the covert, or dissociated, sense of a weak identity.

Superiority, inferiority, and dissociation in recent German history

The response of Germany to the collective trauma of the First World War is an example of a compensatory function. Instead of facilitating a national process of grieving and a reorientation of values, demagogic politicians capitalized on the German cultural and historical tradition with its worship of power and a need to be strong at all times. In this tradition the split between good and bad became the split between strong and weak, and its inflated variant, the split between inferior and superior. Being in a position of weakness will bring out feelings of shame rather than guilt. Such cultural conditions can create either avoidant behavior or outright hatred, both in response to what is experienced as either inferior or superior. As Hannah Arendt (1951) has argued, German anti-Semitism targeted the German Jews for their alleged superiority because of the longstanding role of some of them as a special group with financial ties to the ruling class. At the same time they were targeted as non-Germans, as people without a country, as alien and underprivileged, and seen through the lenses of hatred as inferior and subhuman.

In clinical situations we frequently encounter childhood situations that involve a battle with a parent who acted and felt superior. This is illustrated in the following statement a young man made about his father: "His self-aggrandizement and underhanded boasting used to infuriate me. I don't know why. I was afraid that I couldn't tell him off. He always managed to win, I always felt that I lost." To be the victim in such a situation either induces states of detachment, of depression when the memory of shameful humiliation is dissociated (Bose, 2016), or brings about a state of chronic enragement. In a dissociated state the young person is trapped by the primary need to preserve a benevolent image of the original family, requiring that any need for immediate recognition and for undoing humiliations may then have to be displaced and projected onto the social scene at large.

In his reflections on anti-Semitism, Sullivan wrote of the personal motivation to engage in such prejudice when someone who was mistreated by a parent would identify with the figure of Christ as victim and engage in a "displacement of absolutistic parental authority on to the persecuting Jews" (Sullivan, 1964, p. 82). The original perpetrators in a dysfunctional family often cannot be emotionally targeted. Experiences of humiliation or neglect need to be dissociated, while there persists a vague sense of victimhood together with a chronically resentful self-state that is ready to go after the ethnically or culturally other as a projectively legitimized target. The alternative is to maintain a state of conflict and a shame-avoidant idealizing denial. The deep-seated resentment that is constantly churning needs an uncontestable target. It is the dissociative process itself that drowns out for some the intense hatred toward an abusive perpetrator with the resultant sheltering avoidance. In others it may create a vehement ethnic hatred that pursues the strange other instead of the familial hated other. A similar process may function to maintain a group's or nation's sense of identity when the experience of the original violation or humiliation, for instance a decisive defeat in battle, remains present in the group's or nation's awareness like an open wound. In such instances, a protective and invigorating chronic aversiveness will seek a contemporary target in order to "settle the balance."

The complexity of dissociation is compellingly analyzed in Thomas Kohut's (2012) book *A German generation*. In his analysis of interviews of 62 Germans Kohut portrays how the generation of Germans born around 1900, and identified as the Weimar youth generation, responded to Germany's defeat in the First World War with the desire to create a world that was intact again. They flocked in great numbers to a youth organization that expected them to devotedly embrace the values of discipline, order, and service to the group. As Kohut suggests, "It was crucially important for these Germans to subordinate themselves to the Gemeinschaft. The need to belong to an idealized collective that had defined their lives in the youth movement continued to define their lives in the Third Reich" (T. A. Kohut, 2012, p. 126). As he describes it, "young people from different classes and regions came together to work on behalf of the Volk" (T. A. Kohut, 2012, p. 129).

The members of the youth collective, with their need for ideal experience and purity, accepted the anti-Semitic and racist notions of the National Socialists seemingly without question when they later joined the nationalistic Hitler Youth and *Reichswehr*. In a way they were easy prey because of their idealistic naïvety for the populist calculations of the National Socialists, whose leadership, as Kohut points out, derived from the preceding "front generation" that was " filled with hatred" and blame for the generation of the Weimar Republic that had preceded them. In finding a displaced focus when conceiving of the murder of the Jewish Germans as alleged enemies of the "Volk" their hatred, like the rage of an injured grandiose tyrant, had no bounds.

By contrast, for the other Germans it was not unrestrained hatred but a complex mixture of avoidance, negation, and dissociation that resulted in the Weimar youth generation becoming the bystanders who claimed that they hadn't known or seen what was done to their Jewish neighbors. When Kohut observes that the interviewees avoided "anything [that would] make them feel uneasy, and that they had no capacity or inclination to empathize with Jewish people" (T. A. Kohut, 2012, p. 138), this parallels the individual who dissociates facts about his or her dysfunctional family in an effort to preserve at any cost the needed ideal experience. In a similar sense, bystanding Germans looked away when their Jewish neighbors were humiliated, dehumanized, and deported because they did not want to feel, and could not bear, the shame this represented about themselves and about the country that they needed to continue idealizing.

Diverse forms of hatred

Compared with hatred, dissociation is the alternative, less obvious mode of coping in the encounter with experiences of powerlessness and shame and their undermining effect on the sense of self, especially when the latter is based on inflated standards. This is, however, a self-depleting clinical process that can end in depression. By contrast, hatred can have a more vitalizing effect. It is disappointing that hatred may therefore be for many the primary self-constitutive function when hatred of what is perceived as inferior as well as hatred of what is perceived as superior in self and other serves to preserve a frail sense of identity. An insecure, weak sense of self and identity may often be at the core of a disposition to eruptive aggression, be it as a temporary coping strategy, when rage may provide momentary empowering, or as a rigidly embedded aggressive disposition delivering the ongoing vitalizing effect of chronic rage. The vulnerability of the sense of self is increasingly understood today in various individual development studies (Beebe & Lachmann, 2013) that stress the importance of dependence, recognition, and affirmation of the person by others and that central in that relationship is the importance of being positively valued. It is hard to overestimate what an impact the opposite experience will have, particularly on a young person. The hated other, in a family setting, is likely to become destabilized or in the end may acquire a new relative stability through engaging in self-hatred and developing a negative self-image, or pursue the self-stabilizing strategy of hating the other.

On the level of group and national experience, hatred, in the form of ethnic hatred, will serve to shore up a sense of devalued national or group identity by labeling those who are culturally and ethnically other as hate-worthy and subhuman in an attempt to destroy their dignity and identity. Targeting the other with ethnic hatred, in order to eliminate the threat of otherness, may create the coveted, intense sense of belonging among those joined in hatred. The readiness with which hatred (and, in particular, ethnic hatred) is seized upon derives from its multiple uses in the various self-protective, self-empowering, and identity-enhancing functions. But, in addition to its varied functional motivations, since any emotion requires pertinent symbolic forms to thrive on, it is the sharply targeted hateful ethnic prejudice that ignites hatred and makes it thrive.

Preconceived ideas and their prejudicial derivatives are normally part of what we call identification: they are used to identify oneself and others. Social identity, the identity by which we are recognized by others, is an essential aspect of our personal identity. Preconceived ideas and judgments are part of that process of identification. They consist of generalizations that allow one to achieve a quick orientation while remaining amenable to revision in order to acquire a more complex understanding of the other when more detailed information becomes available. Such flexibility and openness disappear when preconceived notions instead come into contact with chronic resentment. At that point they lose any flexibility they may have had, and become the fuel that feeds the flames. Prejudicial notions are then no longer used for the practical purpose of social orientation but have taken on the function of being the symbolic forms that are very much needed to give shape to the inchoate feeling of hate as well as to keep hate going. Inchoate hatred, in its state of unformulated chronic resentment, looks for a form and container. In such cases, prejudicial judgments will offer the ready-made configurations for the hitherto unformulated smoldering chronic resentment, a pattern that is so effectively exploited by demagogues when they formulate ideologies of hate.

Besides shaping chronic resentment, hating the self and the other may also provide a delusional sense of power and satisfaction of the desire for revenge. Yet, when such satisfaction is not sufficient, ever more violent exercise of power is sought. There may be an immediate reward to be gained from the pursuit of violence, but it is short-lived because the original defeat (or psychic injury) cannot be undone, or, in the case of dissociation, because the original perpetrator cannot be brought into focus or engaged with. In other words, there is no realistic exit from the fire of ethnic hatred until it finally burns out or ends in self-destruction. But there is yet another option whereby hatred takes a turn to the delusional by entering into a hypomanic or even manic self-state. The Italian storeowner I described earlier mentioned such experiences in which his hatred escalated. Another patient, who had suffered in his youth from shaming persecution by his peers for being gay, developed, in order to survive being shamed and hated, a protective shield of compensatory grandiosity with an intensely critical and hating disposition towards his surroundings. Violence was not an option for him, but for a period of several months he entered into a manic state of thinking himself to be the Messiah, and believing that he had control over the minds of other people. Once he had recovered, he developed a more realistic sense of personal value and the capacity to stand up to his own harsh self-criticisms and the judgments of others.

The speed with which hatred can bring about the subjective experience of power and superiority over the hated other can feed delusional self-aggrandizing fantasies and hypomanic excitement. This can easily slide into a manic state in the individual or into the ethnic killing frenzies of past and current history. Just as an individual may fall for hatred because it provides a manic defense against depression and inferiority, or an exciting experience of empowerment, so an entire group or nation may likewise attempt to ward off feelings of national insecurity through ethnic hatred that is whipped into a manic frenzy.

Hatred and the need for recognition

Many conditions of hating the other are driven by the need for recognition of having been hated or otherwise mistreated. This was corroborated in an experience with the patient I mentioned at the start of the chapter. She had difficulty feeling comfortable in her multiethnic neighborhood. She was someone who had spent a lifetime reacting with anger and contempt to ethnic differences while only gradually allowing herself to become aware of the depth of her feelings of having been dismissed and ignored by her parents. At one point in our work together, a scenario emerged between us in which I was not sufficiently available to her when she became seriously ill. The patient focused on me with hatred, berating me as being a cold person and as anxiously hiding behind a defensive professional posture, as having failed to behave with her like any decent human being would have. This confrontation was not made easier by the fact that she was Jewish and I was German. When I finally dropped my defensiveness and accepted the validity of the accusation that I had indeed avoided her, she exclaimed "Now I can claim my self back!" My patient's reaction suggests that the driving force of her hatred was a preconscious search for recognition from the original perpetrator. As her therapist I became an available substitute for the original perpetrator. Once my patient was able to understand her dissociated experiences of having been cruelly and emotionally injured by her family, she began to hate others less.

Of course, outside the treatment room and at the level of groups, such experiences of recognition will seldom be available. A rare example of an attempt at "restorative justice" at the level of group and national experience occurred during the 1990s in the work of the Truth and Reconciliation Commission in South Africa. Through public hearings, the Truth and Reconciliation Commission provided an experience of recognition for at least some of the victims of apartheid. These victims were able to come forth and speak of their experiences. Perpetrators of the apartheid violence were also heard and were given amnesty as long as their crimes were politically motivated and they told the full truth. Yet, as history suggests, once ethnic hatred has broken out in a group or international situation, it is, sadly, rarely possible to break the cycle of hatred begetting hatred. In order to move forward we need to remain aware of the negative imprint of culture and history on our minds. An unflinching look at the burdens that familial and cultural traditions can instill in a person in the form of prejudices and various fantasies of superiority may have some preventative effect in relation to how we see and treat each other. Ultimately I believe that owning the shame over our prejudicial inclinations without denial or dissociation is our only hope for diminishing the destructive impact of prejudicial attitudes and fantasies on our communal lives.

Notes

1 Parts of this essay have previously been published in German (Bose, 1994).
2 Poliakow (1971, p. 66) points out that the "ideal of the German man" became the model on which "Germans of all types tried to mold themselves in increasing numbers … particularly after the Napoleonic wars" and that "secondly Germans with assertive or megalomanic temperaments, similar to that portrayed in their imaginary 'ideal man,' were selected by society and made their mark in public life in ever larger numbers."

References

Adorno, T. W., Frenkel-Brunswik, E., Levinson, D. F., & Sanford, R. N. (1950). *The authoritarian personality*. New York, NY: Harper & Bros.
Arendt, H. (1951) *The origins of totalitarianism*. New York, NY: Harcourt Brace Jovanovich.
Beebe, B., & Lachmann, F. (2013). *The origins of attachment: Infant research and adult treatment*. New York: Routledge.
Bollas, C. (1992) *Being a character*. New York: Hill and Wang.
Bose, J. (1994). Hassen und gehaßt werden. In J. Wiesse (ed.), *Aggression am Ende des Jahrhunderts* (pp. 33–42). Göttingen, Germany: Vandenhoeck & Ruprecht.
Bose, J. (2016). Dissociative process and the depressed patient. *Contemporary Psychoanalysis*, *52*, 51–75.
Fromm, E. (1936) with the collaboration of E. Schachtel, A. Hartoch-Schachtel, & P. Lazarsfeld. *The authoritarian character structure of German workers and employees before Hitler*. Unpublished manuscript.

Haller, M. (1992). Der kollektive Wahn. *Die Zeit*, No. 40, October 2, p. 6.
Kohut, H. (1972). Thoughts on narcissism and narcissistic rage. In P. Ornstein (ed.), *The search for the self Vol. 2* (pp. 615–659). New York: International Universities Press, 1978.
Kohut, T. A. (2012). *A German generation: An experiential history of the twentieth century*. New Haven, CT: Yale University Press.
Lachmann, F. (2000). *Transforming aggression: Psychotherapy with the difficult-to-treat patient*. Lanham, MD: Jason Aronson.
Lichtenberg, J, Lachmann, F., & Fosshage, J. (1950). *Self and motivational systems: Toward a theory of psychoanalytic technique*. Hillsdale, NJ: The Analytic Press.
Lichtenberg, J. D., & Shapard, B. (2000). Hatred and its rewards: A motivational systems view. *Psychoanalytic Inquiry*, *20*, 37–388
Lipton, S. (2014). *Dark mirror: The medieval origins of Anti-Jewish iconography*. New York, NY: Metropolitan Books.
Poliakow, L. (1971). *The Aryan myth: A history of racist and nationalist ideas in Europe*. New York, NY: Basic Books.
Rothstein, A., (1980). Toward a critique of the psychology of the self. *Psychoanalytic Quarterly*, *49*, 423–455
Schaffner, B. (1948). *Fatherland, A study of authority in the German family*. New York, NY: Columbia University Press.
Sullivan, H. S. (1964). *The fusion of psychiatry and social science*. New York, NY: W. W. Norton & Co.

Part III

Confronting the past

Chapter 6

The Stowaway

Reality, the Holocaust and the historical unconscious

Robert Prince

Psychoanalysis and history are both foundational for understanding human identity, nowhere more so than in confrontation with, to use Edmund Burke's (1990) historical term, the "sublime." The sublime, which refers to what is dark and uncertain, subsumes the psychological concept of "trauma." Both the sublime and the traumatic point to the existence of something that actually happened and continues to happen, what is generally referred to as a "fact." Yet facts can be as elusive as they are fundamental, and are often hidden and disguised. Facts are sometimes doubted to exist or seen as constructed. They are interpreted, arranged into patterns, emplotted to create alternative meanings, but, despite a huge range of possibility, there are limits to the permissible (Browning, 1992). There is a finite range of the ways in which a story can be told (White, 1992). There can be distracting noises or thunderous silences, but, to use Eelco Runia's (2010) metaphor, there is a "Stowaway" who, hidden in the shadow that is cast by what happened, and what we say about it, guides a psychoanalytic and historical unconscious.

A theme of historical writing is the location of historical occurrence, i.e. concern for the extent to which it is located in the past or a construction of the present. We have come to appreciate the reciprocity of effect. When the historical subject involves "monstrous behavior ... in utter contradiction to what we regard as our identity" (Runia, 2007, p. 313), its integration into our individual and collective narratives takes time to evolve. Particular details, the facts of the story, may dominate the narrative, move out and back into the shadows, but even then, as they zig and zag, they have clandestine access to the ships' instruments of navigation and propulsion. No matter how powerful the historical story, the telling (the currently fashionable term is transmission) is embedded in its wider surround.

In psychoanalysis unmastered relationships come to be known through enactments in the transference and are illustrated in Freud's trope, "What is not remembered is repeated." In a similar sense, history is subject to variations of Santayana's trope, "Those who do not understand the past are doomed to repeat it." There is an unavoidable reciprocity and even interpenetration between past and present, the former understood through the latter. Attention to vicissitudes in the representation of the "sublime" and traumatic has been especially rich across many fields and sensitive to the temperature of the times, the social, political, and ideological climate (Friedlander, 1992; Hartman, 1996; Spiegel, 2014).

Thus, Holocaust studies in Israel have a trajectory that traces that of national interests, while in Germany the "historians' debate" was linked to political ideology. The nature, perhaps definition, of trauma is that it destabilizes our existent apprehension of the world. It may create an existential crisis in the form of confrontation with a void or it may undermine our capacity for memory, thinking, and symbolization, and thus have its own epistemology, an epistemology of trauma. Psychoanalytic and historical inquiry involve a conflict and courtship between the need to know and the need not to know. Openness to psychohistory depends on the emotional readiness (Bergman, 1982) of the psychotherapist and on the readiness of a culture at a particular moment. When the psychohistorical subject is disruptive of our identity (the preferred stories we would like to tell ourselves about who we are) it is correspondingly more uncomfortable to be conscious of "history flowing through us."

It has been suggested that it takes at least several generations to digest history, and both psychoanalysis and history go through phases in their encounter with the Holocaust, perhaps beginning with shock, then dissociation and a third state of memorialization which serves to establish the boundaries of what can be tolerably said about the subject. Memorialization is a psychic and historical necessity, and has pronounced aspects of being both a "manic defense" serving to replace helplessness with omnipotent control and, from a historical point of view, a form of propaganda. Commemoration functions simultaneously and powerfully to assert identity and deny identity, for example Runia (2007, p. 313) describes the desire to commemorate as one of "the prime historical phenomena of our time" and suggests that "the more we commemorate what we did, the more we transform ourselves into people who did not do it" (p. 320).

Responses to the Holocaust have developed in personal, social and historical contexts. I described in a previous essay (Prince, 2015) the evolution of Holocaust awareness in psychoanalysis and, in a subsequent paper, the vicissitudes regarding the perception of the survivor in the United States. As a small-bore case example of the role of the present moment in shaping what is known about the impact of historical trauma, I would like to use my doctoral dissertation in clinical psychology, *Psychohistorical themes in the lives of young adult children of concentration camp survivors* (Prince, 1974, 1985, 1999). The original intent was psychohistorical; that is, by exploring individuals who were not direct witnesses but were intimately touched by the historical event through their parents, to deepen a sense of the reciprocal relationship between what happens in the outer world and the effects on the inner world.

In retrospect, my aspirations were naïve, which I partly attribute to the effect of trauma on thinking, i.e. the disruption of the instruments of measurement and knowing by confrontation with massive suffering.

A psychohistorical study in its context

The study was conceived at a time that Holocaust representation had not yet made the transition, to use Mintz's description, from "silence to salience" (Mintz, 2001). The student protests in response to the Vietnam War formed the contemporary moral context on which the Second World War, in Hartman's (1996) phrase, "cast the longest shadow." I did have a personal awareness that much about who I was, the identity I wore, came from a fabric made of historical cloth. Woven together were strands of events from family history and from events in my family's world. As a child of immigrants pulled up by the roots and replanted in the loose soil of unfamiliar terrain, I had grown up with a waxing and waning but omnipresent awareness that in my family, which had neither re-created its culture of origin nor integrated into American life, the great marker in time was the "War." Everything happened either before it or after it, my mother came to the United States before it; my father, after. Next to that awareness was the shadow of the Holocaust that as I grew up formed a background for my personal understanding of the world and mysteries/complexity about it. My personal understanding of the Second World War from its cultural representations was as a heroic triumph of good over evil, order over chaos. Each element of my knowledge involved some meditation on human behavior in extremis.

The personal was separate from but certainly affected by the collective. The evolution of collective Holocaust consciousness was complex and episodic (Prince, 2015). It was initially neglected in psychoanalysis (Prince, 2009). The psychological literature on the children of survivors was even sparser and the general thrust, at the time, was that the children of survivors were the product of parental psychopathology no different from children of any parents who carried significant burdens (Prince, 1974). Ironically, subsequent robust research supporting the epigenetic transmission of trauma would conflate the idea of biological transmission for which there is robust evidence with the idea of psychological and cultural transmission.

The reception of survivor memoirs, from the day of liberation, was tortured and produced great bitterness in survivors. There certainly were contemporary milestones that promoted awareness of the Holocaust and fit into national narratives, such as the production *The Diary of Anne Frank* in the 1950s, the Eichmann trial in the early 1960s, and the 1967 Israel–Arab War. But there was not a great deal of discussion about the Holocaust per se. At the time, I could not know that the cultural unfolding of a Holocaust consciousness would lead to the insight that the facts of history, specifically the Holocaust, had a powerful influence on how I saw and experienced the world.

What was at the time controversial in mainstream psychoanalysis that was preoccupied with the internal origins of psychic reality would in the near future be taken for granted.

The immanence of such a consciousness contrasted with the void around it. It is extremely difficult to describe an absence, a lack of interest in the details of genocide, especially in contrast to heroic war movies. In 1961 Raul Hilberg's now classic *The Destruction of the European Jews* was published, subsidized by a survivor family and by a small press with cheap paper and binding. Tony Judt, who famously, and perhaps uniquely, linked changing facts to changing his opinions, captures the times with scenic moments. Describing what came to be recognized as Primo Levi's masterwork, he writes (Judt, 2008) "*Se questo è un uomo*, initially rejected by publishers in 1946 … eventually published, but in just 2,500 copies by a small local press. Hardly anyone bought it." He goes on to write "I can confirm the lack of interest in the Shoah in those years from my own experience, growing up in England – a victorious country that had never been occupied and thus had no complex about wartime crimes. But even in England the subject was never much discussed – in school or in the media." In the 1970s, according to Hartman (1996), history departments began shifting away from regarding the Holocaust as merely a Jewish affair. But, as late as the early 1980s, a Kansas State University historian, George Kren (1983, personal communication), observed that, at that time, "Holocaust studies had not been the road to academic advancement."

My doctoral proposal, which emphasized an attempt to look at the impact of a massive event, the Holocaust, on "psychohistorical figures" was greeted with ambivalence. In retrospect, it was amazing that it was allowed to proceed in the absence of any antecedents, which I interpret as the power of the subject, to its hidden "presence." Though my doctoral program was dynamically steeped, the idea of "capital H" history was nowhere in evidence, and psychological outcomes were attributed to internal dynamics and family systems. It should be stressed that the dominant psychoanalytic approaches of the time had minimal interest in the role of the external world. Nevertheless, the idea of a dissertation about children of Holocaust survivors seemed to pluck a resonant cord, produced an initial affective warmth, but no faculty seemed to have any interest in actually being involved and some responses seemed like they could only be characterized as enactments.

The director of one of the applied psychology programs was enthusiastic and encouraging but broke every appointment to discuss being on the committee. I arrived at the last one to find the doors locked, and saw, through the frosted glass doors of the programs office, that the light was off. Determined to wait, I parked myself in the hall and after a while heard noises. The professor had been there the whole time, apparently waiting to come out of her inner office until she was sure I was gone. I knocked again; I can't remember whether excuses were made, but no meeting was held or rescheduled. For years I thought of this strange incident as another "dissertation story," until it dawned on me that it was a truly a "war story." There was absolutely no antecedent in the behavior of this professor, who was generally liked and respected; nor was there any conceivable explanation for her having to decline participation by going into hiding, except as some enactment having to do with the Holocaust subject. I never suspected her of deliberateness or even consciousness. It would have been easy enough for her to give me five minutes and politely send me on my way, but the behavior represents what Kearney writes in explicating the "Stowaway": "The presence of the past is … a dynamic action, one where the reality of the past acts on us in surprising ways. History sneaks up on us as an unexpected intervention on our consciousness" (Kearney, 2015, p. 307).

The faculty member with the largest reputation was more forthright, agreeing to be on the dissertation committee with the understanding that he was dubious about its viability and that, if I was willing to assume the risks, he would be willing to read it. The committee chair, who had been encouraging at the start, gave absolutely no feedback besides spelling corrections.

The oral defense was, up until the very end, a bad dream. Just before it was to take place, a senior faculty member who was not on the committee, but who had generously offered to attend for support (we had had a warm relationship that included some repartee about our Anglicized Central European names), asked me whether he "had" to be there. A committee member, relatively junior, who minutes before the meeting had sotto voce assured me the dissertation was the most "beautiful" she had ever read, joined in what can only be described as sequential attacks based on my method of searching for shared themes in the mass of interview data. My Ph.D. seemed about to be totally scrapped until the very final approbation by the "outside reader," De Witt Crandell, a psychoanalyst who was also Director of Research Training in Psychiatric Epidemiology at Columbia-Presbyterian Hospital. As harshly confrontational as the committee had been, at the end, really extraordinarily, not a single revision to the 300-page manuscript was required save the addition of five words in the conclusion, stating that the study was "exploratory." I was so grateful that it did not immediately cross my mind that I had been "saved" in another enactment.

In contrast to the previously vibrant engagement with an involved faculty that characterized my earlier graduate experience, the doctoral dissertation was a solitary experience. The exception was "outside" support from Robert Liebert, a psychiatrist and psychohistorian. He generously discussed material from the semi-structured interviews and also used his personal relationships to make introductions to the two towering psychohistorians of the time. One gave me an "interview" which involved a lecture about his work, but seemingly had no interest in the legacy of the Holocaust; the other, a preeminent European émigré, declined to meet me, writing he didn't have time but then added in his letter a peculiar phrase "despite or perhaps *because* (my italics) of the subject."

At the start of the dissertation process, I was very connected, my identity was firmly rooted in the graduate program; indeed, the security I felt gave me the confidence to undertake a risky project. I had survived but was alienated. No connections were left as I emigrated to another country.

On one level, it is understandable that my committee didn't know what to do with the dissertation. It didn't fit in, there was a negligible literature, and an unconventional methodology. I have retrospectively developed sympathy for the plight of the professor who went into hiding rather than directly discuss her participation, and the other who had waxed rhapsodic about the "beauty" of the dissertation only to join a full-throated attack on it. While I certainly do not think it was beautiful, many of the direct quotes from interviewees may have been, and the evocative power of the images of the Holocaust created the "presence" (Runia, 2006) that produced starkly contradictory responses.

Post-dissertation

Since there was so little literature on the subject, I thought the chances for a book were good. I assiduously sent inquiries. Those publishers that responded declined on the basis of anticipating no interest in the subject of the second generation. At the same time, in the Q&A after presentations I was giving, I heard the complaint that there was already too much literature on the subject: it was "overdone." Although many years later there would be room for legitimate if controversial critiques of the pervasiveness and uses to which Holocaust literature had been put (see Maier 1993; Novick, 1999), at that time the literature was still too far too sparse to justify complaints that seemed to translate into "stop afflicting us with this story."

However, after my dissertation was complete I began to get inquiries from other graduate students who were also children of survivors. Helen Epstein published in 1977 a cover story in the *New York Times Magazine* and a subsequent best-selling book (Epstein, 1977, 1978). Ten years later an academic publisher spontaneously contacted me to publish my dissertation in a series in clinical psychology. Twenty-five years later my book was reissued by a trade press. In this context, the dissertation occurred at a point of inflection; I had been, through no fault or virtue of my own, at the leading edge of a generational wave: children of survivors who were coming of age, studying themselves, and making a claim on history. The explanation for this wave is partly suggested by Mintz (2001), who traces the evolution of an image from refugee to survivor, from degraded to exalted, from victim to *tsadik*. Annette Wieviorka suggests that, in the time period this occurred, the survivors had completed the task of rebuilding their lives in a new country and the "chain of generations, doubly broken by the genocide and by emigration, was thus on its way to being reconstituted" (Wieviorka, 2006, p. 102). Spiegel (2009, p. 8) also cites "the maturing of the second generation" as bringing into play new transformations of history through approaches to representation. It was at this time that memoirs, which had been ignored even as they were being urgently produced by survivors as a first priority upon liberation, began to be transformed into collective memory. Within a short period, children of survivors had become a "subject." Longstanding psychoanalytic knowledge and case lore had begun to congeal around a new heading, "transmission."

The substantive criticism of my research, both in the oral defense and in subsequent presentations, one that seemed intense and motivated, was of the primary finding: the heterogeneity of children of survivors. My own simplistic expectation in looking for "psychohistorical themes" is that patterns would emerge that coalesced into traits or that correlations would emerge between the enormous multiplicity of variables and likely results, for example, patterns of communication in survivor families and Holocaust consciousness, or between degree of traumatization in parents and dysfunction in their children. I concluded that, on the contrary, there were radical differences among children of survivors. This was a conclusion that nobody, including initially me, seemed to be comfortable with. Indeed the "five-word revision" required by the doctoral committee implied an investment in further study that would identify these common traits and characterize a second-generation survivor syndrome. The repeated objection to the work, starting with my doctoral committee, was that, if the Holocaust or having survivor parents was so powerful, how could children of survivors be so different from each other across all the dimensions explored in a wide-ranging, unstructured interview?

One interrogation that particularly stands out was at an invited colloquium at the hand of the department chair who had seemed personally affronted and outraged by the psychohistorical approach as well as the observation of diversity. Years later I became friendly with one of the graduate students who had been present. She told me she had discussed with other students his uncharacteristically confrontational behavior and wondered what "had gotten into" him.

The uniqueness of the second generation

In the small sample of "psychohistorical figures" I interviewed between 1971 and 1973 and further supported by the next 40 years of clinical experience, the spectrum of characteristics is startling. On the one hand, it might be argued that there was a sampling bias toward similarity, i.e. a middle-class, educated group. On the other hand, the assumption that they came from similar backgrounds is false. The impact of history on the survivor and on family life was massive, but in different ways. It also involved the variable of life before the war. Parents came from varied cultural, social, and economic backgrounds, which led to complex differences: countries of origin and the socio-economic status of those countries of origin was a significant variable, as was urban vs. rural circumstances, and secular vs. religious. Some led lives of relative privilege before persecution, others led lives of hardship, and their persecution and losses, though massive, had different textures. After all, how does one distinguish, much less represent, the murder of just one loved one with everyone, between indifferent and sadistic brutality, protracted and short duration of physical suffering in a labor, concentration, or death camp, or the different circumstances of rescue and return? And despite the stereotypes of parental communication and the myths of silence, communication was itself varied and apparently little correlated with actual experiences of devastation and loss.

The second generation ranged from those who hold a strong conscious sense of their historical generation to those who reject any identification with survivorhood or history; from feeling completely shaped by history to denying any influence of their parent's survivorhood. They range in character from being narrow, concrete, rigid, and fixed in their views, given to simplistic formulations; to nuanced, complex, individuals, reflecting an ability to take on many different points of view to identify with multiple roles and possibilities, including the conditions under which they could see themselves as becoming bystanders and perpetrators.

Children of survivors described varied patterns of verbal and non-verbal communication and had an extremely wide range of responses to what their parents told them. These responses included horror, pity, shame, a fear of inflicting pain or opening wounds, a desire to avoid, a desire to learn more, perception of parents as severely damaged, and being awed and inspired by perceptions of parental strength, endurance, and integrity. Their perceptions of parents ranged from devaluation to idealization. Their descriptions of parents spanned the dimensions of emotional availability, intrusiveness, overprotectiveness, separation, control, and experiencing parents as limiting or facilitating independence, living vicariously through them, and imposing their worldviews and beliefs. The latter was complicated by different layers of a role reversal, as immigrant parents depended on their children to be the interpreters of a new culture. The strongest evidence of a common theme was a positive one, the experience of complete devotion of parents for their children.

The worldviews of survivors' children include beliefs that could be associated with historical imagery, feelings of personal insignificance, of being a little cog in a huge and indifferent machine, of fears of malevolence, of lack of affiliation and commitment, or strong participation and memberships, having few roots and seeing themselves as living anywhere, ranging from being naïve and dependent to being distrusting and cynical. The children of survivors were also idealistic, committed to helping and healing, and believed they could influence the world. Their identifications were with parents as victim or victor, crushed or resilient, damaged or strong. No character type emerged which could be described as typical of children of survivors. They ranged from those with severe problems in living to those who were extremely well functioning. In terms of the easily stated, they had a wide range of Jewish identification, political and social beliefs, and attitudes toward Israel. Finally, their career orientation ranged widely, with some evidence of a propensity toward social services, healing, and medicine.

Had the complexity of generational identity been considered, diversity would not have been a surprise. The array of shared experiences that might define a generation defies easy categorization. For example, Suleiman, after considering the many different defining influences that could characterize what she provocatively calls the 1.5 generation, child survivors, writes "Maybe there were no generations in the Holocaust, only individuals, each with his or her own unique story" (Suleiman, 2002, p. 284). Not only did I observe the children of survivors to be a varied group, but also my somewhat anxious apprehension, in the early 1970s, that their characteristics were subject to change was confirmed by opportunities to do follow-up studies as well as in the course of clinical encounters. Frie is exactly on target when he observes that "identity is neither fixed nor stable, but linked to the fluid and dynamic shifts of our experiences" (Frie, 2011, p. 136). However, there seems to be a strong prejudice in favour of the safety provided by the belief in fixed states.

The presumption of shared generational consciousness in children of survivors has to take into account the difference in consequences of the impact of relative historical continuity and discontinuity. Children of survivors were marked with the radical disruption of the course of history and exchange between the generations. The essence of genocide is its attempt to eradicate cultural continuity. Berel Lang (1999) highlights the differences between the two generations when he makes the point that the survivor generation has memories of the world that was lost, whereas their children have memories only of a world marked by the Holocaust. The subsequent generation has no such experience or reference. Under some instances they may demonstrate a hunger for such continuity, as reflected by Sebald's (2011) character, Austerlitz, who is in a quest for the story of his life, by Mendelsohn (2006) in an investigation intended to rescue memory by leaving an epitaph on an unmarked grave, by Hirsch and Spitzer (2010) in a physical return to the *lieux de mémoire*, by Foer (2003) in imagination after a failed "heritage tour," and by Spiegelman (1997) when he tries to find historical continuity through interrogating his father. All portray the paradox of the difficulty of finding generational continuity when their subjects are the plowed-under villages of the "Bloodlands" that are represented by the "voids" built into the Jewish Museum in Berlin. It has been remarked that we have the testimony of the survivors but not the dead. Mendelsohn's attempt was to provide that for six of them. He tried to exhume the substance of real people from the shadows cast by numbers.

Lang's (1999) distinction between history and memory is relevant: history is collective while memory is always someone's. Thus unique personal identity, in order to become a generational consciousness, must somehow make a bridge between the personal and the collective. The view from that bridge, when the object of collective memory is the crematoria, is necessarily obscured by smoke. The second generation, unlike the survivor generation, does not, in fact, have memory, but only "postmemory" (Hirsch, 1996), memories that are not their own and are compiled through parental and cultural representations. Their identity is an imbrication of memories that reside in this borderland of ownership, simultaneously not their own and also somehow theirs by inheritance.

The nature of trauma also dictates that the second generation will constitute a diverse population, i.e. trauma is constituted in a cultural matrix and its expression will take different forms. While symptoms of traumatic disorders date to antiquity, Talbott observes that interpretation has changed more than the symptoms of trauma. "Culture," he writes, "provides a framework for understanding" (Talbott, 1997, p. 444). Similarly, Mosse, talking about shell shock, demonstrates that it is "embedded in cultural values" (Mosse, 2000, pp. 101–102). Merridale (2000) links the concept of trauma to that of the self, and suggests that to Russians it may be anti-social. The power of trauma is evident; indeed, it is so powerful that it has a multitude of different effects, thus Shay's (2002) Odysseus, no less traumatized, looks very different from his Achilles (Shay, 1995).

For children of survivors, one of the meanings of the Holocaust has to do with their parents' collective social status shifting from the devalued battered victim to the *tsadik*, possessing special virtues and wisdom. On the one hand, the Holocaust is unique, for example, Langer (1975) distinguishes between violence and atrocity and the incomprehensibility of the Holocaust, while Pinker, citing over 133 million victims of 16 democides before the twentieth century, and quoting the widespread, enthusiastic approbation by various luminaries of world history as well as in the Bible, writes "The shocking truth is most people didn't think there was anything particularly wrong about genocide as long as it did not happen to them" (Pinker, 2011, p. 33). Kohut says that "what separates us from them (the generation of perpetrators and enablers) is 'the grace' of historical experience" (Kohut, 2012, p. 241). The characteristics of children of survivors emerge from and are shaped by the different cultural fragments in which they became embedded. They may identify with heroism or victimization, be proud and triumphant or ashamed and defeated, show assertion or fearfulness as they live in the world. As Frie writes, "the embeddedness of the person in her or his contexts is so profound as to render any absolute distinction of action from context nonsensical" (Frie, 2012, p. 355).

Further, their characteristics, the stories they tell or embody, are totally dependent on who they appear to. As Frie writes in the same essay, "The question of who is listening, which cultural values are at work, and the particular historical backdrop always governs the process of what is or is not said, what is remembered and what is forgotten" (Frie, 2012, p. 337). The accounts of Browning's (1998) "ordinary men" through judicial interrogations are different from Kohut's (2012) analysis of the interviews of a "German generation."

Thus survivors may tell different stories in oral history testimony and therapy offices. As Krystal (1995) writes of survivors: they appear better to sociologists than to psychiatrists.

In light of all the rationales for diversity among children of survivors as a group, the assertion is met with strong feelings. It would seem there is a general investment in seeing them as a homogeneous group. For children of survivors diversity brings up the legitimacy of the claim to a defined generational status. If they share characteristics, the argument for the impact of history is strengthened. For others, diversity suggests shared vulnerability, we are all victims but for "'the grace' of history," to use Kohut's phrase, and differ only in our particular distance from the epicenter.

My emphasis on the heterogeneity of survivors and their children should not be taken as denial of some very important commonalities. The first requires a reverse figure and ground; it is intrinsic not to them but in how they are seen. After being ignored, much like their parents had been, there seems to have been a strongly motivated need to attribute particular characteristics to children of survivors, with a blurring of boundaries between the two generations and their observers. Ironically, one of the traits attributed to survivors and their offspring is difficulty separating, but it would seem that the observers, in a slightly different sense, also have difficulty separating themselves, that is distinguishing their self-states or projections, more charitably hypotheses, from observations. Krystal (1974) suggests that recognition of the affects of others is often either distorted or confused with one's own affects. In this context, the attribution that children of survivors experience their parents' affects or history as if it were happening, or had happened to them, floats somewhere on the stage on which all are players, survivors, offspring, and witnesses. It is in this blurring of roles that the "survivor syndrome" has been extended to the second generation with no less an insistence on the creation of a broad pathography that is based on selective observations.

The generalization from clinical case material is made all the more compelling because much of it is sensitively, often poetically, rendered. One of the more interesting presumptive traits of the first two generations of survivors of the Holocaust is "survival guilt." I would not claim that issues of guilt are not observable in some individuals. Rather I would claim that it has been widely generalized and in truth better fits the narrative and is more consistent with the actions of a culture of bystanders rather than participants. An ironic comparison here might be to the "sullen defensive silence" of the German interviewee who complained about "the guilt that was laid on us" (Kohut, 2012, p. 218).

Like guilt, the "conspiracy of silence" is a popular attribution. Again it is difficult to know who the conspirators are. In the psychological literature it most often seems to refer to survivor families but occasionally to perpetrators, particularly when subject to legal indictment. Rather than silence, the variability of communication, in style and substance, is noted over time and found to depend on the receptivity of the listener. The readiness of a survivor to speak is a function of both participants. This is different from "conspiracy" and is not to deny the affectivity of either the testifying or the witnessing. The suppression of survivor memoirs alluded to earlier is well documented (Greenspan, 2000; Hartman, 1996). Of note, over and over again in survivor testimony, is that well-motivated and trained interviewers can often be seen cutting off survivors eager to tell their story (Kraft, 2002; Langer, 1991).

The enormity of the "monstrous" event is of such magnitude that the witness, no less than the second generation, is in danger of choking on, to use Rosenbaum's (1999) phrase, "second hand smoke." Thus, because the sequelae of historical trauma are dislocation and disorientation, there is a strong need for a coherent, well-emplotted story. The vertiginous spaces Daniel Libeskind created in his design of the Jewish Museum in Berlin cry out for straight lines and solid floors. The arrangement of facts offers multiple possibilities of emplotment (White, 1985, 1992) but some relief must be found in bearable narratives. Thus the official Anne Frank story that minimizes suffering is one of nobility, redemption, and faith in humanity and elides her death (Rosenfeld, 2004). Exegetists of Job tend not to comment that his grief over his sons can never be fully assuaged by the new children he begets after he is "restored," and interpreters of survivor–offspring relations are uncritical of the idea of "replacement children" and that the second generation is shaped by a role of being made into embodiments of their parents' losses.

Trauma as transmitted or trauma as embedded

"Transmission" is another idea that has been eagerly adopted, acquiring canonical status, even before critical scrutiny. Its usage conflates two separate domains of transmission, bio-psychological and historical/cultural. It seems to refer above all to "transmission of trauma," and other aspects of what may be "transmitted," for example values and resilience, may be omitted. It includes transmission of genes altered (Yehuda *et al.*, 2014), i.e., damaged, by stressors, and early interactional and attachment patterns supported by powerful and robust developmental research (Fonagy & Target, 2008). The idea of transmission references the classic formulation of "ghosts in the nursery" (Fraiberg *et al.*,1975), which was preceded by Burlingham's (1951) observation of the sharing of unconscious material which seems to be transmitted in an uncanny and unspecified fashion amplified by Herzog (1982). He concludes that "It seems that the highlights of experiences in which survivor-parents live their past – such as torture, escape, confinement, or starvation – are easily transmitted to children in those phases where the theme of parental trauma coincides with a child's current developmental task" (Herzog, 1982, p. 102). It is also described as a "haunting" (Schwab, 2010; Coles, 2011), and its major thrust is the inducing (the word "impregnating" has also been used) by parents of Holocaust images, memories, narratives, and/or identifications with the parent, lost family members, or perpetrators, and it includes the imposition of generational tasks.

Reflection on what avidly accepted ideas conceal leads to the suspicion that "transmission" leaves out too much of the domain of historical and cultural meaning. It suggests a linear, unidirectional relationship. At its worst, the word seems to imply a communicable disease while omitting the social context in which "transmission" occurs. While on first glance "transmission" would seem to be the mechanism through which "history flows through us," it oddly elides history. If we think of "transmission" in narrative terms, from whose point of view is the story told? Historical contexts "shape not only how it is narrated, but also how it is constructed in the first place" (Spiegel, 2014, p. 166).

An alternative to thinking of trauma as transmitted is to think of it as *embedded* in a total biological, developmental, familial, cultural, and historical context. The passivity of the recipient of transmitted trauma can be contrasted to, for example, the active metabolization of what Erikson describes as "The methods by which historical figures become prototypes of what really counts in his world, i.e., the variables of his group's space-time and the perspectives of its life plan" (Erikson, 1946, p. 359). Analogously, Kohut discusses "concrete historical experiences processed and responded to within different cultural contexts" (Kohut, 2012, p. 240). Erikson and Kohut, generations apart, are capturing the trauma and history as occurring in a bi-directional communicational matrix. Thus children of survivors come to know their parents' trauma through their own experiences of immigrant parents who have a different "native" language, and of not having grandparents, extended families, or national heritages. It is less that the parent's nightmare "transmits" the parent's trauma than it is the child's direct experience in the child's own context. Thinking of trauma as embedded rather than transmitted turns witnessing into something more active than passive; it emphasizes the ongoing participation of all as historical actors in their respective and multiple roles. With a view of transmission as "embedded" it is possible to understand the two discrete traits of children of survivors that are held in common. When children of survivors universally say they "always knew" their parents were survivors and "intend to pass on knowledge" to their own children, they are not claiming that they have been traumatized and plan to pass on trauma but are asserting possession of a heritage, however tragic, that is an important component of their identity. These two observations, lapidary in the context of all their differences, reflect that history, stowed away, has been the bedrock in constituting their identity.

The presence of history

There is a third observation suggesting the hiding presence of history. Though they all do it in their own, unique way, children of survivors do the same thing, namely integrate historical imagery, synthesized from some combination of all the many possible sources, into the narrative of their own lives. In some individuals this process is explicitly conscious, whereas in others it is discernible as it is being explicitly denied. Thus one individual is able to relate the trajectory of life to imperatives from the past (Prince, 1985, 1998), while sufficiently detailed inquiry discloses that, in the very act of vehement denial, another individual designs her life exactly around replication of her apprehension of her father's strategies for survival (Prince, 1980). Thus, for all their uniqueness, as Spiegel (2009, p. 6) describes it, they share belonging to that "second generation of the post-Holocaust world on whose psyche had been indelibly inscribed an event in which it did not participate, but which nonetheless constitutes the underlying narrative of the lives of its members psychologically constituted by history."

Last thoughts: protecting the Stowaway

Implicit in Thomas Kohut's work is the insight that the two terms conjoined as *psychohistory* are inseparable. Our psychological and historical narratives have as their basis something that actually happened, what Kohut (2012, p. 214) calls "concrete historical experience." When I started my inquiry, I had the belief that the objects of my search would be readily identifiable paying passengers. I failed to anticipate that the "facts," be they psychological or historical, would be elusive, located in ever-changing contexts. The differences among children of survivors (and, in one way or another, aren't we all?) could only get more pronounced as history flowed on.

The resistance to psychohistorical "facts" is at least partly motivated by the trauma of postmemory, i.e., facing but not personally experiencing the irreducible fact of past extreme suffering. Indeed, the postmodern disenchantment with the possibility of "truth" may have come from suppression of the knowledge of suffering; the elusiveness of the Stowaway thus reflecting the oldest of psychoanalytic ideas.

If context is all, my dissertation was written at a particular moment in time that was ripe for the emergence of the Stowaway from the shadows. This Stowaway sprang from the ashes of the Holocaust, which itself was partially enabled by the "Big Lie," conscious, instrumentally motivated assaults on "facts." Three quarters of a century later we are confronted with something even more malignant, if that is imaginable: the claim that our world is "post-fact." Despair of ever finding the Stowaway in any hiding place threatens a psychological void (see Prince, 2013) and a historical catastrophe. Despite its difficulty, the necessity of the psychohistorical project was affirmed by George Orwell, who, before the outcome of the Second World War was assured, wrote of "the horrors of emotional nationalism and a tendency to disbelieve in the existence of objective truth because all the facts have to fit in with the words and prophecies of some infallible fuhrer" (Orwell, 2013, p. 232).

References

Bergman, M. (1982). The inner readiness of the therapist to treat survivors and their children. In M. Bergman & M. Jucovy (eds.), *Generations of the Holocaust.* New York, NY: Basic Books.

Browning, C. (1992) German memory, judicial interrogation, and historical reconstruction: Writing perpetrator history from postwar testimony. In S. Friedlander (ed.), *Probing the limits of representation: Nazism and the final solution.* Cambridge, MA: Harvard University Press.

Browning, C. (1998). *Ordinary men: Reserve Police Battalion 101 and the final solution in Poland.* New York, NY: Harper.

Burke, E. (1990). *A philosophical enquiry into the origin of our ideas of the sublime and beautiful.* New York, NY: Oxford World Classics.

Burlingham, D. T. (1951). Present trends in handling the mother–child relationship during the therapeutic process. *Psychoanalytic Study of the Child, 6*, 31–37.

Coles, P. (2011). *The uninvited guest from the unremembered past: An exploration of the unconscious transmission of trauma across the generations*. London, UK: Karnac Books.

Epstein, H. (1977). The heirs of the Holocaust. *New York Times Magazine*, June 19.

Epstein, H. (1978). *Children of the Holocaust.* New York, NY: Putnam.

Erikson, E. H. (1946). Ego development and historical change – Clinical notes. *Psychoanalytic Study of the Child, 2*, 359–396.

Foer, J. S. (2003). *Everything is illuminated.* New York, NY: Harper Perennial.

Fonagy, P., & Target M. (2008). Attachment, trauma and psychoanalysis. In E. Jurist, A. Slade, & S. Berger (eds.), *Mind to mind: Infant research, neuroscience, and psychoanalysis* (pp. 15–49). New York, NY: Other Press.

Fraiberg, S., Adelson, E., & Shapiro, V. (1975). Ghosts in the nursery: A psychoanalytic approach to the problems of impaired infant–mother relationships. *Journal of the American Academy of Child and Adolescent Psychiatry, 14*(3), 387–421.

Frie, R. (2011). Irreducible cultural contexts: German–Jewish experience, identity and trauma in a bilingual analysis. *International Journal of Self Psychology, 6*, 136–158.

Frie, R. (2012). On culture, history, and memory. *Contemporary Psychoanalysis, 48*, 329–343.

Friedlander, S. (1992). Introduction. In S. Friedlander (ed.), *Probing the limits of representation: Nazism and the final solution.* Cambridge, MA: Harvard University Press.

Greenspan, H. (2000). The awakening of memory: Survivor testimony in the first years after the Holocaust, and today. Mona and Otto Weinman Lecture Series, United States Holocaust Memorial Museum. www.ushmm.org/m/pdfs/20040908-greenspan.pdf.

Hartman, G. (1996). *The longest shadow*. Bloomington, IN: Indiana University Press.

Herzog, J. (1982). World beyond metaphor: The transmission of trauma. In M. Bergman & M. Jucovy (eds.), *Generations of the Holocaust.* New York, NY: Basic Books.

Hirsch, M. (1996). Past lives: Postmemories in exile. *Poetics Today, 17*(4), 659–686.

Hirsch, M., & Spitzer. L (2010). *Ghosts of home: The afterlife of Czernowitz in Jewish memory.* Berkeley, CA: University of California Press.

Judt, T. (2008). The 'problem of evil' in postwar Europe. *New York Review of Books.*, February 14.

Kearney, E. (2015). Moved by the past: Discontinuity and historical mutation. *Rethinking History*, *19*, 305–309.
Kohut, T. A. (2012). *A German generation: An experiential history of the twentieth century.* New Haven, CT: Yale University Press.
Kraft, R. (2002). *Memory perceived: Recalling the Holocaust.* New Haven, CT: Yale University Press.
Krystal, H. (1974). The genetic development of affects and affect regression. *Annual of Psychoanalysis, 2*, 98–126.
Krystal, H. (1995). Trauma and aging: A thirty year follow-up. In C. Caruth (ed.), *Trauma: Explorations in memory* (pp. 76–99). Baltimore, MD: Johns Hopkins University Press.
Lang, B (1999). *The future of the Holocaust: Between history and memory.* Ithaca, NY: Cornell University Press.
Langer, L. L. (1975). *The Holocaust and the literary imagination.* New Haven, CT: Yale University Press.
Langer, L. L. (1991). *Holocaust testimonies: The ruins of memory.* New Haven, CT: Yale University Press.
Maier, C. (1993). A surfeit of memory? Reflections on history, melancholy and denial. *History and Memory, 5*, 136–152.
Mendelsohn, D. (2006). *The lost: The search for six of six million.* New York, NY: HarperCollins.
Merridale, C. (2000). The collective mind: Trauma and shell-shock in twentieth-century Russia. *Journal of Contemporary History,* Special Issue: Shell-Shock, *35*, 39–55.
Mintz, A. (2001). *Popular culture and the shaping of Holocaust memory in America.* Seattle, WA: University of Washington Press.
Mosse, G. (2000). Shell-shock as a social disease. *Journal of Contemporary History*, Special Issue: Shell-Shock, *35*(1), 101–108.
Novick, P. (1999). *The Holocaust in American life.* New York, NY: Houghton Mifflin.
Orwell, G. (2013). Letter to N. Willmette. 18 May 1944. In P. Davison (ed.), *George Orwell: A life in letters* (p. 232). New York, NY: W. W. Norton.
Pinker, S. (2011). *The better angels of our nature.* New York, NY: Penguin.
Prince, R. (1974). *Psychohistorical themes in the lives of young adult children of concentration camp survivors* (Unpublished doctoral dissertation). Columbia University, New York, NY.
Prince, R. (1980). A case study of a psychohistorical figure: The influence of the Holocaust on identity. *Journal of Contemporary Psychotherapy*, *11*(1), 44–60.
Prince, R. (1985). *The legacy of the Holocaust: Psychohistorical themes in the second generation.* Ann Arbor, MI: UMI Research Press.
Prince, R. (1998). Historical trauma: Reflections on the Holocaust. In J. Kestenberg & C. Kahn (eds.), *Children surviving persecution: An international study of trauma and healing* (pp. 43–55). Westport, CT: Praeger.
Prince, R. (1999). *The legacy of the Holocaust: Psychohistorical themes in the second generation.* New York, NY: Other Press.
Prince, R. (2009). Psychoanalysis traumatized: The legacy of the Holocaust. *American Journal of Psychoanalysis*, *69*(3), 179–194.
Prince, R. (2013). Facing the void. Paper presented at *The Wounds of History Conference*, New York, New York University.

Prince, R. (2015). The Holocaust after 70 years: Holocaust survivors in the United States. *American Journal of Psychoanalysis*, *75*(3), 267–286.
Rosenbaum, T. (1999). *Second hand smoke,* New York, NY: St. Martin's Press.
Rosenfeld, A. (2004). Anne Frank and the future of Holocaust memory. United States Holocaust Memorial Museum, www.ushmm.org/research/scholarly-presentations/past-lectures-and-symposia/meyerhoff-annual-lecture.
Runia, E. (2006). On presence: Spots of time. *History and Theory, 45*, 305–316.
Runia, E. (2007). Burying the dead, creating the past. *History and Theory*, *46*, 313–325.
Runia, E. (2010). Into cleanness leaping: The vertiginous urge to commit history. *History and Theory, 49*, 1–20.
Schwab, G. (2010). *Haunting legacies: Violent histories and transgenerational traumas.* New York, NY: Columbia University Press.
Sebald W. E. (2011). *Austerlitz.* New York, NY: Modern Library.
Shay, J. (1995). *Achilles in Vietnam: Combat trauma and the undoing of character.* New York, NY: Scribner.
Shay, J. (2002). *Odysseus in America: Combat trauma and the trials of homecoming.* New York, NY: Scribner.
Spiegel, G. (2009). The task of the historian. *American Historical Review, 114*(1), 1–15.
Spiegel, G. (2014). The future of the past: History, memory and the ethical imperatives of writing history. *Journal of the Philosophy of History*, *8*, 149–179.
Spiegelman, A. (1997). *The complete Maus* . New York, NY: Pantheon.
Suleiman, S. (2002). The 1.5 generation: Thinking about child survivors of the Holocaust. *American Imago*, *59*, 277–295.
Talbott, J. (1997). Soldiers, psychiatrists and combat trauma. *Journal of Interdisciplinary History*, *27*, 437–454.
White, H. (1985). The burden of history. In *Tropics of discourse: Essays in cultural criticism* (pp. 27–51). Baltimore, MD: Johns Hopkins University Press.
White, H. (1992). Historical emplotment and the problem of truth. In S. Friedlander (ed.), *Probing the limits of representation: Nazism and the final solution.* Cambridge, MA: Harvard University Press.
Wieviorka, A. (2006). *The era of the witness.* Ithaca, NY: Cornell University Press.
Yehuda, R., Daskalakis, N. P., Lehrner, A., Desarnaud, F., Bader, H. N., & Makotkine, I. (2014). Influences of maternal and paternal PTSD on epigenetic regulation of the glucocorticoid receptor gene in Holocaust survivor offspring. *American Journal of Psychiatry*, *171*, 872–880.

Chapter 7

National nightmare

The legacy of perpetrator trauma[1]

M. Gerard Fromm

In the last footnote to the Introduction of his magnificent *A German generation* (2012), Thomas Kohut quotes a text written in 1969–1970 by his psychoanalyst father: "If the depth psychologist (or the historian, for that matter) is to make a contribution to the understanding of man's role in history and his control over his destiny, then he must try to extend his empathic observation not only to the victims but also to the persecutors, not only to the martyrs but also to the torturers. He must discover the human, the all-too-human, whether in the normal … or in the psychopathological, in the good and in the evil" (H. Kohut, 1991, p. 119).

Kohut is a psychoanalytically trained historian, but he is also a son who learned deeply from his father. Taking up the latter's encouragement to find the all-to-human within the horrific, Kohut proposed that the Austen Riggs Center's Erikson Institute – of which I was the director and he a Board member – convene an interdisciplinary conference, which came to be called "The Legacy of Perpetrator Trauma in Groups and Families." With the help of a number of German colleagues, especially the scholar Hanna Schissler, Kohut invited the key participants from Germany and Austria, and I directed what turned out to be a profound, intellectually stimulating, and emotionally intense two days.

There was a history to the conference theme. For two consecutive years, the Erikson Institute's Fall Conference had studied the transmission of trauma, the clinical relevance of which was becoming increasingly clear. Papers from these conferences were published under the title *Lost in transmission: Studies of trauma across generations* (Fromm, 2012). They joined a literature that began with Selma Fraiberg's classic paper "Ghosts in the nursery" (Fraiberg *et al.*, 1975) and expanded enormously as the suffering of second-generation Holocaust survivors became known and treated.

In succeeding years, we have learned that, as the French psychoanalysts Françoise Davoine and Jean-Max Gaudillière argue in *History beyond trauma* (2004), invoking Wittgenstein, "Whereof one cannot speak, thereof one cannot stay silent." What human beings cannot contain of their experience – what has been traumatically overwhelming, unbearable, unthinkable – falls out of social discourse, but onto and into the next generation, as an affective sensitivity, a strange symptom, a chaotic urgency, in the words of one of our presenters, Gerhard Wilke, "an encapsulated presence," and sometimes an unconscious mission.

The challenge of empathy

This new conference was radically different from the earlier two on the subjects of its focus. As Wilke pointed out in the conference brochure, "psychoanalytic understanding of the working through of such traumatic material is largely based on work done with survivors, émigrés, refugees and their children. What we know less well are the transgenerational phenomena of children of perpetrators" – a generation not guilty by deed but so often caught up in feeling ashamed, guilty, responsible, and horrified by association. In this conference – that Thomas Kohut, and, in some ways, his father, proposed – we hoped to learn about the configuration and dynamics of this particular traumatic history.

In a clinical case conference some time ago, a young male patient told the staff that the hospital "is haunted by the forces of the dead." "They are here as much as there are helping people here," he said. To the degree that a person is unconsciously preoccupied with what may well be a haunting family history – who even at times may represent this hauntedness to and for his family – to that degree, the person's subjectivity is "lost in transmission," sometimes with tragic consequences: the German patient whose grandfather worked in the V-2 program at the beginning of the Second World War and who, years later, hurled himself from his dormitory balcony, thereby becoming a human missile; and the Austrian patient whose suicide attempts always involved the products of his grandfather's pharmaceutical company, itself implicated in a horrific Holocaust history. Erikson Scholar and psychoanalyst Vamik Volkan has discussed this kind of uncanny but stunning intergenerational enactment in a remarkable case history published recently under the title *A Nazi legacy* (Volkan, 2015).

The task of the Legacy of Perpetrator Trauma conference was to explore this phenomenon through the stories of postwar German and Austrian generations. We hoped to help clinicians and scholars revisit and understand more deeply the psychological aftermath of the Third Reich through a consideration of the inner conflicts of those who may carry this psychic burden, on behalf of their families, their society, and, in fact, the rest of us. What might we learn about individual, family, and group dynamics associated with the offspring of perpetrators, and what are the implications of this learning for society?

True to Erikson's conviction that learning occurs in the boundary areas between fields of study, the conference represented a range of disciplines: history, psychoanalysis, psychology, sociology, and others. The tradition of the

Erikson Institute is to hold *working conferences*, by which we mean that the presenters do not have the answers to the questions of the conference, except perhaps for themselves; that learning occurs through active dialogue among presenters and members; and that sometimes how we talk about something – the process dimension of the conversation – illuminates more deeply what we are talking about. In this conference, that process dimension was inescapable. We were dealing with an extremely serious subject and highly charged material. Members' joining this conference represented an act of courage because it inevitably meant encountering genuinely disturbing feelings, and inevitably challenged us to think more deeply, more discerningly, and, as Heinz Kohut suggested, more empathically about those feelings.

Freud spoke about every family's "archaic heritage" (Freud, 1939, p. 38), and one task of transmission turns out to be the generational struggle to resist the dissociation of that heritage, to recognize, in Davoine's and Gaudillière's phrase, the "cut-out unconscious" (Davoine & Gaudillière, personal communication) – cut out, that is, from the official narrative, whether that narrative is the family's or the society's – and to bring its full, tragic story into social discourse. How the unconscious gets "cut out" – and an astonishing 1930s dream journal kept by a woman named Charlotte Beradt (1968), to which I will return later, may open a window onto that process – leads to one set of questions. How it gets re-inscribed, if you will – the profound task of telling the story – is where the conference began.

The danger of love

The conference was structured around three presentations, with considerable time for general discussion. The first theme to emerge was a simple but powerful one: how to love when the object of that love is implicated in horrific crimes. Alexandra Senfft, a freelance journalist, whose personal story, *Silence Hurts: A German Family History* was published in 2008, put it in hypothetical form: "What if my grandfather had taken me onto his lap and I had begun to love him?" (This and other quotes come from the presentations and discussions at the conference.) Other similar, not at all hypothetical, statements spoke to the visceral experience of trying to contain the good and the bad at the same time, of vomiting out at the moment of taking in, of genuine love and horror at the feeling of loving.

It was as though it fell to the next generation to at least attempt to integrate what they experienced with their parents and what they also knew about them, an integration that the parents themselves seemed not to make at all. Rather the perpetrator generation, the generation of "knowing and not knowing," seemed essentially to be living out that old definition of schizophrenia, that is, the split personality, and living permanently in what Melanie Klein (1946) called the paranoid-schizoid position, the place where at all costs good and bad must be kept separate. The maturational effort toward what Klein called the depressive position, that is, the task of holding the good and bad in the same space toward some sort of integration, fell to the next generation. It was a profoundly difficult emotional assignment.

Part of the integrative task that fell to the children of perpetrators included feeling the guilt and shame of their parents' actions, which they themselves had warded off. Their children's responses took more than one form. We heard examples of essentially manic efforts at reparation, not necessarily directed to the victims of the Nazis, but to other suffering people in far-off countries. By "manic" I don't only mean frenetically active and obsessively preoccupied; I also mean what is termed a "manic defense," that is, manic reparation in the service of keeping at bay the very feelings of guilt motivating it. We noted as well friction between this generation and their children when the latter did not want to continue the reparation project but rather hoped to go on with their own lives. That wish, understandable as it is, is of course not at all easy to accomplish, not only because of their parents' pressure to continue the reparative mission, but because of the larger task of individuating from the chaos of such immense family disaster.

Another form this effort to process parental perpetration took, in the second and third generations, was identification with the victims, sometimes very literally and to a quasi-psychotic degree. Vamik Volkan in his recent book *A Nazi legacy* (2015) tells the story of a man who in his sleep leaves his bed to frantically open windows night after night. Though this man's troubles were many and complex, this particular stubborn and mysterious symptom was eventually understood in relation to his Nazi grandfather, who murdered Jews by gassing them inside a school bus. His victims – *like his grandson years later* – frantically tried to open windows.

Alexandra Senfft structured her presentation around two questions: her mother's question, "Why did they kill my father?," and her own, "Why did my mother die?" In the story, Ms. Senfft's mother loved her own father and was devastated when he was hanged for war crimes when she was 14. Over time, as she learned about his Nazi career and his role in deporting 65,000 Jews, she became increasingly depressed and alcoholic. In a family context where her own mother refused to believe, or to speak about, what had happened and who admitted no guilt or shame at all, Ms. Senfft's mother spiraled into madness.

Or perhaps into a mad sanity. In her alcoholic state, she would panic about being closed in and scream for help. Davoine and Gaudillière, in *History beyond trauma* (2004), report clinical work in which psychosis and trauma go hand in hand. They are convinced that the psychotic patient is madly conducting a research into the rupture between his family and the social fabric, a rupture brought about through trauma and betrayal. Beyond her screaming about the suffocating silence of her family, was Ms. Senfft's mother also living out her fragmented imagining of what her father's victims might have experienced? And was that part of her tragic death, self-inflicted while drunk, in scalding water?

There was one more thing Ms. Senfft's mother did while drunk, much more in the direction of an active transmission: She talked to her oldest child and, as Ms. Senfft said, "I let her." Frightened of "becoming" her, Ms. Senfft needed to know why her mother had died, one year after her own mother did, and boxes of letters left to her became a way into that terrible story. Like another presenter, Marcus Carney, whose award-winning documentary *The end of the Neubacher project* (2007) tells the story of his mother's family and its involvement in Austrian National Socialism, Ms. Senfft took up the task of inscription of a cut-out history, the task of "how to give my mother a voice."

But she then encountered the same terror her mother felt, the terrifying dilemma of exploding the silence or sinking into it. In a sense, by taking the risk of learning and then speaking the truth of her family history, she found herself in another transmission role: destroying the family myth, she *became the perpetrator*: the one who inflicts on her family, *for the first time*, the horrific images and feelings that have been so strenuously split off and kept at bay. The psychoanalyst Donald Winnicott in a paper called "Fear of breakdown" came to a remarkable intuition: "The patient needs to 'remember' ... but it is not possible to remember something that has not yet happened, and this thing of the past has not happened yet because the patient was not there for it to happen to" (Winnicott, 1974, p. 105). It's as though Ms. Senfft's family had dissociated themselves so thoroughly from their own lives that, in a very powerful sense, they were at risk of experiencing *in the future, at her hands* the trauma of what they had already done.

Ms. Senfft experienced enormous and sustained family resistance to her writing her book. She was criticized, seen as having something terribly wrong with her, and shunned. "Drive carefully" after one such family meeting had a menacing ring to it. Ultimately she lost her family when her book came out, though, crucially, not her whole family: her father supported her throughout the project. As she said, "I don't know what I would have done if he had turned against me." And, in a sense, her mother was there too, as the "open wound" of her family that "nobody treated," until her daughter did by writing her story.

The word "therapist" has an ancient Greek root in the word "therapon," the second-in-combat, the one who *attends to the burial ritual of the warrior*. In a sense, this is the role that Ms. Senfft served for her mother. In his enigmatic statement that the symbol is "the murder of the thing" (Lacan, 1977, p. 104), the psychoanalyst Jacques Lacan evokes the varying levels at which inscription – and the witnessing embedded in it – destroys something. He also refers to its role in a person's fundamentally separating from the traumatic context: the way that inscription on a tombstone allows leaving the dead – and the trauma leading to the death – because now one knows where to truly find them.

A delegated life

Another presenter, Gerhard Wilke, a sociologist and organizational consultant, referred to present-day Germany as a "post-traumatic society." Today's understanding of PTSD includes three major elements: overwhelming exposure to horror, manifested in the symptom triad of flashbacks, dissociation, and hyper-arousal; the experience of sudden serious loss; and what has come to be called "moral injury." Coined by the VA psychiatrist, Jonathan Shay (2014) and broadened by Brett Litz (2014), moral injury refers to a deep sense of betrayal of "what's right," committed by someone in legitimate authority or by oneself, in a high-stakes situation: the devastating emotional legacy of witnessing or participating in something that fundamentally violates one's most basic sense of moral order. All three elements occur simultaneously and with extraordinary intensity in perpetrator families.

Wilke captures one aspect of the second and third generations' sense of themselves in the statement that "We live a delegated life." From his point of view, his generation is always representing someone to someone else, and, in one way or another, is implicated constantly in working out something for someone else. This is part of the perhaps naïve but urgent longing for "one's own life." Wilke attempted to get some grasp on this phenomenon for himself personally by leaving Germany for London, from which vantage point two things happened. First, he was constantly seen as a Nazi, which he actually found useful; in the safer, more playful context of London, he could dare to face the Nazi in himself. But his former countrymen did not have the luxury of this perspective from a distance, so the second thing that happened was Dr. Wilke's dedicating himself to helping them achieve it, as best he and they could. He does this through consulting to their work lives (Wilke *et al.*, 2005) and helping them see – not an easy task, to be sure – the playing out of war trauma in their daily relation to authority, to ordinary assertiveness, to their need for order, and so on.

Following Wilke's presentation, we had set aside a considerable length of time for conference discussion. The first half of that time was to be a space for volunteer members to express freely what they had experienced in the conference – and where those experiences had led them in their associations – to which Wilke consulted; the second half was to be a more reflective and integrative conversation for everyone, to which both he and I were to consult. But first, the opportunity was to simply bring out whatever members were carrying emotionally from the presentations and discussions so far. This was obviously not an easy task, even if it promised some degree of relief, learning, and even intimacy. As I had from the very beginning of the conference, I told myself once again to try to "hold the whole thing," meaning that I was keenly aware of how critical it was for the staff to contain this process, to manage boundaries, and to be present as sensible authority.

In the first discussion, members were very attentive to the presence of two Holocaust survivors in their midst. Nevertheless – or perhaps because of this – the unfolding conversation was extraordinary in its emotional scope and detail. Stories about members' families came out, many associated with wartime experiences. References to the conference material included very personal reactions, sometimes of feeling things from both sides. Anxiety ebbed and flowed, and, at one point, in the midst of the unstructured opening up of experiences, one of the Holocaust survivors spoke with feeling about "needing a framework" for what was happening. Not long thereafter, the second Holocaust survivor began to speak at some length and rather theoretically about trauma. Interesting as his comments were, the effect was to interrupt the expression of what members were carrying and how it linked to their personal experiences.

Wilke consulted to what might be the group's need, via this member's discourse, to protect itself from the intensity of feeling that had been emerging. Despite this intervention, members seemed to defer to the Holocaust survivor who had been speaking, and indeed his comments, again very astute but conveyed almost as a lecture, continued at some length, limiting the opportunity for other members to speak about their experiences. Eventually, one German member and Wilke again intervened with the speaker in ways that some members felt to be too confrontational. And suddenly, just as this part of the group discussion was coming to an end, we were back to the old roles of German perpetrator and Jewish victim. Sadly, a framework of sorts had fallen into place, and the flow of conversation – if not of history, to pick up on one of Kohut's concepts – had stopped.

In the broader reflective discussion that followed, the group tried to process what had happened with only partial success. Feelings were still running high and tended toward polarized positions. The group did its best to reflect on the events of the first discussion and at least allowed members' different perspectives to be articulated. The hypothesis I found myself with, and offered to the group, was that, as this powerful conversation was coming to a close – and therefore as we were all about *to be silenced permanently*, this discussion group being the last conference event – there was something unbearable about, in Heinz Kohut's terms, the effort to "extend (our) empathic observation" such that we might end up on the wrong moral side of history, not to mention being stuck with unbearable identifications. The old roles – and the sense of being back to square one – disappointing as they were, were nevertheless reassuring. We knew where, in a projective sense, to leave the good and the bad. Though it was hard to know what members did with my intervention and indeed how they actually understood what had happened, it seemed to me that the potential learning from and about the group's process was invaluable.

The destruction of dream life

"What haunts are not the dead, but the gaps left within us by the secrets of others." This quote from the Hungarian psychoanalyst Nicholas Abraham begins a recent book – part legal treatise, part Holocaust history, part family study – by Phillipe Sands (2016). As we have seen so far, one generation's secrets become the next generation's gaps, and also their hauntedness. But a remarkable dream journal from the 1930s suggests the ways that, in the context of terror and destructive group processes, the earlier generation attempted to keep secrets from itself, leading to profound, collective dissociation and the licensing of horrific destructiveness. A natural experiment in what Gordon Lawrence (1991) called "social dreaming," the journal illuminates the steady assault on a person's inner life and the way that massive social trauma and malignant authoritarianism turn an essential privacy into dangerous secrecy, even from the self.

In his remarkable analysis of Freud's Irma dream – the foundational dream in psychoanalytic dream theory – Erik Erikson noticed a group process. Freud's intellectual ambition for his new science of psychoanalysis – an ambition that was the "cornerstone of his identity" and an "almost obligation to his people" (Erikson, 1954, p. 169) – came up against something having gone dangerously wrong in his patient's treatment. In the face of this set of anxieties – guilt for harming his patient, fear of failing to meet the internalized aspirations of his ethnic group, fear of persecution by jealous colleagues – Freud, in his dream, defensively joins his professional group and blames someone else for the trouble. Erikson notes how "infantile wishes to belong to and believe in organizations providing for collective reassurance against individual anxiety ... easily join other repressed childhood temptations – and force their way into dreams" (Erikson, 1954, p. 158).

As I have argued elsewhere, "Adaptation requires that we 'see' the Other on whom we depend so fully throughout development, and psychic change relies to some extent on our seeing the Other whose conflicts speak to and through us. In certain contexts, ... envisioning the Other may move beyond the familial environment to larger social realities ... (E)ach dreamer is potentially a 'seer' of his or her 'people' and of the relationship to that Other. This has been described (Lawrence, 1991) as 'social dreaming.' In my own terms, I consider it an aspect of "unconscious citizenship" (Fromm, 2000, p. 289) But what if the Other is all-powerful and ruthlessly dangerous? And what if that Other sees that you see it?

This is the framework from which I would like to reflect on the earlier question about how the unconscious may become "cut out" and on the remarkable journal mentioned above. Throughout the 1930s, the journalist Charlotte Beradt kept a notebook, which was published in 1968 with the title *The Third Reich of Dreams*, in which she recorded the dreams of ordinary, "nonpolitical" German citizens, just after National Socialism came into power. Here is one of those dreams: "It was about nine in the evening. My consultations were over, and I was stretching out on the couch to relax with a book, when suddenly the walls of my room and then my apartment disappeared. I looked around and discovered to my horror that as far as the eye could see no apartment had walls anymore. Then I heard a loudspeaker boom, 'According to the decree of the 17th of this month on the Abolition of Walls ...'" (Beradt, 1968, p. 21).

This is the dream of a middle-aged doctor, who that day, in response to the block warden's apparently casual, half-joking observation that he had no flag outside his apartment, thought to himself "Not on my four walls" (Beradt, 1968, p. 22). The consequence in his dream is that his walls and all others are abolished. The physical boundary between private and public life no longer exists, just as, during the day, the boundary between private thought ("Not on my four walls") and public communication (no flag) did not exist either. Stunned by this experience, the doctor wrote his dream down, only to be accused of doing so in the next night's dream.

Beradt thus documents the penetration of the totalitarian Other into private life, including the private life of dreaming. She thereby raises for us questions about the effect of such serious boundary disturbance, and presumably both sleep and dream deprivation, on a terrorized group. From a different context, the psychoanalyst Christopher Bollas, considering the problem of sexual abuse, argues that the invading Other "electrifies the dream process" itself (Bollas, 1989, p. 175), rendering it too charged with anxiety to be at all useful in the processing of wishes and the development of symbolic functioning. In this vein, the epigram to Bruno Bettelheim's Afterword to Beradt's book is "Sleep no more. Macbeth doth murder sleep" (Beradt, 1968, p. 149).

Here is another dream on this theme: "I dreamt I was talking in my sleep and to be on the safe side was speaking Russian (which I don't know, and anyway I never talk in my sleep). I was speaking so that I would not even understand myself and so no one else could understand me" (Beradt, 1968, p. 52). The dreamer dreams in a language that not only those around her but even she herself cannot understand. As I wrote elsewhere, "If dreaming represents an effort, albeit ambivalent, to process important inner and outer life events, what does it mean to dream in order not to understand yourself?" (Fromm, 2000, p. 294).

What I believe we see here is "a desperate effort not only at safety but at anything that would feel like a boundary; the dreamer's demand that she have a private life is paid for by her keeping that private life from herself" (Fromm, 2000, p. 292). Beradt is remarkably attuned to the humor and the profound absurdity in these dreams, which she also sees in the dreams of many young Germans in which they express shame and horror at having hair of the wrong color or the wrong kind of nose. Beradt is astonished and also amused by the utter silliness and arbitrariness of these physical ideals, which are bought into, however, with a teenager's deadly seriousness and enforced with brutality, either by the State or by one's peers.

A third dream on the theme of the public and the private: "In place of the street signs which had been abolished, posters had been set up on every corner, proclaiming in white letters on a black background the twenty words people were not allowed to say. The first was 'Lord,' the last was 'I'" (Beradt, 1968, p. 23). In this dream of an educated young woman, reference points, represented by street signs, are abolished. Given the words that have been censured, the more fundamental reference points of "Lord," representing a higher power or a moral order, and of "I," that is, personal subjectivity, are forbidden as well. The disoriented dreamer is left in a terrorized dyadic relationship with the unseen authority behind the posters. Hence this woman's comments, to some degree like the previous dreamer, that "To be on the safe side, I must have dreamt this dream in English" (Beradt, 1968, p. 23).

Jacques Lacan returned Freud's foundational description of the trajectory of clinical psychoanalysis – "Where Id was, there Ego shall be" (Freud, 1933, p. 80) – to its original German: "Where It was, there I must come to be" (Lacan, 1977). This last dream suggests that the totalitarian process perversely reverses this trajectory: "Where I was, only It will be," with "It" referring to the dominant–submissive pairing between the State and its subjects. There is no Third (Muller, 1996), through which to ground the pair in a larger symbolic and moral order. As Beradt puts it, these dreams were "dictated ... by a dictatorship." She suggests that this "(d)ream imagery might thus help to describe the structure of a reality that was just on the verge of becoming a nightmare" (Beradt, 1968, p. 9).

Beradt adds that "The dreams we are concerned with were not produced by conflicts arising in their authors' private realm, and certainly not by some past conflict that had left a psychological wound. Instead they arose from conflicts into which these people had been driven by a public realm in which half-truths, vague notions, and a combination of fact, rumor, and conjecture had produced a general feeling of uncertainty and unrest. These dreams may deal with disturbed human relations, but it was the environment that had disturbed them" (Beradt, 1968, p. 15). She records many dreams in which this social dimension of fear, uncertainty, and miscommunication plays out with predictable results. In many dreams, she observes a "chorus" who intone statements like "There's not a thing one can do" (Beradt, 1968, p. 72), or whose silence accuses the dreamer of a costly and misguided refusal to join.

Indeed, so many dreams include, to the dreamer's shock, "silent and expressionless faces" (Beradt, 1968, p. 25), there being no human response at all when the dreamer expects and desperately needs one. In a sense, these dreams foreshadow the child development research of many years later having to do with the "still-face experiment" (Tronick, 2007), in which the mother is instructed to break the communicative rhythm of looks, smiles, and sounds with her infant, and instead present a "still face" for a short time. After efforts to re-engage mother – to restore what Erikson would call "basic trust" in this intimate social process – the infant invariably withdraws into what looks like hopelessness and reflexive shame.

If one essential function of the dream-work is overcoming trauma-induced helplessness, Beradt shows us dreams in which a collapse analogous to that in the still-face experiment occurs, and terrorized helplessness is recurrently justified. In one dream, the dreamer is "no longer able to speak except in chorus with my group" (Beradt, 1968, p. 87); and another person dreams "I was saying, 'I don't *have* to always say *no* anymore'" (Beradt, 1968, p. 119). About this last quasi-delusional contortion seemingly in the direction of freedom, Beradt comments that "Amid all the 'musts' of life under totalitarian rule, this almost touching magic formula, 'don't have to,' demonstrates once again what effort it costs to be against the state when freedom is a burden and bondage comes as a relief" (Beradt, 1968, p. 119).

Beradt calls this group process the "imperceptible and undramatic ... transition from suggestion to autosuggestion" (Beradt, 1968, p. 119), as insidious as it is terrifying. Erikson writes that "Where the human being despairs of an essential wholeness, he re-structures himself and the world by taking refuge in totalism" (Erikson, 1959, p. 133). By totalism, he means "a Gestalt in which an absolute boundary is emphasized. Nothing that belongs inside must be left outside; nothing that must be outside should be tolerated inside" (Erikson, 1959, p. 133). Beradt's book documents this despair of an essential wholeness and the subsequent disastrous splitting and re-structuring. As I noted elsewhere, "(r)elentlessly, we see the ethnosyntonic but ego-dystonic conflict resolved in favor of membership rather than identity or conscience. The totalitarian outcome is the self-alienated subject rather than the citizen, and the destruction of dream life – one space for self–other confrontation – is at the heart of the totalitarian method" (Fromm, 2000, p. 293).

In the name of the father

The title of this volume, *History Flows through Us*, comes from the final chapter of Thomas Kohut's *A German generation* (2012). In my contribution, I have tried to illuminate some of the intergenerational, dream, and group processes by which this flow works to shape individual feelings, attitudes, and behaviors. The title of Kohut's concluding chapter is "The authority of historical experience," with the word "authority" connoting, to my mind, not only the power historical experience unconsciously exercises over people but also the set of rights or claims one generation makes on the other. It seems to me, as I have argued elsewhere (Fromm, 2012), that the transmission of trauma from one generation to the next reflects a complex authority issue. To some degree, the experience of the next generation has been "authored," if you will, by the unspoken, indeed unspeakable, traumas in their parents' histories, and some of these children – Ms. Senfft's mother perhaps – are lost in this transmission.

Others, like Ms. Senfft herself, may have been especially, if unconsciously, "authorized" to carry the parent's trauma into the future. "She talked to me, and I let her." This may take the form of a symptom, of an "unthought known," in Christopher Bollas' apt phrase (Bollas, 1987), or of an urgent question: for example, "Why did my mother die?" In one way or another, such transgenerational experience "must come into being as emotional understanding if the [person] is ultimately to take authority for his or her own life as distinct from that of the traumatized parent" (Fromm, 2012, p. 113). Ms. Senfft's story suggests that the authority of one generation's historical experience – and its raw, if unconscious, power over the next – can be mitigated by that next generation's finding the authority – and, to be sure, the courage – to become its author, and to somehow inscribe this "archaic heritage" (Freud, 1939, p. 38) into the larger human discourse.

Ms. Senfft needed her father to find this authority, and fathers are a major part of the story Kohut tells in *A German generation*. He argues that the defeated, humiliated, and lost fathers of the First World War – from the PTSD perspective, a set of profound losses, horrific shocks, and moral injuries – set the experiential stage for the next generation's profoundly powerful peer relationships – indeed, their driven merger with the collective – which in turn made them vulnerable to, indeed hungry for, the return of a powerful, idealized father. Beradt reports a dream in which the phrase "In the Name of …" is proclaimed over the radio repeatedly, but its last word is "Führer" (Beradt, 1968, p. 40). In this dream, Hitler supplants all fathers, including the Heavenly One.

In the Preface to *Young man Luther* (1958), Erikson – the son of a German Jewish woman and a Danish Gentile father whom, to his great pain, he never knew – concludes with "a memory which had been utterly covered by the rubble of the cities and by the bleached bones of men of my kind in Europe. In my youth, as a wandering artist, I stayed one night with a friend in a small village by the upper Rhine. His father was a Protestant Pastor; and in the morning, as the family sat down to breakfast, the old man said the Lord's Prayer in Luther's German. Never having 'knowingly' heard it, I had the experience, as seldom before or after, of a wholeness captured in a few simple words, of poetry fusing the aesthetic and the moral …" (Erikson, 1958, p. 10). Once again, we encounter the longing for wholeness and its being found, however temporarily, through a father.

Thomas Kohut concludes his introductory chapter with a memory too: "My own interest in history can be traced back to fishing trips with my father in rural Wisconsin when I was very little. I do not recall us ever catching anything, but I vividly remember listening with rapt attention as my father told me stories of the Persian and Peloponnesian wars as we sat in a little rowboat in the hot sun on a lake …" (T. A. Kohut, 2012, p. 18). Barely 15 years after his escape from Vienna, Heinz Kohut and his son are together, alone on a boat, safely separate from other people, warmed by the sun, waiting for nature to offer something special from its depths, telling and listening to stories of long-ago and far-away wars. From this comes a life's vocation, a story of too close a war, and our gratitude that some transmissions – or should we say trans-missions – are more profoundly generative than others.

Notes

1 A different version of this chapter was published in 2017 in Organisational and Social Dynamics, 17, 111-126, and is included in this volume by permission of OSD's editors.

References

Beradt, C. (1968). *The Third Reich of dreams*. Chicago, IL: Quadrangle Books.

Bollas, C. (1987). *The shadow of the object: Psychoanalysis of the unthought known*. London, UK: Free Association Books.

Bollas, C. (1989). The trauma of incest. *Forces of destiny: Psychoanalysis and human idiom* (pp. 171–180). London, UK: Free Association Books.

Carney, M. (2007). *The end of the Neubacher project.* A documentary film written and directed by Marcus J. Carney.

Davoine, F., & Gaudillière, J.-M. (2004). *History beyond trauma.* New York, NY: Other Press.

Erikson, E. (1954). The dream specimen of psychoanalysis. In R. P. Knight & C. R. Friedman (eds.), *Psychoanalytic psychiatry and psychology: Austen Riggs Center* (Vol. 1, pp. 131–170). New York, NY: International Universities Press.

Erikson, E. (1958). *Young man Luther*. New York, NY: W. W. Norton and Company.

Erikson, E. (1959). The problem of ego identity. In G. S. Klein (ed.), *Psychological issues* (pp. 101–171). New York, NY: International Universities Press.

Fraiberg, S., Adelson, E., & Shapiro, V. (1975). Ghosts in the nursery. *Journal of the American Academy of Child Psychiatry, 14*, 387–421.

Freud, S. (1933). The dissection of the psychical personality, Lecture XXXI. *New introductory lectures on psycho-analysis. S.E. 22*. London, UK: Hogarth Press.

Freud, S. (1939). *Moses and monotheism. S.E. 23.* London, UK: Hogarth Press.

Fromm, M. G. (2000). The other in dreams. *Journal of Applied Psychoanalytic Studies, 2*, 287–298.

Fromm, M. G. (2012). *Lost in transmission: Studies of trauma across generations.* London, UK: Karnac Books.

Klein, M. (1946). Notes on some schizoid mechanisms. *International Journal of Psycho-Analysis, 27*, 99–110.

Kohut, H. (1991). On leadership. In P. Ornstein (ed.), *The search for the self: Selected writings of Heinz Kohut* (Vol. 3, pp. 103–128). New York, NY: International Universities Press.

Kohut, T. A. (2012). *A German generation: An experiential history of the twentieth century.* New Haven, CT: Yale University Press.

Lacan J. (1977). *Écrits: A selection*. New York, NY: W. W. Norton and Company.

Lawrence, W. G. (1991). Won from the void and formless infinite: Experiences of social dreaming. *Free Associations*, *2*, 259–294.
Litz, B. (2014). Clinical heuristics and strategies for service members and veterans with war-related PTSD. *Psychoanalytic Psychology, 31*(2), 192–205.
Muller, J. (1996). *Beyond the psychoanalytic dyad.* London, UK: Routledge.
Sands, P. (2016). *East West Street: On the origins of genocide and crimes against humanity.* New York, NY: Knopf.
Senfft, A. (2008). *Schweigen tut weh: Eine deutsche Familiengeschichte.* Berlin, Germany: List.
Shay, J. (2014). Moral injury. *Psychoanalytic Psychology, 31*(2), 182–191.
Tronick, E. (2007). *The neurobehavioral and social–emotional development of infants and children.* New York, NY: W. W. Norton and Company.
Volkan, V. (2015). *A Nazi legacy.* London, NY: Karnac Books.
Wilke, G., Binney, G., & Williams, C. (2005). *Living leadership.* Harlow, UK: Pearson Education Limited.
Winnicott, D. W. (1974). Fear of breakdown. *International Review of Psycho-Analysis*, *1*, 103–107.

Chapter 8

Not as one would like to imagine

Psychoanalysis during and after the Third Reich

Emily Kuriloff

The German psychoanalyst Uwe Peters speaks of his nation's impoverished "intellectual life" at the hands of the Nazis. In an effort to help his non-German readers empathize with his regret, he invites them to imagine the richness within the greater German-language community, if only the Jews were still there:

> The entire development of ego psychology (Anna Freud, Heinz Hartmann, Rudolf Loewenstein, and Ernst Kris), which indeed was initially formulated just before the emigration, [would have] taken place in [Austria]. Rudolf Lowenstein would have analyzed Jacques Lacan in Berlin and not in Paris. Heinz Kohut and Otto Kernberg would have developed their theories of narcissism in Vienna and not in Chicago and New York.
>
> (Peters, 1988, p. 55)

Or would they have? Peters' reverie reveals the conceit of a psychoanalysis that transcends geography, culture, and temporality. Ironically, as he laments the loss to his nation, he trivializes the seismic effects of Nazism on those analysts who survived but whose ideas were invariably influenced by their forced displacements to Paris, New York, Chicago, etc. As this discussion attempts to illustrate, the story of German psychoanalysis during and after Nazism is a painful reminder of the ways in which the ideas and spirit of a terrible time and place can challenge psychoanalytic self-reflexivity, identity, and agency.

The "Aryanization" of psychoanalysis?

When the Nazi regime initially took over in 1933, both Jewish and non-Jewish analysts tried to compromise with the Reich in order to preserve analytic work and community. "It is on record," Wallerstein reports, "that Ernest Jones counseled the group (stripped of its majority Jewish members who were stepwise pushed out) to do its best to maintain its psychoanalytical presence and functioning, for who knew, after all, how long Hitler would last." (Wallerstein, 1987, p. 33). To make clear the situation in which these people found themselves, Wallerstein wonders what any analyst would do if they were

> trained psychoanalysts, with life, family and career solidly in Germany, with its culture and language, with Ernest Jones the IPA president advising that we not panic and flee, but stick together to maintain the flame of psychoanalytic reason against the demonic and irrational forces threatening to engulf us? ... How many would have dared to join the protests ...?
>
> (Wallerstein, 1987, p. 33)

There were some protests. When Edith Jacobson, the politically leftist Jewish analyst, was arrested in 1935 because of her connections with patients opposing National Socialism, Felix Boehm and Carl Müller-Braunschweig, two leaders among the "Aryan" analysts, initially wrote a letter in opposition to her incarceration. But then they attempted to rescind the document. According to German psychoanalyst Regine Lockot, (1985), Anna Freud understood their change of heart, which was based on their fear for the survival of their flagship institute should it openly align itself with the left. While Ms. Freud privately shared her apprehension for Jacobson, she concurred with the German analysts' "pragmatism." Neither, perhaps, could any analyst imagine the full measure of the destructive potential of Nazi ideology and praxis; it was and remains beyond mentalization. Indeed, Jacobson herself had chosen to return to Berlin after having left early in Hitler's reign, and was smuggled out of the country following her furlough from prison due to severe medical illness.

While Jacobson was spared, psychoanalysis in the Reich did not remain unsullied. Käthe Dräger, a non-Jewish German who resisted, and was persecuted by the Nazis, explains that "A chronicle of the years 1933–1945 would be easier to write if we could tell the tale today: At a certain point in the development of the situation, the 'Aryan' analysts simply said 'no.'" Alas, as Dräger implies, those who remained – generally – said "yes" (Chasseguet-Smirgel, 1987, p. 435). But what did saying "yes" mean? In 2001 historians Eileen and James Goggin published a rather polemical deconstruction of praxis during the Third Reich, *Death of a Jewish Science* (Goggin & Goggin, 2001) in which they claim the complete eradication of what had previously been psychoanalysis in Germany. The Goggins make two essential arguments throughout their book. The first is that individual experience, expressed via free association, becomes a travesty in an unfree, totalitarian state. The second is that the doctors who remained at the Göring Institute were more or less in cahoots with a medical agenda that had at its core "the joint principles of healing and extermination" of undesirables.

Leaning heavily upon a compilation of documents from before, during and after the Nazi period entitled "Here life goes on in a most peculiar way" (Brecht *et al.*, 1985), Goggin and Goggin take to task historian Geoffrey

Cocks' 1985 landmark volume on the period, *Psychotherapy in the Third Reich*, particularly his claim that, as a result of Matthias Göring's leadership of the former Berlin Psychoanalytic Institute, work continued, and in some ways even thrived under Hitler (Cocks, 1985, pp. 15–17; revised edition, Cocks, 1997). They challenge Cocks' criterion of "institutional continuity" as synonymous with the survival of psychoanalysis during the Third Reich, accusing him of neglecting what went on *inside* the consulting rooms that remained open between 1933 and 1945.

Cocks counters the Goggins' argument by noting that nobody "really" knows what went on inside the institute's consulting rooms at the time. Some analysts, Cocks points out, particularly the notably antifascist John Rittmeister, spoke of achieving "scientific advancements" in their work there. Cocks goes on to challenge the Goggins' monochromatic characterization of those who remained behind, suggesting that

> their collaboration with the Nazi regime was not one-dimensional. It was composed of a variety of motivations along a sliding – and often extremely slippery – scale of general morality and professional ethics, the result being their functional support of the regime as well as the defense and advancement of a discipline that was suddenly growing – incompletely before 1945 – into a profession through the integration of their work into various state, party and private institutions (e.g. private health insurance; applied psychology in industry, education and the military; the medical service of the Luftwaffe).
>
> (Cocks, 2001, p. 212)

Such "official" support for psychoanalysis did indeed enhance its visibility and popularity, initiating an institutional and social trend that persists in Germany today. Cocks also claims that, because it was Matthias H. Göring, cousin to the infamous Fieldmarshal, who was appointed head of the "Aryanized" establishment, his assumed loyalty afforded him independence from government oversight. Indeed, few of the institute's psychoanalysts were members of the Nazi party, and M. H. Göring did not require that they join.

If Cocks reckons that the Goggins' conclusions are excessively damning, there are other assessments that tend toward the opposite extreme, presenting an idealized view of those who remained. The American interpersonal analyst Rose Spiegel (1975), for instance, writes that non-Jewish, German analysts protected the Berlin institute from fascism during Hitler's reign. Spiegel bases her argument on interviews with middle-aged German doctors, individuals whom Spiegel and her analytic associate Gerard Chrzanowski had first encountered at a conference in Mexico. That Spiegel's subsequent study based itself solely upon these former Göring Institute analysts meant that she was relying on information from individuals who "were vulnerable to defensive distortion, if not outright cover up" (Goggin & Goggin, 2001, p. 23), rendering her conclusions questionable.

Arthur Feiner, another interpersonal psychoanalyst who was to collaborate with Speigel and Chrzanowski on a never-to-be-published volume on the topic (Chrzanowksi, 1997), did have a more complex view of the study, a difference missed by Goggin and Goggin in their critique of this research. That is, Feiner recognizes the need to dissemble, but also the analyst's desire to preserve psychoanalysis at all costs. He ends his comments as follows:

> It has been argued long ago that sometimes men try to carry out unjust laws so as to weaken their severity. It is perhaps just a deceitful rationalization to ease their consciences. The moral implications of the facts presented here may have to be faced by all of us. As Earl Wittenberg (1984) commented, they, in Berlin, were like we are. I may have left you with more troubling questions than when I began.
>
> (Feiner, 1985, p. 544)

Either/or views of German psychoanalysis among those in the profession may reveal how people struggle to integrate aspects of self and other conflict with our identity. For instance, Spiegel writes that part of what motivated her to study the members of the Göring Institute was the hope that she would not have to accept that analysts accepted Hitler in their midst. Instead she wanted to believe, as she puts it, "that in the vortex of Nazism, somehow human decency had somewhere, somehow survived." (quoted in Goggin and Goggin, 2001, p. 21). Her "wish" is certainly understandable, particularly when evil has become entwined with that which has been otherwise esteemed as good – in this case, psychoanalysis itself.

Goggin and Goggin (2001, p. 173) take the view that it was not until the 1970s that a new generation of non-Jewish German analysts really began to "come to terms with their Nazi roots." Those before them had reportedly closed their eyes, and so made it difficult for younger analysts to ask questions or express feelings about the past. Rather than the classical trope of the fear of opening the door to the primal scene, one German analyst reports that both his patients and his colleagues were "more afraid of opening the door to the gas chamber" (Speier, 1993, quoted in Goggin and Goggin, 2001, p. 174).

Given a culture of silence, and the jockeying for position of not one, but two, German psychoanalytic societies that ensued in the immediate postwar period, it is not hard to understand that as late as 1977, when the International Psychoanalytic Association proposed holding a future annual meeting in Berlin, the offer was rejected by analysts who felt that the German groups had not adequately addressed their past. (Ehrlich, 2009). When the proposal was renewed in 1985, the international analytic community was more amenable to meeting on German soil, yet many of the analyst-émigrés who thought they might attend found returning to Hitler's ex-capital too painful to contemplate.

Thus, Hamburg, a port city with a tradition of more progressive politics dating from the 1920s, was chosen.

Times were indeed changing. Beginning in the early 1980s, West German historians and analysts had gained access to original source material from the Berlin Institute archives that had previously been unavailable; the new materials allowed greater exploration of the times. The psychoanalyst Regine Lockot, whose work I will address later in this chapter, became a chief investigator.

Lockot compares the theoretical rifts within psychoanalysis to the divisions that created the Berlin Wall, the former involving a number of players, events, and motives. The analyst Carl Müller-Braunschweig had been president of the Deutsche Psychoanalytische Gesellschaft (DPG) after the war. He opposed the development of what he saw as revisionist analytic ideas by his colleague Harald Schultz-Hencke. At the first meeting of the International Psychoanalytic Association (IPA) in 1949 in Zurich, Schultz-Hencke presented these ideas, assuming that Müller-Braunschweig supported his presentation. As Lockot tells it, without the foreknowledge of Schultz-Hencke, Müller-Braunschweig instead provoked a confrontation after the talk, juxtaposing his reportedly "pure" views to those of the Neo-Freudian Schultz-Hencke. Müller-Braunschweig hoped this would provoke Schultz-Hencke to leave the DPG, but Schultz-Hencke refused to do so. Müller-Braunschweig thus secretly founded the Deutsche Psychoanalytische Vereinigung (DPV). Without any further examination of the history or differences between the groups, including, most notably, Müller-Braunschweig's complex yet clear involvement with the Nazis, the IPA accepted the DPV as the only legitimate institute for membership – and the DPG was "out" by 1951.

Lockot understands these developments as more than the usual power struggles that occur in all groups. She also described them to me as enactments from the past:

> There's always a furnace of theoretical discussion … On the surface it's given the label of "theoretical differences" or "political differences" but it's really finger pointing to rid oneself of guilt; underneath the confrontation is the wish to blame the other person so as not to confront your own responsibility, not to integrate the parts of yourself and your past you refuse to accept, the German past that is hard to accept.
>
> (Lockot cited in Kuriloff, 2014, p. 76)

In their book exploring the "Nazareth" Tavistock group relations conferences between German and Israeli analysts, H. Schmuel Ehrlich and his colleagues also take on the deeper meanings contained in the struggles between the DPV and the DPG. "Both groups," according to Ehrlich (2009, p. 168) were "in a collective German state of denying an incredible depression, marked by the imputations of having betrayed Freud and having adapted to the Nazi ideology during the twelve years of dictatorship." Supporting

Lockot's formulations regarding the conflict's latent meaning, Ehrlich goes on to argue that

> What was even more important was the not clearly understood significance of the DPV's recognition by international psychoanalysis in Amsterdam in 1951. The DPG's non-recognition seemed like an international condemnation of its members and increased the enmity against the rival. The DPG seemed to have been allotted the depressing burden of the German past for both psychoanalytic groups. Now DPV members, on the other hand, could entertain the semi-conscious illusion of being on the side of persecuted psychoanalysis, and therefore belonging to the persecuted ones.
>
> (Ehrlich, 2009, pp. 169)

Because I was going to Germany for a family vacation, I contacted Regine Lockot, and she responded "You are certainly welcome in Berlin." In particular, she invited me to participate in her forum, a discussion group of fellow professionals interested in the topic of analysis and the Holocaust. Lockot had taken it upon herself to distribute my manuscript to all members, and I had received more than one helpful, often self-disclosing, response beforehand as a result. One analyst revealed that her father's military service during the Second World War in a Jewish Ghetto or camp had led to his psychic collapse and subsequent psychoanalytic treatment, contributing to the development of her own interests.

Both Lockot and her group had much to say about Berlin. In addition to her historical acumen, Lockot was generous with her feelings, helping to create what she aptly termed a "private space" for testimony and witnessing. Elaborating on the silence of the German analysts in the first decades after the war, she shared the roots of her involvement in the research: "For me, when I started to be interested after the war, there was more to it than shame, guilt, or avoidance. I did not feel able, as a non-Jew, to engage this, as if I had no right, it was not fair of me – it was not my story. When I started my research, I felt I needed to clear up what happened in Germany among the Germans first" (Kuriloff, 2014, p. 82).

Later, when Lockot began to interview Jewish analysts, her youthful enthusiasm was not matched by adequate sensitivity. She shared this with me, too:

> I had some contact with Anna Freud – I had an appointment with her in London but it was cancelled because it was the same day that Dorothy Burlingham died. Since I had time, I contacted Paula Heimann instead. She asked me to send written questions ... But I was naïve, and lacked awareness ... I asked inappropriate questions ... For instance, I asked about analysts' involvement in the early Nazi Euthanasia project. To this

> Heimann replied to me something like, "Its too much to explain," adding, "If you want to get back your questions, please send postage ..."
>
> (Kuriloff, 2014, p. 82)

Since then, she offered, she had come to appreciate the deeply personal and complex feelings of all involved.

I was impressed by Lockot's openness regarding her struggles with her research. Her disclosures helped me to accept, even to correct, my own difficulties. Indeed, in her later edits to my manuscript, she regretted that I could not read German, for then I would have known the tone and content of the long-unavailable eyewitness accounts she had uncovered during the 1980s. She wanted me to detect that "special feeling" for what happens to people when "horror has been dealt as if it is the most normal thing in the world, and normality is made horrifying" (Kuriloff, 2014, p. 83).

Subsequently, I presented this material at a conference at the William Alanson White Institute in New York, where psychologist and analytic candidate Katarina Rothe (personal interview, 2012) had other interpretations based on her own research (Rothe, 2009, 2012) on postwar anti-Semitism in Germany. Rothe, who was formally an Assistant Professor at the University of Leipzig, explored contemporary attitudes toward the Third Reich's "final solution" via interviews with non-Jewish Germans. When she reviewed the transcripts of these discussions, she was struck by the unmentalized enactments between herself and her subjects. In fact, her own fantasies and feelings were part of her data, revealing a pattern she refers to as "poles of accusation," or an oscillation between the roles of victim and victimizer, between interviewer and interviewee. Rothe then concluded that "projective identification" – the placing of unwanted, unbearable affects in the other – is often the prototype for relatedness between generations of Germans when they encounter the specter of National Socialism.

At my invitation, Rothe put her psychoanalytic expertise, and her researcher's ear, to the conversations between myself and Lockot. That is, she explored a possibility that she had already confirmed in her published research; that non- Jewish Germans tend to deposit (or "project," as the psychoanalyst would put it) their psychic guilt and shame onto the other. What is more, Rothe also replicated what she had noted in the interactions with her research subjects – that past trauma is too disruptive to the individual's equilibrium, too overwhelming to consciously own and manage mentally. Rather, the past repeats itself in our present actions that remain out of awareness, insidiously haunting both Jews and Germans. Put differently, both of us were unwittingly swept up in an interactive matrix from an unbearable past, "projecting" and playing out polarities. Was Lockot "unconsciously enacting a role reversal" when she spoke of fellow Germans' "horrifying experiences," Rothe wondered? Who, Rothe continued, was in fact the victim of horror? Was it the Jew or the German? At this juncture Rothe stopped herself midsentence in order to observe that now she, a non-German Jew, was becoming Lockot's accuser, a recursive pattern in lieu of herself owning the identifications associated with cruelty and destruction. She then revealed to me that "I only became aware of my latent accuser position in the course of doing my study." And there was more. She added "I only became aware of this personal defense against the transmitted shame and projected 'guilt' feeling in my own family even later" (Kuriloff, 2014, p. 83). Such "transmitted shame and projected guilt" referred to the moment when Rothe discovered that her grandfather, who had previously been idealized in the family as a brave, fallen soldier, was instead an avowed National Socialist.

Never holding herself above the fray, Rothe continued to deconstruct the conversation with Lockot. The "special feeling" to which Lockot referred – inaccessible to me because I have no German – reminded Rothe of the "phantasm" of the elevated German people during the Reich – the *Volksgemeinschaft*. This, she explained, was the innately superior, special group to which the inferior *Untermenschen*, the Jews, could never belong. As troubling as her research felt to me, I was at the same time relieved and moved by this conversation between myself, a Jewish grandniece of many murdered family members, and Rothe, the non-Jewish granddaughter of a Nazi. There were some similar moments of recognition between myself and Lockot as well. For example, at one point in our conversation I asked Lockot how she felt about Berlin's new Jewish Museum. We shared our admiration for Daniel Libeskind's brilliant architecture – his uneven walkways, a staircase leading nowhere, the engulfing Holocaust "tower." But then Lockot added "They should have kept it empty." Feeling understood, I shared my sense that the museum's exhibits objectify Jews and Jewishness as an alien, even an extinct people. Then I went further, quipping "Hitler got his wish – he had been saving religious articles in Prague, hoping to create a museum for a '*Judenrein*' world." Lockot nodded in agreement. There were other, similar moments of recognition between myself and Lockot as well. At one point, she shared her personal reaction upon visiting the site of the Wannsee conference, a suburban Berlin villa where the top SS officers had decided to implement the "final solution to the Jewish problem": I saw the exhibits – some photos in which Nazis are smiling and laughing as they taunt and humiliate Jews. These disturbed me very much. And I thought, "This is sadistic pleasure" (Kuriloff, 2014, p. 84).

I found myself assenting to the idea that sadism is a part of being human, and added that sadomasochistic patterns can become entrenched in families, as well as subcultures, and passed down from generation to generation. The capacity to acknowledge sadism has long been identified by psychoanalysts as a useful step towards self-control, as opposed to "acting out." Madame

Janine Chasseguet-Smirgel, for instance, suggests that the inability of the postwar second generation of Germans to take responsibility for what happened in their nation is connected to a denial of such impulses. Chasseguet-Smirgel (1988) critiqued a 1984 volume of essays by German analysts edited by Jean-Luc Evard entitled *Les années brunes: psychanalyse sous le IIIe Reich* (*The brown years: Psychoanalysis under the Third Reich*) by noting the absence of any discussion of sadism, and the authors' inability to see their patients' identifications with the aggressors who were their fathers and forefathers. She gave the following warning: "One would hope that all analysts would agree that we all have *Hitler in uns*, and that only by integrating this diabolical part of oneself is it possible to disentangle oneself from it" (Chasseguet-Smirgel, 1988, p. 1061).

Lockot of course acknowleged Germany's culpability, although until the 1960s most Germans avoided the topic entirely. As I walked amidst the many commemorative plaques, museums, and monuments acknowledging the Shoah in twenty-first-century Berlin, I wondered why they were not built earlier, for instance during my first visit in 1980, when I not only noted the dearth of formal gestures of recognition, but was confronted by an unapologetic, middle-aged anti-Semite while I drank beer in the Munich tavern at which Hitler launched his first putsch. Contrary to the postwar thesis of the German analysts Alexander and Margarete Mitscherlich that excessive guilt rendered post-Nazi Germans unable to mourn, and thus to recognize and acknowledge their crimes outright (Mitscherlich & Mitscherlich, 1975), the historian Thomas Kohut (2012) introduces the opposite possibility: mourning, he reckons, must proceed from a capacity to feel guilt and responsibility. Kohut studied transcripts of interviews with "ordinary" Germans who were enthusiastic National Socialists, noting the pride and optimism evident in these interviews, and the remarkable absence of any mention of the loss not only of the war, but also of their esteem in the eyes of the world. All of this is denied, disavowed, perhaps not even present in conscious memory. Kohut thus posits that, in order for Germans to accept their murderousness, they must first feel their narcissistic injury. Put differently, Germans must mourn the loss of esteem and power in order to accept the carnage and destruction, and the guilt for what they have wrought.

What, then, of the shame and guilt of non-Jewish German psychoanalysts? Let us consider one prominent member of the Berlin Institute as a case in point. Tasked by M. H. Göring to lead the ideological campaign as a part of the ongoing program of "Aryanization" (Lockot, personal communication, 2010), Dr. Carl Müller-Braunschweig seemed more compliant than eager. Moreover, his appointment was acceptable to an unenthusiastic but realistic Sigmund Freud. In addition to the logic that Müller-Braunschweig's presence would protect the community from obvious dangers, Freud and Müller-Braunschweig both feared the influence of analysts not loyal to Freud's theory as control was being wrested from the founders. According to Cocks (1985) this is why the overtly anti-Nazi analyst Harald Schultz-Hencke was not particularly favored by Freud and his group for a central role in the transition. Indeed, after the war, and despite a record relatively unsullied by participation in fascism, Schultz-Henke's theoretical beliefs left him outside the circle, as Lockot notes in her description of the reorganization of psychoanalysis after the Second World War.

As Müller-Braunschweig, the chosen one, and Sigmund Freud's heir apparent – his daughter Anna Freud – toured the institute to plan for its "Aryanization," she began to weep, prompting Müller-Braunschweig to write her a comforting follow-up letter in which he expressed his hope that psychoanalysis in Vienna would maintain its independence from National Socialism (Lockot, personal communication). The letter's contents were indeed discovered by the authorities, who had been monitoring the activities of the prominent Miss Freud. As a result, Müller-Braunschweig was humiliated, not allowed to set foot in the institute, and permitted to work only from his home office (Lockot, personal communication). Not unlike the earlier noted hypothesis put forward by Kohut, the historians Goggin and Goggin (2001) similarly view the public nature of this punishment – this humiliation – as contributing to what they characterize as Müller-Bransweig's ever-increasing desire for approval from the Nazis. That is, rather than critically acknowledge what the Nazis were actually doing, he became more invested in shoring up his sense of self and esteem. Thus, evidence reveals that his anti-Semitic views, for instance, deepened in the years ahead. Anna Antonovsky, an Austrian émigré and psychoanalyst, concurs, noting just how far he went: "Müller-Braunschweig's 1942 study plan for the Göring Institute clearly lists the teaching of the theories of heredity and race and names among the lecturers Herbert Linden, the director of the euthanasia program for the untreatable mentally ill." (Antonovsky, 1988, p. 228). Furthermore, his writing describes psychoanalytic treatment as a means to help the individual not to become more fully herself, but instead to feel a part of the "*Volk*," or the superior Aryan group whose separate subjectivities were rejected as deviant, and dangerous to their compliance with loyalty to Hitler.

What, then, are we to make of the psychoanalytic community's participation, even half-heartedly, in the Third Reich? Some of the analysts at the Göring Institute seemed to have made a space for themselves to practice as usual, but many doctors also became "handmaidens" (Goggin & Goggin, 2001, p. 209) to the principles of the regime, including their participation in the "curing" or killing of homosexuals. Their complicity disposes of the conceit of the neutral professional, possessed of an analytic identity transcending culture and circumstance. As Bernd Nitzschke (1991, cited in Goggin & Goggin, 2001, p. 210) puts it, such an ideal only helped some of the German analysts who remained in the Reich to rationalize going along with, and even embracing, National Socialism.

What traction, then, does the individual analyst, or the analytic institute/society, possess to resist this pull of context? What is the "cash value" in Freud's revelation of the regressive pull of the group, or the archaic identifications associated with group leaders, if the analyst is invariably influenced, seduced, or changed by their context? Consider here Frosh's (2005) insight regarding the irony in the Nazi attempt to remove the Freudian Jewish "taint" from psychoanalysis. Frosh says that, in doing so, these "Aryans"

> jettisoned many of the elements of Freudian thought that might have protected them from conforming to Nazi demands ... Freud (1930) famously theorized the individual as always opposed to society, always discontented within it; on a personal level, and despite considerable ambivalence, he identified his own Jewishness as a major, even necessary, spur to achievement precisely because it set him outside the social norm. "To profess belief in this new theory," he wrote, called for "a certain degree of readiness to accept a situation of solitary opposition – a situation with which no one is more familiar than a Jew."
>
> (Freud 1925, p. 222). (Frosh, 2005, p. 268)

Shall we embrace this stance in future? Chasseguet-Smirgel (1987, p. 435) turns what may seem an academic question into a more urgent one by evoking a postwar context, thereby alerting us that we are in perpetual danger of behaving as German-identified analysts did in the 1940s, particularly in the midst of tyranny. She describes what happened in Eastern Europe within the decade after Hitler's demise:

> When the Communists came to power in an eastern European country, they asked the analysts to declare that psychoanalysis was a "piece of capitalist putridity," after which they would be allowed to work and retain their Party membership. Quite a number signed this declaration. The authorities then said: "You see, they say so themselves," and decided to dissolve the Society. The interesting thing is that apart from a few émigrés, no one remembers this story any longer.

As Edgar Levenson (1989) would put it, perhaps the psychoanalytic process – and the psychoanalyst – need to be less concerned with the question "What does it mean?" and should instead ask, always and repeatedly, "What's going on around here?"

References

Antonovsky, A. (1988). Aryan analysts in Nazi Germany. *Psychoanalysis and Contemporary Thought*, *11*(2), 213–231.

Brecht, K., Friedrich, V., Hermanns, L. M., Kaminer, I. J., & Juelich, D. H. (eds.) (1985). *"Hier geht das Leben auf eine sehr merkwürdige Weise weiter ..." Zur Geschichte der Psychoanalyse in Deutschland.* Hamburg, Germany: Kellner. (English translation by H. Ehlers, *"Here life goes on in a most peculiar way ..." Psychoanalysis before and after 1933.* London, UK: Goethe-Institut.

Chasseguet-Smirgel, J. (1987). Time's white hair we ruffle: Reflections on the Hamburg Congress. *International Review of Psycho-Analysis, 14*(3), 433–444.

Chasseguet-Smirgel, J. (1988). Review of J.-L.Evard (ed.) *The brown years. Journal of the American Psychoanalytic Association, 36*(3), 1059–1066.

Chrzanowski, G. (1997). Eulogy for Rose Spiegel, M.D. *Contemporary Psychoanalysis, 33*(2), 177–183.

Cocks, G. (1985). *Psychotherapy in the Third Reich: The Göring Institute.* New York, NY: Oxford University Press.

Cocks, G. (1997). *Psychotherapy in the Third Reich: Second edition.* Oxford, UK: Oxford University Press.

Cocks, G. (2001). Death of a "Jewish science"? Psychoanalysis in Nazi Germany. *Psychoanalysis and History, 3*(2), 211–225.

Ehrlich, H. S. (2009). Central and emergent themes. In H. S. Ehrlich, M. Erlich-Ginor, & H. Beland (eds.), *Fed with tears – Poisoned with milk: The "Nazareth" Group Relations Conference* (pp. 160–174). Gießen, Germany: Psychosozial.

Feiner, A. H. (1985). Psychoanalysis during the Nazi regime. *The Journal of the American Academy of Psychoanalysis and Dynamic Psychiatry, 13*(4), 537–545.

Frosh, S. (2005). Jung and the Nazis: Some implications for psychoanalysis. *Psychoanalysis and History, 7*(2), 253–271.

Goggin, J., & Goggin, E. (2001). *Death of a Jewish science: Psychoanalysis in the Third Reich.* West Lafayette, IN: Perdue University Press.

Kohut, T. A. (2012). *A German generation. An experiential history of the twentieth century.* New Haven, CT: Yale University Press.

Kuriloff, E. A. (2014). *Contemporary psychoanalysis and the legacy of the Third Reich. History, memory, tradition.* London, NY: Routledge.

Levenson, E. A. (1989). Whatever happened to the cat? Interpersonal perspectives on the self. *Contemporary Psychoanalysis, 25*(4), 537–553.

Lockot, R. (1985). *Erinnern und Durcharbeiten: Zur Geschichte der Psychoanalyse und Psychotherapie im Nationalsozialismus [Remembering and working through: On the history of psychoanalysis and psychotherapy in National Socialism].* Frankfurt am Main, Germany: Fisher Taschenbuch.

Mitscherlich, A., & Mitscherlich, M. (1975). *The inability to mourn: Principles of collective behavior.* New York, NY: Random House.

Peters, E. W. (1988) The psychoanalytic exodus: Romantic antecedents, and the loss to German intellectual life. In E. Timms & N. Segal (eds.), *Freud in exile: Psychoanalysis and its vicissitudes.* New Haven, CT: Yale University Press.

Rothe, K. (2009). *Das (Nicht-)Sprechen über die Judenvernichtung. Psychische Weiterwirkungen des Holocaust in mehreren Generationen nicht-jüdischer Deutscher. [(Non-)Speaking about the extermination of the Jews. Psychical aftermaths of the Holocaust in several generations of non-Jewish Germans].* Gießen, Germany: Psychosozial.

Rothe, K. (2012). Anti-semitism in Germany today and the intergenerational transmission of guilt and shame. *Psychoanalysis, Culture & Society, 17*(1), 16–34.
Spiegel, R. (1975). On psychoanalysis in the Third Reich. *Contemporary Psychoanalysis, 11*(4), 472–492.
Wallerstein, R. S. (1987). The terms of the dialectic. In J. Chasseguet-Smirgel (ed.), *Maintenance of the Psychoanalytical identity and functioning in a world of flux* (pp. 21–59). London, UK: International Psychoanalytical Association.

Part IV

Bridging psychoanalysis and history

Chapter 9

Psyche and history

Kaiser Wilhelm II and his role in German politics reconsidered

Ute Daniel

On the morning of December 28, 1918, a Saturday in the midst of the political turmoil following the abdication of the German Kaiser Wilhelm II six weeks before, Harry Graf Kessler visited the deserted imperial palace in Berlin. Kessler, a patron of the arts and a vigilant observer of Wilhelminian politics, recorded in his diary his impressions of the private rooms of the Kaiser and his wife, which were stuffed with all sorts of tasteless knick-knacks:

> Nothing but amazement, that the poor, horrified, fanciless creatures who preferred this trash and lived their futile lives in the precious surroundings of the palace among lackeys and fawning courtiers could make world history. Out of these surroundings came the world war, or at least what the Kaiser can be blamed for in connection with the world war: out of this tawdry ... illusory world came his judgements, plans, combinations and decisions ... I do not have pity on him, only, on second thought, I feel horrified and joint guilt, that this world was not spoiled long ago.
>
> (Kessler, 2006, p. 712)

Apparently, Kessler, an aesthete, was shocked by the contrast between the banal furnishings of the Kaiser's rooms and the large-scale consequences that originated from them. Though he didn't blame Wilhelm alone for the catastrophe of the Great War, he believed that the emperor's narrow-mindedness was instrumental in bringing it about.

In some ways, Kessler's sort of amazement persists today. The role of Wilhelm II in the politics of the German Empire and in the events leading up to war in 1914 is a recurring theme in historical research (Hull, 1982; Röhl & Sombart, 1982; Cecil, 1996/97; Röhl, 1998, 2002, 2004, 2014; Clark, 2000; Reinermann, 2001; Mommsen, 2002; Winzen, 2002; Mombauer & Deist, 2003; Kohlrausch, 2005; Daniel, 2005; Geppert, 2007; König, 2009; Bösch, 2009). These questions may linger on for another century. I do not claim to end the dispute in the following essay. My aim is more modest. I try to make it plausible that in order to understand the role of the Kaiser in the course of events from his enthronement in 1888 to the outbreak of the First World

War we need to take a closer look at the interdependence between him and his surroundings. Those surroundings were not the private rooms that Kessler toured in December 1918 but the private and public events in which Wilhelm took part in his youth and during his reign before 1914. By understanding those events and their reverberations, one perceives more clearly the intricacy and ambiguity of Wilhelm's role in his Prussian–English family and the German realm. And perceiving the many facets of Wilhelm's role allows us, I hope, to ask questions that are not as obsolete as they may seem; above all, whether Wilhelm really was the powerful ruler who led his country and the world along the path that he had chosen for them.

My discussion has two parts. The first is my rough sketch of Wilhelm's rise and fall in the public's eyes. The second is a summary of Thomas A. Kohut's psycho-historical analysis of the young Wilhelm, which was published a quarter of a century ago and still challenges historiography (Kohut, 1991). Together the two parts provide, I hope, a picture of the German Kaiser as a part of the political scene and his private environment, which a richer understanding of the German *Kaiserreich* requires, i.e., one that does not reduce the *Kaiserreich* to the playground of Kessler's "poor creature."

Wilhelm II as the symbol for Germany's encirclement

At the peak of the Agadir Crisis of 1911 – an escalation of the struggle between France and the German Empire for influence in Morocco – Baroness Spitzemberg, a very well-informed aristocrat of Baden, wrote in her diary

> Oh the Kaiser! He is held by everyone to be an extremely cowardly person, someone without courage or vigor ... He shies away from responsibility, from disruptions in his way of living, from work, from sacrifice of all kinds ... The *Post* [a Berlin newspaper] published positively treasonable comments, which culminated in calling the Kaiser a coward and docile with foreigners ... [A] declaration of war would be received with an enthusiasm as great as in anno 1870. What will come of all of this?
> (Vierhaus, 1960, pp. 531f)

At the time that Baroness Spitzemberg recorded these devastating judgments, the image of Kaiser Wilhelm II had already undergone breathtaking changes, especially in the eyes of the nobility, the bourgeois elite, and large sections of the press (see Daniel, 2005). When, two years after becoming Kaiser in 1888, Wilhelm dismissed Otto von Bismarck – the absolutely dominant figure in the politics of the German Empire since 1871 – as chancellor, his claim that he would govern the realm himself was well received. Bismarck was thought to be too old to live up to the new challenges of the imperialistic age. And since he took the arena of German foreign policy to be the European continent, he wasn't really interested in world politics. A young

Kaiser eager to play a role in the "scramble for Africa" symbolized for many Germans a modern regime.

At first, Wilhelm met expectations, especially in 1896, when he sent the famous "Kruger telegram" to Paul Kruger, the President of the Transvaal Republic, congratulating him on having defeated the Jameson Raid, an attempt to trigger an insurrection in the South African Boer Republic, that was supported by the Prime Minister of the British Cape Colony, Cecil Rhodes. The telegram caused indignation in London, but Berlin's upper-class and conservative newspapers welcomed it as a token of a vigorous anti-British policy. And in March 1898, Wilhelm's plans to construct a German fleet began to be realized when the Reichstag passed the first Naval Law, followed in 1900 by the second one. The resulting buildup, which was popular among the German middle and upper classes, began the Anglo-German naval arms race, which produced the two most conspicuous of the naval buildups that were proceeding in several countries, for example, also Russia, France, and Japan, before 1914.

But, soon, the conflict between Great Britain and the South African Republic that led to the outbreak of the Boer War in 1899 was to tarnish the Kaiser's reputation among the upper classes and the leading political periodicals of the *Kaiserreich*. It was not only in Germany that this war aroused a wave of resentment against England, but only in Germany was the monarch a member of the British royal family. Wilhelm's mother, Victoria, was the daughter of Victoria, the Queen of the United Kingdom of Great Britain and Ireland, and Edward VII, the son and successor of Queen Victoria, was his uncle.

So, as anti-British feelings increased, suspicions mounted that Wilhelm's loyalty was split between his mother's and his father's countries. For years, Bismarck, the former chancellor, and his family and followers had been spreading allegations of the Kaiser's pro-British inclinations. Now, Wilhelm himself, apparently unable to understand the dynamics of the new era of mediatized politics, nourished them. At the end of 1900, a Boer delegation led by Paul Kruger had come to Germany to plead for German assistance against the British. In their search for support Kruger and his entourage had been touring Europe accompanied by international media hype. Newspaper commentaries and novels; books for children and religious tracts; cartoons, poems, and anti-capitalist pamphlets spread the narrative of the greedy British Goliath attacking the Boer David. On December 1, 1900, a huge crowd gathered at Cologne's main train station to cheer Kruger and his entourage. However, the Kaiser did not share the enthusiasm for the Boers, and he refused to receive the delegation. Newspaper commentators asked rhetorically how it could be that a great power like Germany could allow London to decide who it would receive. Even the liberal *Berliner Tageblatt* (of December 6, 1901) was of the opinion that the Kaiser's refusal humiliated the Germans.

Worse things followed. At the beginning of 1901, Queen Victoria died, and her grandson traveled to London and stayed until Victoria's funeral on February 5. Consequently the celebration of his birthday on January 27 in

Germany had to be canceled, and he was also absent from January's celebration of the bicentennial of the Prussian state. While in London, Wilhelm decorated Field Marshal Frederick Roberts, who had led the victorious British forces against the Boers, with the Order of the Black Eagle, the highest Prussian order of chivalry. That was too much, especially in conservative Prussian eyes. On the Kaiser's return from England, the *Kreuzzeitung*, a conservative newspaper that usually supported the Prussian throne, published an editorial that came close to withdrawing its support for Wilhelm:

> People don't understand why, as it is said, His Majesty the Kaiser … bestowed this inimitable distinction on the English commander against the Boers … In our opinion, great attention should be paid to their expressions, the more so as they express the people's profound feelings … We feel obliged to comment when it is to be feared that the Monarch and the nation don't understand one another. The fear of such a misunderstanding unfortunately becomes manifest when a deep disagreement between the spirit of the nation and the actions of the Monarch emerges.
>
> (*Neue Preußische Zeitung/Kreuzzeitung*, February 8, 1901, evening edition)

Wilhelm's reputation in his own realm would never recover from the harsh criticism he endured at the time of the South African War. And he himself, though unaware of what he was doing, prevented the criticism from dying down. Some years later, in 1908, the *Daily Telegraph* published an interview with Wilhelm in which the Kaiser divulged that he had ordered his leading officers to work out a British plan of campaign against the Boers and had sent it to London – a plan, Wilhelm claimed, that the British had more or less followed. The interview's publication caused a political crisis in Germany, where another of Wilhelm's blunders, namely, the first Moroccan Crisis of 1905–1906, was still well remembered. The Kaiser had visited Tangier in March 1905 in order to demonstrate Berlin's unwillingness to tolerate French meddling in Morocco, which was in violation of the Madrid Convention of 1880. His action was meant to reassure German proponents of colonial expansion and to demonstrate to Paris and London that from now on the established imperialistic powers would have to reckon with the German Empire.

As it turned out, though, the demonstration backfired. During the international conference on the Moroccan question, which met in Algeciras from January to June, 1906, both Great Britain and France made it clear that they would not accept Germany's claim to a share in the domination of northwestern Africa. Not even Italy, which had been in the Triple Alliance with the German Empire since 1882, stood firmly by Germany's side. As diplomats and newspaper commentators from different countries and contrasting political affiliations agreed, the conference had shown the international isolation of the German Empire. In Germany, this failure in imperial politics was seen as devastating to Germany's reputation and aroused Germans' fears. Their worst geopolitical nightmare, namely, the "encirclement" of Germany by France, Great Britain, and Russia, seemed to have come true, and not because Germany had really tested its strength but because it had failed to exert itself by not pursuing a military solution. The idiom of encirclement now became omnipresent in Germany. And in the eyes of Germany's elites the culprit was the emperor, whose lack of strength and resoluteness had brought about the feared encirclement. Friedrich von Holstein, the leading civil servant in the German Foreign Office, who thought it fatal to Germany that the Kaiser lacked the nerves of his grandfather, Kaiser Wilhelm I, concluded "That's the worst of it. Step by step foreign countries realize that His Majesty gives in when heavily pressured, and that will be a danger in the years to come. The pressure is going to be exerted anew." (Holstein, 1932, p. 245).

Though Holstein feared pressure exerted on Germany from outside, it was internal pressure that was increasing. As usual, Maximilian Harden, the eloquent editor of the journal *Die Zukunft* and one of the harshest critics of Wilhelm II, sounded the sharpest note. His editorial of April 1906 was entitled "Wilhelm the peaceful." At the core of Harden's commentary was an explicit threat: "If a German Kaiser is so non-belligerent that not even the threat of being humiliated would make him unsheathe his sword, then the German people should forge their destiny themselves" (Harden, 1906, p. 12).

In sum, Wilhelm II, who in retrospect looms as the trigger-happy militarist paving the way to 1914, had since 1900, with his erratic actions, his lack of determination to strengthen Germany's position in the world, and his supposed pride in his English ancestry, seemed to his subjects just the opposite. In the German view, the Kaiser exuded not strength and security but weakness and vulnerability. According to this perspective, the greatest possible hazard for the future of Germany sat on its throne. As was to be expected, this felt lack of leadership radicalized the nationalistic right wing in Germany much more effectively than any feelings of national strength could have.

Wilhelm II and the Germans: A Study in Leadership reconsidered

A quarter of a century has passed since Thomas Kohut published his book on the German Kaiser, *Wilhelm II and the Germans: A study in leadership* (1991). In that book, Kohut wanted to demonstrate that

> Psychoanalysis, with its exploration of individuals in their depth and complexity, is fully compatible with the historian's similarly intensive exploration of the human past. Furthermore, psychoanalytic methodology (its mode of observation, conceptualizations, and interpretations) that explains what has been empathically understood is fully compatible with historical understanding and explanation.
>
> (Kohut, 1991, p. 6)

For Kohut, therefore, a psychoanalytic model is especially appropriate to a study of Wilhelm II and his role in history. Since then, much more has been written on Wilhelmine Germany than can be listed here, a huge academic literature in which the Kaiser figures prominently, though in different roles.

As a historian I have two reasons to look back in this volume and reflect on Kohut's work. First, I want to get a present-day perspective on an eminent psychoanalytic model for writing history, a model that claims that historical explanations based on historical agents' empathic understanding are compatible with, and in some cases even superior to, established forms of historical understanding and explanation. Second, I want to assess the challenge that Kohut's psychoanalytic interpretation of Wilhelm II still poses to established historiography today, when historical knowledge of the period is richer and more sophisticated than it was at the beginning of the 1990s.

So, what does Kohut do in his book on the Kaiser? He tells two stories: the politicization of Wilhelm II's personality (Part I) and the personalization of politics in Wilhelmine Germany (Part II). He centers both stories around three hypotheses. His first thesis, which connects the two stories and is the book's recurrent theme, is that a special kind of entangled history comes into being in 1858 with the marriage of Friedrich, the heir to the Prussian throne, and Victoria, the daughter of Queen Victoria, namely, the history of the political as well as personal interconnections of Germany and Great Britain. Victoria's and Friedrich's eldest son, Wilhelm, was to be the personification of this entanglement in an epoch in which both countries – their monarchs and leading politicians as well as the press and its readers – had to cope with one another in such highly politicized contexts as colonialism, armament, and economics.

The book's first part, "The Politicization of Personality," argues for the second thesis, that the politicization of Wilhelm's personality, which began before his conception, so to speak, enabled him to be a "mirror image" (Friedrich Naumann) of the Germans. Through his relationship with his parents, he developed a conflicting (national) identity – partly English, partly Prussian/German – which he could not integrate into a consistent whole. Prone to self-doubts and anxieties, he was very sensitive to how those around him responded to himself: "Wilhelm's disjointedness enabled him to respond to the variety of often contradictory interests confronting him as Kaiser and to reflect back the diverse natures and aspirations of the Germanies and the Germans that made up his environment" (Kohut, 1991, p. 119).

In the second part, "The Personalization of Politics," Kohut substantiates his third thesis, that Wilhelm came to symbolize Germany at his time (which the present-day term "Wilhelmianism" continues to substantiate). He was a "transference figure" (Kohut, 1991, p. 119) for many of his subjects insofar as they projected their anxieties and hopes onto him. That was possible because Wilhelm himself experienced the same anxieties and hopes, especially in his ambivalent feelings toward England and his obsession with national self-aggrandizement.

That is an admittedly very rough sketch of Kohut's overall argument. So, how does he argue in detail for these conclusions? And what methodological role does empathy play in his historical explanation? At the heart of Kohut's approach is his focus on the interdependences among people. Empathy for him does not constitute, as it does for many biographers, an analytical perspective on how an individual sees the world of history. So, just as he claims, the book is not a biography (Kohut, 1991, p. 5). It is more. It uncovers the interrelationships between its protagonist and the people with whom he interacts, and investigates the dynamics that pertain to these interactions. That may not sound spectacular, but it is. For historians mostly shy away from the burden that they would impose on themselves were they to try to understand not only their protagonists but also the people with whom they were interrelated. In the first part of the book, Kohut does exactly that with Wilhelm's family, especially his relationship with his parents. The second part looks at the Kaiser's interrelationships with friends, diplomats and politicians, the press and public opinion, and his subjects as he perceived them. To give only one example, in the chapter entitled "The Legacy of Maternal Possessiveness," the reader learns how Wilhelm learned to adopt patterns of behavior that he had acquired in response to Victoria's possessiveness. Wilhelm broke away from her with difficulty, but he had to cope with his powerful attraction to her throughout the rest of his life. But the reader also learns a lot about how Victoria perceived her eldest son and why she perceived him that way. Victoria wanted him to emulate her father, Prince Albert, who was her idol, and tragically rejected Wilhelm because he failed to live up to her expectations. In the course of this relationship with his mother, Wilhelm learned to behave in ways that were later typical when he was Kaiser, e.g., sudden outbursts because of hurt feelings and a dependence on the approval of others.

It is Kohut's rich detailing of perspectives, his focus on interpersonal dynamics, and his careful attention to the ambiguities of actions and perceptions that make the book exceptional. Kohut brings his hypotheses, which I've broadly described above, to life through his in-depth explorations of individuals' relationships with one another. What makes this approach possible is the abundance of source material, which Kohut interprets with great care, and which, because it is impossible to summarize, explains why any summary must be inadequate.

What kind of Kaiser, and what kind of Wilhelmine Germany, does Kohut describe in the pages of his book by means of his psychoanalytic approach? And do his conclusions still make an important contribution to the state of the art? My answer to the last question is "Yes, more than ever." Owing to the impact of John C. G. Röhl's work, especially his stupendous three-volume biography of Wilhelm II (Röhl, 1998, 2004, 2014), current research often understands the Kaiser in a way that mirrors his self-perception, *viz.*, that he was a genuine sovereign whose rule constituted a "personal regime" ("*persönliches Regiment*"). According to Röhl, the upshot was that Wilhelm exerted his power in ways that made him crucial to the outbreak of war in 1914. According to Kohut, too, Wilhelm's was a "personal regime," but not because he exerted the influence that Röhl ascribes to him. Rather, such power and influence was only what Wilhelm's contemporaries attributed to him in perceiving him as the symbol of the Reich. Thereby, foreign governments saw him as a decisive force, and Germans "invested the Kaiser with emotional authority" (Kohut, 1991, p. 171). Such attitudes had multiple consequences in Germany and abroad, which is only another way of saying that they influenced the course of history. Thus, *contra* Röhl and others, it was the perception, not the fact, of the Kaiser's power – the image of the Kaiser's "personal regime" – that exerted its influence on events. In fact, it is precisely such perceptions of power that still today are key to understanding those events, as we see in Röhl's explanations of the *Kaiserreich* and its role in world history and the outbreak of the First World War.

Kohut's Kaiser, and this is the answer to the first question, was far from a forceful leader. He was too irritable and uncontrolled, too susceptible to manipulation, and too unfocused. But Kohut does not take that to mean that he was not influential. Insofar as his volatility was an impediment to the formulation of a consistent German foreign policy, he exerted significant negative influence. And his determination to build a powerful navy, in order to strengthen the Reich's, and Wilhelm's, standing *vis-à-vis* Great Britain, was willful enough to get the High Seas Fleet built. As Wilhelm saw it, the new fleet would both force the British to treat Wilhelm, and the Reich, with respect and be instrumental in forging an Anglo-German alliance, the ultimate expression of esteem between equals. It was this respect from his mother's country, not its defeat by German warships, for which Wilhelm longed.

From Kohut's point of view, Wilhelm the fleet-builder was the core of the symbolic Wilhelm who mirrored the German nation. He "reflected with particular clarity those who dominated the stage in Wilhelminian Germany, who set the tone, determined the pace of daily life, and established the order of the day. Those Germans invariably saw themselves as representatives of a more dynamic, enterprising, and aggressively modern generation than the one they were impatiently thrusting aside" (Kohut, 1991, p. 229). But, in the end, Wilhelm proved too inconsistent, too ambivalent, to live up to these expectations. In fact, the interview that he gave to the *Daily Telegraph* in 1908 shattered the mirror into pieces. Here Wilhelm presented himself as an Anglophile who had sent to London plans for fighting the Boers, the enemies of the British in the Boer War of 1899–1902 who were idolized in Germany. Now German suspicions that the Kaiser, the grandson of Queen Victoria, was a security risk, which had been growing since 1900, came to the fore.

As I mentioned above, this interview, given the widespread fears of Germany's encirclement by an alliance led by London, proved to be one of the Kaiser's most serious misjudgments. It deprived German elites of the symbol that had stood for their desires to participate in what was then called "*Weltpolitik*" and pursue a foreign policy of self-aggrandizement, and, worse, it made the Kaiser a symbol of the very opposite, namely, that the inimical forces that threatened to surround the nation were already inside its borders, indeed, sitting on the thrones of Prussia and the Reich. As a consequence of this radical change in the perception of the Kaiser, Wilhelm's fall from grace precipitated the self-radicalization of politics that was part of German history prior to 1914. In this sense Kohut's development of historical and psychological insights into the Kaiser's actions avoids reductionist explanations (Röhl, 2004, 2014) of the First World War. His scholarship explains a far more complex history, the entanglement of historical, political, and psychological factors that led to the July crisis of 1914.

References

Bösch, F. (2009). *Öffentliche Geheimnisse. Skandale, Politik und Medien in Deutschland und Großbritannien 1880–1914*. Munich, Germany: Oldenbourg.

Cecil, L. (1996/97). *Wilhelm II* (2 Vols.). Chapel Hill, NC: University of North Carolina Press.

Clark, C. M. (2000). *Kaiser Wilhelm II*. Harlow, UK: Longman.

Daniel, U. (2005). Einkreisung und Kaiserdämmerung. Ein Versuch, der Kulturgeschichte der Politik vor dem Ersten Weltkrieg auf die Spur zu kommen. In B. Stollberg-Rilinger (ed.), *Was heißt Kulturgeschichte des Politischen* (pp. 279–328). Berlin, Germany: Duncker & Humblot.

Geppert, D. (2007). *Pressekriege. Öffentlichkeit und Diplomatie in den deutsch-britischen Beziehungen (1896–1912)*. Munich, Germany: Oldenbourg.

Harden, M. (1906): Wilhelm der Friedliche. *Die Zukunft*, *27*, 6 April 1906, 1–12.

Holstein, F. von (1932). *Lebensbekenntnis in Briefen an eine Frau*. Ed. H. Rogge. Berlin, Germany: Ullstein.

Hull, I. (1982). *The entourage of Kaiser Wilhelm II: 1888–1918*. Cambridge, UK: Cambridge University Press.

Kessler, H. Graf (2006): *Das Tagebuch, Band 6: 1916–1918*. Ed. G. Riederer. Stuttgart, Germany: Cotta.

König, A. (2009). *Wie mächtig war der Kaiser? Kaiser Wilhelm II. zwischen Königsmechanismus und Polykratie von 1908 bis 1914*. Stuttgart, Germany: Franz Steiner.

Kohlrausch, M. (2005). *Der Monarch im Skandal. Die Logik der Massenmedien und die Transformation der wilhelminischen Monarchie*. Berlin, Germany: Akademie.

Kohut, T. A. (1991). *Wilhelm II and the Germans: A study in leadership*. New York, NY: Oxford University Press.

Mommsen, W. J. (2002). *War der Kaiser an allem schuld? Wilhelm II. und die preußisch-deutschen Machteliten*. Berlin, Germany: Propyläen.

Mombauer, A., & Deist, W. (eds.) (2003). *The Kaiser: New research on Wilhelm II's role in imperial Germany*. Cambridge, UK: Cambridge University Press.

Reinermann, L. (2001). *Der Kaiser in England. Wilhelm II. und sein Bild in der britischen Öffentlichkeit*. Paderborn, Germany: Schöningh.

Röhl, J. C. G. (1998). *Young Wilhelm: The Kaiser's early life, 1859–1888*. Cambridge, UK: Cambridge University Press.

Röhl, J. C. G. (2002). *Kaiser, Hof und Staat. Wilhelm II. und die deutsche Politik*. Munich, Germany: Beck.

Röhl, J. C. G. (2004). *Wilhelm II: The Kaiser's personal monarchy, 1888–1900*. Cambridge, UK: Cambridge University Press.

Röhl, J. C. G. (2014): *Wilhelm II: Into the abyss of war and exile, 1900–1941*. Cambridge, UK: Cambridge University Press.

Röhl, J. C. G., & Sombart, N. (eds.) (1982). *Kaiser Wilhelm II: New interpretations. The Corfu papers*. Cambridge, UK: Cambridge University Press.

Vierhaus, R. (ed.) (1960). *Das Tagebuch der Baronin Spitzemberg, geb. Freiin von Varnbüler. Aufzeichnungen aus der Hofgesellschaft des Hohenzollernreiches*. Göttingen, Germany: Vandenhoeck & Ruprecht.

Winzen, P. (2002). *Das Kaiserreich am Abgrund. Die Daily-Telegraph-Affäre und das Hale-Interview von 1908. Darstellung und Dokumentation*. Stuttgart, Germany: Steiner.

Chapter 10

Fathers and sons

The Kohut odyssey

Geoffrey Cocks

The career of Thomas Kohut, a historian and psychoanalyst by training, not only was influenced by that of his famous father, but also, in some fundamental ways, paralleled it. The historical contexts of the early lives of Kohut father and son were very different. The father was born in Vienna in 1913 as the only son of Felix, a businessman, and Else Kohut and into what would soon become the violent eclipse of the Austrian Empire during the First World War. The son was born in Chicago in 1950 and thus into the bright and powerful light of an ascending America in the wake of the Second World War. Heinz studied medicine and became a psychoanalyst. Tom's course was different: "like lots of first-year college students, I imagined I was going to medical school" (Elovitz & Cocks, 2005, p. 50), but, while also undertaking postgraduate training as a psychoanalyst, Tom became a historian. Yet, in becoming a historian, Tom realized a wish of his father's. Heinz once told Tom that, had he not become a physician, he would have chosen to be a historian. For Tom's 25th birthday in 1975 Heinz sent him a photograph accompanied by words freighted with great pride and perhaps also some ambivalence and sense of paths not taken:

> I am happy about the fact that you are enjoying your work [in history graduate school], that you are fascinated by your favorite teacher, that your skill and knowledge are expanding ... I hesitated about the photograph. But someday you will be teaching and then you can look at the picture and see me there, reading, as some kind of forerunner.
>
> (H. Kohut, 1994, p. 320)

In bringing psychoanalytic insights into history Tom was, moreover, one of the historians of his time who recognized that psychoanalysis and history are kindred disciplines. Both disciplines are historical in aim and in method. Both psychoanalysis and history seek to understand the past and its influence on the present. Both are idiographic rather than nomothetic, that is, both use case studies to detail events and contexts as lived, experienced, and recalled. Both use not only the human capacity for objective reasoning, but also subjective insight into the lives of other human beings at other times and other places. And both analyst and historian rely on the inescapable ability of one human being to "resonate" emotionally with another, even – for history – at a distance. Heinz Kohut's own self psychology laid just such special emphasis on the scientific and therapeutic value of empathy for analysis.

The curve of life

Heinz's last paper, "Introspection, empathy, and the semicircle of mental health" (H. Kohut, 1991), was edited and presented posthumously by Tom on November 7, 1981 at the Chicago Institute for Psychoanalysis on the occasion of the fiftieth anniversary of the institute's founding. The image of the semicircle comes from the post-Homeric story of Odysseus and his infant son Telemachus. Odysseus, reluctant to leave his wife and son to fight against Troy, feigns insanity by sowing his field with salt. One of the Greek delegates, suspecting a ruse, throws the baby in front of the plow. Odysseus describes a semicircle around Telemachus, demonstrating his mental health by saving his son's life. Kohut saw this story as affirmation of the self's commitment to the next generation as an extension of the self. He did not regard the individual, like Freud did, as trapped by a constant circular struggle between selfish drives and social prohibitions. For Kohut, the dynamic life of the self was as much, if not more, one of interdependence, nurture, and growth. He conceived of life as having a curve from beginning to end that represents a developmental trajectory beyond childhood conflicts into the time of one's own life and the space of others' lives.

I first met Tom at the Pacific Coast Branch Meeting of the American Historical Association at Occidental College in August 1987. Both Tom and I were – and are – historians of Germany – he had studied with Otto Pflanze at the University of Minnesota – and also both identified at the time with "psychohistory," the then-popular though also controversial application of psychoanalytic methods to the study of history. Tom had trained as a research psychoanalyst at the Cincinnati Psychoanalytic Institute and practiced as a psychotherapist, while I had taken a field in psychohistory at UCLA with historian and psychoanalyst Peter Loewenberg. It was in Los Angeles that Tom asked whether I would be willing to edit his father's correspondence. He told me that he thought my book on the history of psychoanalysis and psychotherapy in Nazi Germany, *Psychotherapy in the Third Reich: The Göring Institute* (1985), made me an appropriate choice for this task. By this he no doubt meant my expertise in the time period during which his father had lived the first half of his life, the subject matter of medical psychology, and my knowledge of German. The combination in my work of his father's field of study and the regime that had forced Heinz from his homeland must also have played a part in Tom's decision.

Tom also said that he thought my ability to be objective about psychotherapists and psychoanalysts working for Hitler showed a degree of "empathy" (*Hineinfühlung*) useful both generally and specifically in treating the personal and professional lineaments of his father's life and career. I don't recall how intentional it was on my – or our – part that the correspondence opens with a letter of 1923 from Heinz to his father and closes with one in 1981 from Heinz to his son. But a mutual feeling of generational solidarity in carrying on the realization of parental hopes and aspirations for their progeny was certainly, I think, generated – or strengthened – between Tom and me after both my father and Tom's mother, Elizabeth, died during the production of the volume.

Like Odysseus, Heinz's father was taken away by war. Heinz was left with a controlling and paranoid mother who bred insecurity and self-doubt in her son, an only child. Tom led me to see that his father's own childhood experience is reproduced in the seminal case study in self psychology "The two analyses of Mr. Z.," which was published in 1979, just two years before Kohut's death. Tom and his mother were convinced that "Mr. Z." is in fact Heinz and that the two analyses are in fact Heinz's own training analysis with Ruth Eissler and a later self-analysis. It was this case – and this life – that embodies the distinction Heinz drew between Freud's "Guilty Man," the son of a seductive mother and a forbidding father, and Kohut's "Tragic Man," the son of an unempathic mother and an absent father. Both father and son, Heinz believed, were fleeing from the compensatory and fearful psychological control and domination of the mother.

That Heinz's own son would be an only son must have recalled the problems of his own childhood. But it also recalled the importance – psychoanalytically informed on the part of both mother and father – of a nurturing family environment for Tom. There is considerable evidence for this in Heinz's correspondence. Although, given his fame and his responsibilities, Heinz was away from home a great deal, annual vacations from 1951 on in Carmel-by-the-Sea, California (where Heinz nonetheless spent considerable time writing) were high on the list of family priorities. Over the last 20 years of his life, moreover, Heinz wrote to Tom regularly and took great pleasure in Tom's education generally and his subsequent career as a historian in particular. In late 1967 he notes in a letter to Anna Freud that in high school

> Tom is working hard and consistently this year – he is especially enjoying a course on Melville which is given on a high level of scholarliness and by a teacher who, I believe, combines enough similarities with the father and yet enough striking differences from him to make him a fine object of idealization for an adolescent.
>
> (H. Kohut, 1994, p. 182)

In 1979 he wrote an old friend from Vienna about his still ambivalent feelings about his German origins and then links these feelings to Tom:

> ... the older I get, the more I feel some strange nostalgia – for Germany. I wouldn't dare tell this to many people. But the only times when, in recent years, I have felt thoroughly "at home" was when I was in Germany and/or with German friends. Not any real yearning for Austria, or for Vienna – despite their being so nice to me in recent times. I wonder why? ... But down deep it gives me enormous pleasure that Tom studies modern German history, that he speaks German accent[-]free and that he is spending his second full year in Germany now.
>
> (H. Kohut, 1994, pp. 386–387)

Particularly meaningful to Heinz was his participation with Tom in a psychohistory conference in Chicago in 1980. More generally, Heinz also placed an emphasis on the importance of the younger generation both in the psychoanalytic profession and in public life. Although he and Tom sometimes clashed violently over the war in Vietnam and Heinz worried about the costs of Tom's militancy on his "chances for a productive and happy future" (H. Kohut, 1994, p. 217), Heinz identified with the idealism of youthful protestors. He dedicated *The restoration of the self* (H. Kohut, 1977) to "G and his generation," August ("Gustl") being Tom's middle name from Heinz's Viennese analyst August Aichhorn and from his favorite Gymnasium history teacher, August Hornung. To put it in classical terms, Tom, who in the early 1970s gained conscientious objector status with the draft, might have represented for Heinz both Telemachus and Odysseus – "the first would-be draft evader in literature," Heinz wrote (H. Kohut, 1978, v. 4, p. 562). Tom was not only the son, but also a father who, unlike Odysseus and Felix, did not go off to war, abandoning (again) the son to the mother.

The circle of life

Tom too would eventually return to the era of Heinz's childhood in his own work as a historian. He has recalled that "[d]espite my father's background, I never had much interest in Austrian history" (Elovitz & Cocks, 2005, p. 51). Tom's original interest in history had been the Second World War, at the other pole of his father's life in Europe, but ultimately more compelling, among other reasons certainly, was the world war that accompanied his father's first years. It was an undergraduate professor at Oberlin College, Robert Neil, who first inspired Tom to study Kaiser Wilhelm II of Germany. Tom's doctoral dissertation was a psychological study of Wilhelm, the man most identified with the central German role in the events that sent Heinz's father off to war. It is perhaps psychologically significant as well that Tom chose this subject for his dissertation in spite of Pflanze's reservations. Pflanze advised against the topic because he feared that a work of psychohistory would not help Tom get a job as a historian. This was the case even though Pflanze in the early 1970s had revised his own longstanding research on Bismarck along psychoanalytic lines, which was precisely the reason why Tom chose to study with Pflanze. In any case, this study of a difficult and destructive leader was not simply a labor of love, an indication that Tom's reasons for choosing it were overdetermined. Tom even begins the book that came out of this dissertation, *Wilhelm II and the Germans*, with the acknowledgment that studying "Kaiser Wilhelm II for fifteen years has been a trying experience" (T. A. Kohut, 1991, p. vii).

Tom's second book, *A German generation* (T. A. Kohut, 2012), likewise engages the history of the First World War since it is a longitudinal psychodynamic study of "62 Germans who were all born around the outbreak of the First World War" (Elovitz & Cocks, 2005, p. 52). In this book Tom has returned to his original interest in the history of the Second World War, and to its cause, the Nazi regime in Germany, which brought an end to his father's life as an Austrian and European Jew after the Nazi annexation of Austria in March 1938. For Heinz, the Anschluss marked the loss of another father, Freud, to whom Heinz and a friend waved farewell at the Vienna train station on the afternoon of June 4, 1938. As he recalled it in a letter to Kurt Eissler in 1952,

> I saw Freud on the day of his final departure from Vienna, in 1938. The information that he would be leaving, the Railway Station (Westbahnhof?), and the time of the train's departure came to me through Aichhorn with whom I was in analysis at that period. Aichhorn told me that Freud had requested that the fact and, at any rate, the details of his leaving be kept secret and that he didn't want any friends to come to the station. Aichhorn suggested, however, that there would be no harm in my going there if I kept myself in the background. A friend of mine and I arrived at the station about 15 minutes before the train was to leave. It was a beautiful, sunshiny day. The station was rather empty and there was no evidence of any surveillance by the police. We located Freud quickly as he was sitting at the window of his compartment, facing the rear of the train. We kept about ten steps back of Freud's part of the train and, therefore, could not see anyone else in the compartment. Next to Freud's window, on the station platform, stood a crying woman in simple dress (we assumed it was a maid of the Freud household) who was spoken to, apparently in an attempt to console her, by a lady of Freud's party (Anna Freud?). Freud's face was calm and, almost as if he were embarrassed by the emotional scene, he seemed to pay no attention to it. My friend recognized Professor Marburg, the Neurologist, in the same car. When the train began to move we walked up toward Freud and lifted our hats. Freud looked at us, took off his traveling cap, and waved to us.
>
> (H. Kohut, 1994, pp. 64–65)

Soon enough Heinz too was forced to leave his homeland. He had received his medical degree in November 1938 but had had to take his medical exams under the dark press of events resulting from the Nazi Anschluss of Austria into the Greater German Reich. The consequences for Jews in Austria were disastrous. In autumn the Nazis decreed that those Jewish medical students who were in their last year could take their oral exams, but only on an accelerated schedule. In early October Heinz learned that he would have to take eight examinations within a period of four weeks starting immediately. A month later he and his mother had to hide during the anti-Semitic riots that began in Germany and Austria on November 9. While waiting to emigrate, Heinz worked as a clerk at the Rothschildspital, the hospital of the Jewish Community. In March 1939 Heinz was on a train through Germany on the way to a transit camp in England, where he worked in the first-aid station. An affidavit from a friend's business partner in Chicago allowed him to get a visa to the United States, where he arrived in early 1940. His mother left Austria in February 1940 and arrived in Chicago in March.

All these threats and outrages were further blows to Heinz's self-esteem, rendering him all the more susceptible to feelings of narcissistic injury and tellingly disinclined for as long as he lived "to talk about particular chapters of my early life" (H. Kohut, 1994, p. 11). The Anschluss also seemed to justify the paranoia of his mother "that was the complement to her desire to control those around her" (H. Kohut, 1994, p. 12). As Charles Kligerman expressed it at Kohut's memorial service in Chicago in 1981, the "rise of Hitler and the destruction of the idealized Viennese world in which he had become *persona non grata* were tremendous blows to his self-esteem" (Kligerman, 1985, p. 12). Such feelings were aggravated by the fact that Heinz was raised in a thoroughly secular Jewish family environment and so regarded himself as Austrian rather than Jewish. He told Tom that he was therefore unable to comprehend why he had to leave Austria since he did not regard himself as having a Jewish identity: "all of a sudden, these bullies came along who claimed they were the real Germans and I was all of a sudden a foreigner and didn't belong" (Quinn, 1980, p. 124). All his life, consequently, Heinz remained deeply ambivalent about Austria, saying of his first return to Vienna in 1957 that he was thereby "playing with psychological fire" (H. Kohut, 1994, p. 325).

Tom's method of extensive interviews with his subjects in *A German generation* drew from his psychoanalytic training and the psychoanalytic milieu created within his family by his mother's and his father's professional lives. All of Tom's scholarship is of course marked by its intellectual debt to psychoanalysis and to his father's self psychology. His work is also distinguished by its depth of analysis in addressing fundamental issues of historical method and historical subject matter. In his essay of 1986 in *The American Historical Review*, Tom argues with great precision and clarity for the indispensability of psychoanalysis in the task of explaining the psychological dimension of past human experience (T. A. Kohut, 1986). He had also phrased this argument with effective emphasis in the introduction to *Wilhelm II and the Germans*:

> In contrast to the psychology of the simple (that is, measurable) human experience, psychoanalysis, with its exploration of individuals in their depth and complexity, is fully compatible with the historian's similarly intensive exploration of the human past. Furthermore, psychoanalytic methodology (its mode of observation, conceptualizations, and interpretations) that explains what has been empathically understood is fully compatible with historical understanding and explanation.
>
> (T. A. Kohut, 1991, p. 6)

In the footnote to these words, Tom cites his own "Psychohistory as history," though only after his father's essay, "Psychoanalysis in a troubled world," from the second volume of *The Search for the Self* (1978). In the introduction Tom proceeds to consider various psychoanalytic models, including the object-relations school used by Judith Hughes to study the Kaiser in *Emotion and high politics* (1982). His own choice is self psychology, appropriate for the obviously narcissistic Kaiser Wilhelm. Tom's analysis focuses on Wilhelm's "self-certainty" as compensation for feelings of rejection and weakness (aggravated by a withered arm) stemming from his childhood. Tom discovers – in striking parallel to the familial environment of Heinz's first and early years of which perhaps Tom was therefore mindful – that "Prince Wilhelm's childhood and adolescence were characterized by maternal anxiety and paternal neglect." It was the response to his "mother's confusion about him ... [and her] emotional unreliability" that led to the "unrestrained grandiosity ... depression ... [and] inconsistency of Wilhelm's self" (T. A. Kohut, 1991, pp. 15, 30, 47). This compensation took the form of aggressive behavior, a need to be the center of attention, and displays of martial vigor and costume. (While Heinz too loved being the center of attention and was a brilliant *raconteur*, his grandiosity needless to say was genial rather than bumptious.) This habitual behavior of Wilhelm's extended well beyond his immediate circle as the Kaiser continually sought out the adoration of the German masses. Known as the "traveling Kaiser" (*Reisekaiser*), he constantly attended ceremonies all over Germany at which he, dressed in one of his many elaborate uniforms, would occupy center stage. Tom here is extending the emphasis in his father's self psychology on human interdependence to examine and analyze not just the needs of the leader, but the need among his followers for such displays of confidence and power. Many Germans, inflamed by highly organized mass media propaganda directed by, and for the benefit of, the Imperial armed forces, sought some measure of personal and national empowerment as compensation for feelings of endangerment and persecution at the hands of the established powers of Europe. This is brilliant psychohistory – and brilliant history – in that it links in a dynamic and multi-causal manner the biography of the individual with the broader human experience of time and place.

"It happened once, exactly like that"

Tom's unique status in the world of psychoanalysis as well as being a member of the guild of historians has also given him the opportunity to tell psychoanalysts what history can do for them. In 2003 he published "Psychoanalysis as psychohistory" in *The Annual of Psychoanalysis*, in which article Tom discusses the interviews he has conducted with Germans of his father's generation. These, Tom argues, demonstrate "that the influence of history on the psyche is at least as significant as the influence of the psyche on history" (T. A. Kohut, 2003, p. 226). The impress of his father's – and his family's – history is consciously explicit in the vignette with which he begins his essay:

> Let me begin with a personal anecdote. Some years ago, my family and I visited a friend and her daughter in Brussels in Belgium. The woman we visited is a commissioner in the European Economic Community and is approximately 10 years older than I am, born, I would think, around 1940. She comes from a Jewish family and survived the Holocaust, with her parents and siblings, by hiding in Brussels. During our visit, we made a walking tour of the city and, turning a corner, came upon a small construction site in the sidewalk. There was a hole in the pavement, about a yard deep, with a wooden walkway over it and a railing. But when our Belgian friend saw this construction site, she cried out in a panicked voice, "Watch out! Be careful! It's dangerous!" In reality the construction site was not dangerous, not even for our children. But her reaction, her panic-stricken reaction, was so familiar to me. My father could have – would have – reacted in the same way. He too survived the Holocaust, fleeing Austria as a young man in 1939. And I must confess that I too have this panicky reaction at times. The world is bright and colorful, the sun is shining [like the day in 1938 Freud left Vienna]. But then out of the corner of the eye one glimpses a little spot of gray, and suddenly one is seized with a terrible anxiety that this little spot will suddenly cover the whole colorful scene in black. From our contemporary perspective, the source of this so exaggerated reaction is not difficult to identify. It was produced by the historical reality of the Holocaust. It happened once, exactly like that. The world was bright and colorful, the sun was shining. But suddenly one found oneself in the middle of a lethal situation. What today seems such an unrealistic and inappropriate panic was, back then, a realistic and appropriate reaction to a situation of extreme danger. The relatives of my father, his aunts and uncles, who did not have his panic-stricken reaction and remained in Austria, were all exterminated.
>
> (T. A. Kohut, 2003, p. 225)

To put it another way, as filmmaker Stanley Kubrick (1928–1999), another keen and anxious Jewish observer of modern history, once did, "Gentiles don't know how to worry." Tom's empathy here is not just the product of an observant and humane mind, but also of reasoned employment of emotions born of his own history, that of his family, and that of Jews in our time. At the same time, however, just as Tom evenhandedly – and very wisely – concludes in this essay that "the psyche and history mutually shape one another" (T. A. Kohut, 2003, p. 226), here and in his most recent book he does not give in to teleology and the fatalistic or even morbid reductionism that is so tempting for historians when peering into the abyss of 1933 to 1945 in Germany and Europe. No historian can write history blind to the future of that history. This is especially so in the history of Germany after 1914, the year in or around which Tom's interviewees were born. The elephant – or, rather, the dictator – in this room of history is particularly large and menacing, particularly when it comes to the motivations and actions of the youth toward which Hitler and the Nazis directed so much of their appeal. The history of German youth – and the widespread German youth movement – in the 1920s and early 1930s is not simply one of being precursors of Nazism. Rather, as Tom documents, it has its own history, one that placed a premium on collective belonging and one that for its own reasons developed in ways that flowed into Hitler's Germany and became part of that larger and deadlier phenomenon of a *Volksgemeinschaft* dedicated to war against, and extermination of, "the Other." In other words, there are continuities in German history to and through 1933 and 1945 that render Nazi Germany neither the culmination nor the interruption of a broader national, continental, and human history.

Tom's conscientious and skillful study of the German "Generation of '14" has allowed him once again to demonstrate the insight and empathy that have always been a hallmark of his scholarship. And his interdisciplinary familial and professional background too contributes to his ability in this instance to use history as a means to critique one of the great psychoanalytic studies of Nazism. In 1967 West German psychoanalysts Alexander and Margarete Mitscherlich, colleagues and friends of Heinz and Betty, "published an extraordinarily influential essay" (T. A. Kohut, 2012, p. 230), "The inability to mourn – and connected with it: a German way of loving." The Mitscherlichs argued that postwar Germans bore the burden of great unconscious guilt over the Nazi past. But the Mitscherlichs also assumed that Germans had to feel guilt over Nazi Germany, an assumption that was based on the Mitscherlichs' and others' own conviction that Germans should and must feel and be guilty over that past. Tom, however, invokes the need for empathy and sympathy in understanding that Germans' investment in aspects of the Third Reich represented for them after the war not guilt, but loss:

> Whereas the Mitscherlichs argued that the inability of Germans to face their unconscious guilt prevented them from mourning the loss of the Third Reich, I would invert their formulation to argue that the inability of Germans to mourn the overwhelming losses they had suffered, including the loss of the Third Reich, prevented them from experiencing guilt

> over its crimes. And whereas the Mitscherlichs argued that the inability of Germans to face their unconscious guilt prevented them from mourning the victims of National Socialism, I would argue that the inability of Germans to mourn their own overwhelming losses prevented them from mourning the losses of others – including those inflicted by Germans.
>
> (T. A. Kohut, 2012, p. 231)

Tom's critique demonstrates the importance of historical evidence won through psychoanalytically informed interviews. Deftly employed empathy wins historical insights connected with the words, memories, and feelings from the experiences of participants in this history. *A German generation*, like *Wilhelm II and the Germans*, is admirably and characteristically both fully informed and fully unencumbered by theory, as pride of place goes to a clear and compelling historical focus on people, experiences, and events. At the same time, the interdependence of human emotional experience that in turn is a hallmark of psychoanalytic self-psychological theory fills this most recent of Tom's psychohistorical works with familial meaning as well as scholarly distinction. The same emphasis on the psychodynamic connections between and among human beings is likewise reflected in the four entries in the bibliography of *A German generation* of works authored by Kohut father and son.

References

Elovitz, P., & Cocks, G. (2005). Thomas A. Kohut: Historian with a psychoanalytic world view. *Clio's Psyche, 12*(1), 49–56.

Hughes, J. (1983). *Emotion and high politics: personal relations at the summit in late nineteenth-century Britain and Germany*. Berkeley, CA: University of California Press.

Kligerman, C. (1985). Memorial for Heinz Kohut, M.D., October 31, 1981. *The Annual of Psychoanalysis, 12–13,* 12.

Kohut, H. (1977). *The restoration of the self.* New York, NY: International Universities Press.

Kohut, H. (1978). *The search for the self: Selected writings of Heinz Kohut, 1950–1978.* New York, NY: International Universities Press.

Kohut, H. (1991). *The search for the self: Selected writings of Heinz Kohut, 1979–1981.* New York, NY: International Universities Press.

Kohut, H. (1994). *The curve of life: correspondence of Heinz Kohut, 1923–1981.* Chicago, IL: University of Chicago Press.

Kohut, T. A. (1986). Psychohistory as history. *The American Historical Review, 91*(2), 336–354.

Kohut, T. A. (1991). *Wilhelm II and the Germans: A study in leadership.* New York, NY: Oxford University Press.

Kohut, T. A. (2003). Psychoanalysis as psychohistory or why psychotherapists cannot afford to ignore culture. *The Annual of Psychoanalysis 31*, 225–236.

Kohut, T. A. (2012). *A German generation: An experiential history of the twentieth century.* New Haven, CT: Yale University Press.

Quinn, S. (1980). Oedipus vs. Narcissus. *New York Times Magazine*, November 9.

Chapter 11

Psychoanalysis and history at the crossroads

A dialogue with Thomas Kohut

Roger Frie

How can the fields of history and psychoanalysis benefit and learn from one another? When all is said and done, how do we make sense of the interaction between history and the human psyche? These are the kinds of questions that have occupied Thomas Kohut and guided the contributions to this volume. Given the collegial nature of this book, I felt it was important to conclude by bringing Kohut's own voice to bear. The final chapter begins with my discussion of Kohut's understanding of the connections between history and psychoanalysis and ends with an extended dialogue between us. I consider Kohut's approach to psychohistory and its parallels with psychoanalytic thinking and practice and then turn to his emphasis on empathy, particularly its relevance for understanding the German generation's perpetration of, and complicity in, the Holocaust. This discussion sets the stage for our dialogue, in which Kohut reflects on the interaction between history and psychoanalysis and expands on the themes of German history, the Holocaust, and the importance of empathy.

Bridging psychoanalysis and history

For many readers, the surname "Kohut" will evoke the ideas and spirit of Heinz Kohut, the originator of self psychology. Thomas is the only son of Heinz and Betty Kohut, who were both psychoanalysts. He was born in 1950 in Chicago, the city where he also spent his childhood and grew up in a social milieu that counted among its members the major psychoanalysts of the time. As Kohut describes it,

> Virtually all of my parent's friends when I was a child were analysts and I remember being fascinated by them and by the conversations I overheard when I was little. I knew so many of the famous second-generation analysts. I still recall being swung in the air by Ernest Jones and meeting Marie Bonaparte in Paris when I was six or seven. I was extremely close to Marianne Kris and to Anna Freud, who were like grandmothers to

> me ... That early milieu was decisively important and created what now seems like a magical childhood, associated with central Europe.
>
> (Elovitz & Cocks, 2005, p. 50)

Kohut's childhood world was populated by Austrian-Jewish and German-Jewish émigrés and refugees, survivors of Nazi Germany's perpetration of the Holocaust. This psychoanalytic and central European milieu forms the backdrop for Kohut's focus on the psychological dimensions of German history.

Kohut was introduced to the burgeoning field of "psychohistory" when he was a graduate student. Peter Gay, one of the best-known representatives in the field (see Gay, 1985), became an important mentor and Kohut (2000) later published an essay "The creation of Wilhelm Busch as a German cultural hero, 1902–1908," in a *Festschrift* in honor of Gay. Psychohistory, as it was initially practiced, referred to the study of "historically significant figures ... in order to explain how their political attitudes and actions in adulthood could be understood as attempts to solve psychological problems encountered in childhood (T. A. Kohut, 2012, p. 1). Kohut's investigation of the influence of the individual psyche on history culminated in the publication of his book *Wilhelm II and the Germans, A study in leadership* (T. A. Kohut, 1991). One of Kohut's early objectives was to elaborate the role of psychoanalysis for history. He was particularly concerned with approaches to psychohistory that reduced human experience to psychological theorizing. In his important essay "Psychohistory as history," Kohut (1986, p. 338) wrote "Too often when employing the psychohistorical method, the historian comes to the past with an understanding and explanation already in hand; the understanding and explanation do not emerge from the past itself but are the products of a theoretical model." The parallels with psychoanalysis are unmistakable.

Psychoanalysts are renowned for their stalwart belief in the "rightness" of their own theory. Each school of psychoanalytic theory and practice wields a particular point of view, and, in so doing, often denies the validity of what other schools have to say. As a result of their long years of training, psychoanalysts may become very good practitioners of their own theoretical approach but limited in their ability to appreciate the veracity of other viewpoints. Once we believe in the truth of a theory it easily morphs into a worldview, with the result that we see and interpret human experience through the lens of that particular outlook.

In the same essay Kohut is concerned with what happens when the psychohistorian imposes his or her theoretical beliefs onto the person being studied. According to Kohut,

> There is a difference between the historian whose contemporary concerns influence his choice of subject and whose contemporary assumptions color and even facilitate his explanations and the psychohistorian who accepts uncritically the historical validity of contemporary evidence and

> uses it as a substitute for evidence from the past. Although the present may distort or inform the historian's understanding and explanations, he still attempts to transcend the limitations of his own time and to put himself as much as possible into the context of the past. By contrast, when employing the psychohistorical method, the psychohistorian applies the standards of the present onto the past without attempting to take differing circumstances into account.
>
> (T. A. Kohut, 1986, pp. 339–340)

When the historians or psychoanalysts interpret human experience through the reductive lens of theory, they inevitably rely on universal explanations. This "one size fits all" kind of thinking overlooks the variability of individual experience, cultural context, and the importance of historical relativity. As Kohut observes, "Even the basic psychological experiences that we share across time, given our common humanity, are certain to be expressed in a different psychological language and in response to different historical circumstances – differences that must make us regard the attempt to impose a psychological model on the past with considerable skepticism." Turning directly to the practice of psychoanalysis, Kohut (1986, p. 344) states that "theory in analysis should never be imposed from without on the patient."

For Kohut, the psychohistorian, like the psychoanalyst, must always be able to perceive the subject of study from multiple perspectives. In this context he also points to the relevance of empathy:

> The comparable relationship between general and particular in history and in the clinical practice of psychoanalysis reflects the fact that both disciplines, to the extent that they seek to understand human feelings, thoughts and actions, share what the philosopher Wilhelm Dilthey defined as the methodology of the human sciences – that is, knowing by empathic understanding. The essential element in the psychoanalytic and historical understanding of human beings is, in Dilthey's well-known phrase, "the rediscovery of the I in the Thou." In both disciplines *the investigator feels or, perhaps better, thinks his way inside the experience of the other when he understands him … empathy is our ability to transcend subjective responses and to experience although to a necessarily attenuated degree, the experience of the another*. In other disciplines understanding is achieved when the investigator puts himself in the place of the other and imagines why – given the time, place, circumstance, and experience of the other – it makes sense that he felt, thought and acted as he did.
>
> (T. A. Kohut, 1986, p. 344, my emphasis)

Kohut's emphasis on empathy is a thread that runs throughout his writing. It is also a theme that illustrates the connection to his father, Heinz Kohut, and the interests of psychoanalytic self psychology more generally. Kohut builds on the affinities between the practice of history and psychoanalysis when he states:

> Just as the historian understands an event of the past as being the product of a multitude of causal factors, historically comprehensible only from many different perspectives, so the psychoanalyst understands his patient in many ways, from many different points of view ... And, just as the historian focuses on a particular past event and seeks to understand it in depth on its own terms, so the psychoanalyst focuses on the experience of his particular patient and seeks to understand him in depth and in terms of his own unique language and experience.
>
> (T. A. Kohut, 1986, p. 343)

Over time Kohut's examination of the psyche's influence on history has shifted to a focus on how history shapes the psyche. Kohut now sees the impact of the historical environment on the psyche as equally significant. In the same sense, Kohut has moved from studying historically significant figures, such as Kaiser Wilhelm II, to studying ordinary individuals and the way in which these persons are shaped by history. As Kohut states, he is concerned with the "study of experience, less what the people of the past did and more what they thought and felt ... not of elites necessarily but also especially of ordinary people" (Elovitz & Cocks, 2005, p. 56). This shift in his work is especially apparent in such publications as "Psychoanalysis as psychohistory or why psychotherapists cannot afford to ignore culture" (T. A. Kohut, 2003) and in his book *A German generation: An experiential history of the twentieth century* (T. A. Kohut, 2012).

Lived experience across generations

Kohut's focus on the lived experience of persons illustrates the relevance of psychoanalysis for his work as a professional historian. Kohut's approach to studying lived human experience is integrative in nature. His aim is to account for the mutual influence of psyche and history, or, differently stated, the inherent interaction between person and context (see Frie & Coburn, 2011). In line with the recent sociocultural turn in psychology, Kohut (T. A. 2012, p. 1) states that "Psychologically we are constituted in no small measure through our experience of the environment. That environment is constituted by history. Therefore history constitutes our psyches." From the perspective of psychoanalysis, this suggests that the workings of the individual mind cannot be understood apart from the social, cultural, and historical contexts in which we live out our lives (Frie, 2014).

Kohut's book *A German generation* (2012) examines how history shaped a group of middle-class Germans who were members of the generation of perpetrators and bystanders that supported the Third Reich and unleashed the horrors of the Holocaust. The book tells the story of their lives and shows how this generation was psychologically influenced by a series of historically engendered losses over the course of the century. It is highly readable, devoid of theoretical jargon, moving, and provocative. Kohut takes his readers on a journey of thinking and imagining oneself into the events and lives of this group of Germans in order to grasp why they may have acted in the way they did. His work, in other words, is fundamentally empathic in nature.

The German generation described by Kohut was profoundly influenced by traumas and dislocations throughout the course of their lives. They were born in the years before the First World War, and their parents had been participants in the First World War. Following the Armistice in 1918 Germany endured many years of political and economic crises that fundamentally challenged the short-lived democratic Weimar Republic. Against this background, the German generation embraced the utopian promise of the Third Reich, the community of the "*Volk*," and its ideology of racial purity. After 1945 the psychological effects of the defeat of Nazi Germany and the loss of the *Führer*, along with the wartime traumas and privation of the immediate postwar years, went unacknowledged or were denied. Questions of guilt and responsibility for the Holocaust, if they arose at all, came later and often only in response to the widespread reproach of their children, the second generation, some of whom rebelled against their parents in the late 1960s because of their silence about the past, or their unquestioned support of the Nazis.

Kohut's book is based on the transcripts of interviews carried out by three German academics with 62 members of this generation during the mid-1990s. In a move that is common in psychoanalytic case writing, but has been questioned by some historians, Kohut condenses the 62 interview transcripts into six composite interviews. According to Kohut, it was the extensive overlap in the individual experiences of the group members that made this step both possible and necessary. During their adolescence the group had all belonged to the Youth Movement, then, during the Third Reich, they belonged to the Reich Work service, and finally, during the postwar years, to the Free German Circle. Kohut's book is likewise divided into three corresponding historical periods, roughly before, during, and after the Third Reich. In each case the composite interviews are followed by a detailed analysis and an essay that intersects with current historiography.

The group members' turn to the collective, the *Volksgemeinschaft*, compensated them for their losses over time, but also impeded their ability to empathize with others. Their lack of empathy was powerfully at work in their perception of their Jewish neighbors and in their anti-Semitic attitudes. Kohut suggests that the absence of empathy can have devastating consequences. Shaped by ceaseless Nazi propaganda, most of the 62 either directly supported the regime's anti-Semitic policies or conveniently looked away when confronted with the results. Kohut shows how the group members' individual and collective sense of morality and capacity for empathy was fundamentally altered as they engaged in a stance of simultaneous seeing and not-seeing. As Kohut observes, "The interviewees seem to have experienced the Third Reich in an intensely visual way, what was seen and, crucially, what was not seen in Nazi Germany take on particular importance ... they did not perceive the persecution of Jewish people and the entire extermination project, although they speak at length about this absence" (T. A. Kohut, 2012, p. 137). Examples of "looking away" and of "vanishings" were commonplace among the interviewees. The persecution, deportation, and, finally, extermination of the Jewish people was quite simply "not seen" even though their disappearances were everywhere in evidence.

Kohut suggests that the interviewees actively avoided registering what they saw around them, because to do so might have caused them to feel uneasy and, in turn, could have led them to feel empathy. "Given what these interviewees conceded they knew, it took an act of will for them not to have known what was going on. In a sense they had to avert their eyes to avoid seeing what was right in front of their noses" (T. A. Kohut, 2012, p. 139). Drawing on the work of the sociologist Kai Erikson, Kohut suggests that the interviewees were unable or unwilling to integrate what they saw into consciousness, thus drawing a distinction between individual perception and socially constructed knowing:

> The role played by society in integrating perception into consciousness is especially significant in a community as intense, as controlling, and ultimately as tenuous as the National Socialist Volksgemeinschaft. That is to say, there was a mutually reinforcing relationship between social consensus and knowledge during the Third Reich ... Acknowledging the Final Solution would have asserted the "I" against the "we" and alienated the knower from the Volksgemeinschaft, a racial community in which Jews and their persecution were to be eliminated from consciousness. For if the persecution of Jews was acknowledged, then Jews were acknowledged. And if Jews were acknowledged, then they could be experienced as human beings.
>
> (T. A. Kohut, 2012, p. 141).

"What Germans 'knew,'" Kohut explains, "was, in part, a product of social consensus, and accepting what was commonly known was a condition for membership in the community" (T. A. Kohut, 2012, p. 141). Kohut thus shows how the intense need for belonging informed a specific way of knowing, and more specifically a way of seeing, and how this in turn led a group of "ordinary" Germans into complicity with the crimes of the Nazis. The conclusion is chilling: "It seems important to remind ourselves that what ultimately separates us from those who carried out and enabled the genocide is historical experience" (T. A. Kohut, 2012, p. 240).

A future-oriented approach

Kohut's argument for the importance of empathy cannot be overestimated, especially given his own family background. For Kohut the question of historical trauma and the shadow of the Holocaust is very real:

> Although neither of my parents identified themselves as Jewish, both, according to Nazi racial criteria, would probably have been victims of the Final Solution had they been living in territory controlled by Germany during World War II. Although from a German American family, my mother appears racially to have been a quarter Jewish, on her mother's side. And my father was racially wholly Jewish. Indeed, my father escaped the Holocaust only by fleeing Austria in 1939, and four of his five uncles and aunts, as well as cousins, perished in the genocide.
>
> (T. A. Kohut, 2012, p. 16)

Despite his "abhorrence" of National Socialism and the awareness of his own potential "victimhood" given his Jewish heritage in relation to the Nazi past, Kohut's objective is to "reduce the intellectual and emotional distance separating us from them, in part by thinking our way inside their unique historical circumstances, in part by recognizing that on some level they were as we are and that we have within us the capacity to be as they were" (T. A. Kohut, 2012, p. 17).

In order to recognize a shared humanity with others, Kohut maintains that we need to ask ourselves whether the "German generation" is so very different from us, or whether it is the historical circumstances that make them appear so different. In a passage that may be challenging for some of his readers, Kohut writes

> We share human nature with the perpetrators and their complicit bystanders. Two specific aspects of human nature seem particularly relevant in the context of National Socialism and the Holocaust. Although the intensity may vary from person to person, or indeed from culture to culture, all human beings have the need to belong to the group and to exclude others from it, a need that centrally motived the genocide, in my view. And all human beings have the capacity to dehumanize others by closing off empathy for them, a capacity that enabled the genocide to be carried out.
>
> (T. A. Kohut, 2012, p. 240)

Kohut wants to narrow the distance between "us and them" and thus to help us grasp our ongoing potential for dehumanizing attitudes and behaviors in the present. He is imagining himself in the place of ordinary Germans in order to try to understand their motivations and their experience at the time.

Kohut's attempt to understand suggests the need for all of us to reflect on why human mistreatment continues, despite our knowledge of the Holocaust. This understanding is essential so that we don't fail in the same way that countless Germans during the Third Reich did. In this sense we might say that Kohut's approach to integrating history and psychoanalysis is future-oriented. In order to develop a meaningful personal and political awareness in the present and future, we need to better understand the crimes of the past.

Dialogue with Thomas Kohut

R.F.: It is a pleasure to be able to discuss your interdisciplinary work in history and psychoanalysis. Before we turn to your scholarship, I'd like to begin by asking you a few questions of a more personal nature.

Many readers may identify your surname with that of your father, Heinz Kohut (1913–1981). With this in mind, I'd like to quote a passage from the end of the Introduction of your most recent work, *A German generation: An experiential history of the twentieth century*:

"Empathy ... connects us emotional and intellectually to others, allowing us to recognize ourselves in those who initially seem different, even alien. Empathy is at the heart of the historical method and at the heart of history's appeal, the pleasure we derive from learning about people in the past, very different from us and like us at the same time. My own interest in history can be traced back to fishing trips with my father in rural Wisconsin when I was very little. I do not recall us ever catching anything, but I vividly remember listing with rapt attention as my father told me stories of the Persian and Peloponnesian wars as we sat in a little rowboat in the hot sun on a lake near Dousman. This book is based upon stories and presents stories, the stories of people and their lives set against a historical backdrop nearly as dramatic as the one that framed the stories retold by Herodotus and Thucydides and retold again by my father to me." (T. A. Kohut, 2012, p. 18)

In this touching passage you make a direct connection between your father and the development of your own work as a historian and psychoanalyst. Could you reflect on the nature of this connection, which is both personal and intellectual in scope?

T.K.: I think my interest in history can be connected with my father two ways, one related to what he did and one related to who he was. Regarding the former, my father was deeply interested in history, a fact reflected not only in the stories he told me on my childhood fishing trips but also in his own work, which very frequently engaged with historical themes. His work that expressly relates to history has been collected and published in the volume *Self psychology and the humanities*, edited by Charles B. Strozier (see H. Kohut, 1985). I also believe that my father's engagement with history can be seen as underlying or at least powerfully influencing the development of his ideas that eventually took the form of self psychology. Self psychology is based upon the premise that human beings are psychological products of their environment, indeed that the self is formed through the internalization and transmutation of the responses of the environment. Not simply in infancy but throughout our lives we are in fact never fully psychologically autonomous, according to self psychology, but remain connected to the environment (the concept of the selfobject): to a certain extent, we experience our environment as part of ourselves and ourselves as part of our environment. Since our environment is to a not insignificant degree historically determined (that is, shaped by forces that transcend the individual and the individual's unique situation), history can be said to shape the self. In a sense, then, my focus on the psychological impact of history on human beings follows logically from a basic, perhaps *the* basic, premise of self psychology. Moreover, not only what I study but how I study it, the psychological approach I take to the past, the empathic approach I take to the past, comes from my father – as well, I should add, as from my mother. In relation to human beings, whether in the present or in the past, I seek to think my way, to imagine my way, inside their experience – their past history, their present-day circumstances, and their expectations for the future. Indeed, in history the fact that I generally seek to empathize not with human beings who are sympathetic but those who are unsympathetic to me, whose feelings, thoughts, and actions are both reprehensible and difficult to understand, can be traced back to my father. In 1969–1970 he wrote in "On leadership" (H. Kohut, 2011) that it is precisely those people who have committed the most heinous acts, referring explicitly to the Nazis, whom we need to try to understand empathically. Thus, in the book from which the passage you quoted above comes, I sought to empathize with Germans who were sympathetic to National Socialism, to try to understand their enthusiasm for the Nazi racial collective of the *Volksgemeinschaft*, in short, I sought to empathize with Nazis. It is no accident that my middle name is "August" after my father's analyst, August Aichhorn, and his Gymnasium history teacher, August Hornung. I suppose you could say that my scholarly career, which has been devoted to understanding the psychological dimension of the past, was already preprogrammed in my middle name. The more personal reason I became a historian I think had less to do with my father's interest in history and more to do with who my father was – or rather was not. My father was not like the fathers of my friends. He was not really an American. Despite his love of the United States and intense patriotism, he remained very much a European, a central European, a Viennese. In some ways he was a fascinating person, in part because of his intellect and personality but also because he was "foreign" or at least different from the world in which I grew up. The fact that, because of the trauma of the Holocaust, the world from which he came and in which he grew up was rarely discussed in the family made that world fascinating to me. My interest in German history reflects my father's central European background, I think. I was curious to understand both the world from which he came and curious also perhaps about why he had been forced to leave the world to which he was obviously still deeply attached.

R.F.: Reflecting on the interdisciplinary connections you make between history and psychoanalysis, I wonder whether you might discuss what it was like for you to grow up as the son of a psychoanalyst and a psychoanalytic social worker. Your father and your mother, Betty Meyer Kohut (1912–1992), a social worker who trained psychoanalytically in Vienna during the 1930s, interacted with other well-known German and Austrian refugee psychoanalysts. Can you describe this intellectually stimulating environment? What it was like for you as a child? What is it like now looking back at this remarkable time in psychoanalytic history?

T.K.: This past academic year-and-a-half I spent in Oxford and in Vienna. While we were in Oxford, we visited the Freud Museum in London. In Vienna, I was the "Fulbright Freud Visiting Scholar of Psychoanalysis" at the Freud Museum in the Berggasse. The last time I had been at what is now the Freud Museum in London, I was a teenager and had been invited to lunch by Anna Freud and Dorothy Burlingham. What I had experienced as Anna Freud's home was now a museum, a "part of history." In the exhibition at the London museum there were displays in cases of objects I had seen when they weren't historical artifacts but household items. There is a film running constantly at the London Freud Museum. Numerous psychoanalysts and other people I had met or known when I was a child were to be seen in the film. In the Freud Museum in Vienna there was an exhibition about early, important, and influential women psychoanalysts, again including Anna Freud. As you can tell from my invitation to her house in Hampstead, I knew Anna Freud well. She stayed with us in our apartment in Chicago when she received an honorary degree from the University of Chicago. I became quite close to her. She even wrote a letter supporting my application to be a conscientious objector during the Vietnam War. And I didn't just know Anna Freud, I met Marie Bonaparte and was swung up in the air by Ernest Jones when my parents took me to the meeting of the International Psychoanalytic Association in Paris in 1956. At various meetings of the American Psychoanalytic Association, I vividly recall meeting Heinz Hartmann and Erik Erikson. In addition to Anna Freud, I was very close to Marianne Kris. Until he broke with my father over what would become self psychology, Kurt Eissler annually sent me that year's set of Austrian stamps. It is really quite a strange experience for me to realize that my past, at least in psychoanalytic terms, has become "historical," that I knew people who are now remembered in museums and that I had visited places that have now become museums. That psychoanalytic past does seem very far away to me, but it is very much part of me nonetheless. Perhaps as a result, it makes me uncomfortable when people today dismiss psychoanalysis or when psychoanalysts themselves use the word "psychodynamic" instead of "psychoanalytic," as if the word psychoanalysis reveals them to be anachronistic. Still, we are now living at a time when psychoanalysis has been deeply integrated into the way most of us view and understand ourselves and the world, including into numerous not explicitly psychoanalytic forms of psychotherapy, and perhaps as a result the notion of a psychoanalytic "movement" to which those analysts that I knew as a child saw themselves belonging is no longer relevant. That "movement" had energy and hope but it also was ideological, intolerant, and could reject heretical or dissenting members with a cold brutality that I got to experience firsthand when close friends of my father like Eissler rejected him and his work after the publication of *The analysis of the self*.

R.F.: Was it this central European background that led to your eventual focus on German history?

T.K.: I found the Central European world of my father deeply fascinating. I can remember as a small child listening with rapt attention to conversations (often in German) that took place in our apartment in Chicago or on vacation in Carmel, California with the friends of my parents, virtually all of them European émigrés. I realize now that most, though not all, were Jews, but they seemed to embody Europe, European culture, the educated, humanistic tradition so much associated with central Europe. It seemed a magical world to me. Part of my fascination with that world, perhaps, stemmed from my unconscious or barely conscious awareness that that magical world was connected with terrible darkness. Perhaps I was drawn to the magic *and* to the darkness. As a child, I was obsessively devoted to Tolkien's *The Hobbit* and *The Lord of the Rings*, both books presenting worlds of magic and wonder and of terrible darkness. In reading those books over and over again, I used to live in those worlds of wonder and of terror in my imagination. As I said earlier, as a historian I attempt to think and perhaps even feel myself back into the experience of the people of the past. In relation to the Third Reich, that meant thinking and feeling my way back into the world of Nazi Germany, "Mordor" if you will. When I was working on *A German generation* there was an extended period of time in which "I inhabited in my mind the world of the Third Reich, and the world of the Third Reich inhabited me." I wrote in the book that I found this a "difficult and upsetting experience." It *was* difficult and upsetting, but perhaps there was something exhilarating about that experience as well. Certainly, in working on the book there was an attempt to master that history psychologically, a history deeply connected to the history of my family. It's no accident that it was only relatively late in my career that I was able to think my way into the experience of Germans during the Third Reich. My Master's thesis on the Prussian Land Tax Reform of 1861 and my dissertation and subsequent book, *Wilhelm II and the Germans*, both related to nineteenth-century Germany (see T. A. Kohut, 1991). It was only in middle age, well after my father's death, that I turned to the Nazi period and attempted to empathize with Nazis and those many Germans who supported them. That's no accident and is connected with my increasing ability to come to terms with and explore my own family background, the family background of my father, in which the Holocaust played such a central role and which was covered by a cone of silence in my family growing up. I still find it easier to empathize with Nazis and their supporters than I do to imagine my way inside the experience of their Jewish victims. That is still too close, too painful, too upsetting, and ultimately too frightening to me. Nonetheless, I have very recently begun to learn about the history of my Austrian relatives, all Jews, many killed in the Holocaust. Perhaps someday I will be able to write and teach about German and Austrian Jews, but I'm not quite there yet.

I guess the point is that one cannot separate one's personal history from the history one studies. When one works on a historical topic, one also works on oneself. That's part of what makes historical work deeply rewarding and also at times deeply difficult to do. Although that may make historical work sound self-absorbed, it is nevertheless the case that one's historical work can speak not only to oneself but also to others, and not just to other historians, who are wrestling with the same or similar personal issues. In the case of *A German generation*, I have received a number of messages from people, non-historians, who have found my book relevant to their own efforts to explore and process the history of their families. The personal issues I was seeking to explore in my work are the same or similar to the personal issues that they are seeking to explore in theirs. I think, Roger, that applies to you as well. Our two books (T. A. Kohut, 2012; Frie, 2017) are related to one another, speak to one another, and their conversation is in fact what has brought this conversation about.

R.F.: Perhaps what also connects our two books is the application of psychoanalysis to the study of history. You trained as a psychoanalyst in Cincinnati from 1981 to 1984 around the same time you completed your Ph.D. degree at the University of Minnesota and you have always maintained the importance of psychoanalysis for the field of academic history. Could you reflect on your development as a professional historian and the role that psychoanalysis has played for you? Do you still practice psychoanalysis alongside your work as a historian?

T.K.: As part of my training as a "research candidate" in Cincinnati, I worked as a psychotherapist at the Veteran's Hospital and at the University of Cincinnati Central Psychiatric Clinic. Following my graduation from the

Institute, I worked for about a year in private practice with a psychiatrist friend and colleague. When I got the job at Williams College in 1984, I gave up psychotherapeutic work and became a full-time historian. Over the course of the years that I have been at Williams, my connection to psychoanalysis and psychology grew increasingly tenuous. There is no question that my entire worldview and way of dealing with people remained and remains deeply psychoanalytic – not that I'm analyzing other people all the time. Instead, I seek always to understand where others are coming from, what *their* experience is, how the world looks to them. That's the approach I take to the people of the past, and it's the approach I take to the people in my life. It's an empathic approach. That approach is certainly something that comes out of my psychoanalytic education in Cincinnati, but even more, it comes out of my family background. My psychoanalytic approach to people in the past and in the present, my empathic approach to them, comes ultimately from both my parents, from the way they viewed and tried to make sense of the world. Professionally, my psychoanalytic education and family background affects not only what I teach but how I teach as well. I'm not primarily a lecturer; I'm a discussion leader. I want my students to speak in class. My role is to ask questions, to listen to the responses of the students, and to respond to their answers, frequently by posing another question. And central to that teaching style is an ability to listen, to understand, and to make connections, all of which I would describe as central to psychoanalytic treatment. I try to be sensitive to the experience of students in class, to read their faces and body language and tone of voice, as a way of trying to keep them engaged in the class, to make them feel included, and able to negotiate the occasionally upsetting historical topics we consider. My empathic approach and my efforts to be sensitive to other people were probably especially important in my work as Dean of the Faculty at Williams. When problems arose, I sought not to determine the "objectively correct" solution but first to understand the subjective experience of those involved. My solutions to problems (generally arrived at collaboratively) sought to reconcile the subjective experiences of those involved in an issue in a way compatible with the institutional interests of the college.

Since 2001, I have reconnected more directly with psychoanalysis as a result of my association with the Austen Riggs Center in Stockbridge, Massachusetts. Since that date, with one brief interruption, I have been a member of the Board of Trustees at Riggs, and for much of that time a member of the Council of Scholars that advises the Erikson Institute at Riggs. The Erikson Institute in significant part engages in clinical and socio-cultural and historical work that is related to the work I do myself and to which I am personally and professionally committed. Reflecting the name and the work of Erik Erikson, the Erikson Institute explores issues where the clinical and the cultural (in an anthropological sense) come together, to explore how insights developed in intensive work with troubled patients can give us insight into the broader socio-cultural and historical context and how our understanding of the broader socio-cultural and historical context can deepen our understanding of troubled patients, whose lives like our own are embedded in that context and who cannot be fully understood independent of that context. I greatly value my connection with Riggs and through it my reconnection with psychoanalysis. Just as in my scholarship and in my personal life I have in the last decade or so connected or reconnected with history and family history relating to the Holocaust, through my connection with Riggs I have reconnected with psychoanalysis both professionally and personally. It feels on several levels as if circles are closing for me. That's a nice feeling.

R.F.: Can you speak to the current status of the field of "psychohistory" and suggest some key texts that readers, who may be unfamiliar with this kind of work might examine to learn more about it?

T.K.: "Psychohistory" had its heyday in the 1970s when a number of interdisciplinary forms of history, like quantitative history, micro-history, economic history, and women's history, emerged and sought to establish themselves as independent historical subfields. Obviously, some of these subfields still exist; others, like psychohistory, have more or less disappeared. But I would regard the disappearance of those subfields not so much as a sign of their failure as of their success. They generally, and psychohistory in particular, have been integrated into standard historical scholarship. A great many historians, particularly cultural historians and historians of experience, engage in what used to be called "psychohistory." There are very few books, including my own, that I would describe as exclusively or even mainly psychohistorical. They are simply history books that focus on human beings and seek to know and understand the people of the past and that are keenly sensitive to the psychological dimension of history. The original psychohistory was highly dependent on the use of psychological and especially psychoanalytic theory in its attempts to understand past people. Contemporary cultural history and the history of experience are perhaps less explicitly theoretical and more empathic. Countless historians today seek to understand the experience of past people in ways that are profoundly sensitive to psychological experience, from Peter Gay's magisterial *The bourgeois experience from Victoria to Freud* volumes to Lyndal Roper's *Oedipus and the devil* and *Witch craze*. Indeed, every single historian contributor to this volume can be described as a psychohistorian in that sense. Geoffrey Cocks' (2012) work is probably the most explicitly psychological, indeed psychoanalytic, both in subject matter and approach, as in most recently his book about the experience of health and illness in Nazi Germany,

The state of health. Dorothee Wierling's historical writing is profoundly empathic and psychologically sensitive, as in her recent work, *Eine Familie im Krieg* (Wierling, 2013) on the experience of the family of Lily and Hermann Braun, their son, Otto, and their family friend, Julie Vogelstein, during the First World War. Alexandra Garbarini's (2006) work on Jewish diary writers during what we now call the Holocaust, *Numbered days*, and many of her subsequent articles are attempts to define and to understand how Jews sought to understand, process, and bear witness to the incomprehensible – cognitively and psychologically. Alon Confino's work, particularly his recent *A world without Jews* (Confino, 2014) is centrally concerned with fantasy, with the role played by the Nazi imagination in motivating and giving life to the Holocaust, as the Nazis sought to realize their fantasy of creating both a present and a past without Jews, a "world without Jews." Finally, Ute Daniel is one of our profession's most articulate and effective practitioners and (in her book *Kompendium Kulturgeschichte*, 2001) advocates for a cultural history where the historian seeks to think and imagine him- or herself inside what Reinhart Koselleck called the "space of experience" and the "horizon of expectation" of the people of the past.

R.F.: In my experience, many (though by no means all) psychoanalysts view the humanities as separate from the work of clinical psychoanalysis. I have always been curious about this distinction. I came to psychoanalysis by way of an academic background and profession in the humanities, at a time when psychoanalysis was widely read and discussed in academia. Once I began my psychoanalytic training, and later retrained as a clinical psychologist, I observed that my psychoanalytic teachers and colleagues often separated clinical psychoanalysis from its wider applications. Thus, while my fellow academics were fascinated by psychoanalysis, my fellow psychoanalysts and psychologists did not necessarily see the humanities as relevant to what they did. Has this been your experience as well? And how do you think this phenomenon can be explained?

T.K.: I fear that your observation about clinicians is generally the case. They tend to rivet their gaze on the clinical situation, fearing perhaps to leave their comfort zone in order to learn about unfamiliar things in unfamiliar ways. Indeed, one of the most exciting things about the Erikson Institute at the Austen Riggs Center is that it seeks to bring the humanities and social sciences to bear on clinical work. Ideally, the Erikson Institute is not only a place where the insights gained from working intensively with individual patients are "applied" to the broader social, cultural, and historical context, but also a place where clinicians, through interaction with scholars in the humanities and social sciences, learn to see things in their patients – and in themselves – that they otherwise would have overlooked. Although one might think that social, cultural, and historical issues that are psychologically important will come up in therapy independent of the therapist's knowledge of the social, cultural, and historical context, a therapist's ability to recognize and understand those issues is dependent on the therapist's sensitivity to the extent and to the ways in which the social, cultural, and historical context shapes the self – including, I might add, the self of the therapist. Indeed, the fact that therapist and patient often share the same social, cultural, and historical context can mean that both fail to appreciate its influence. Thus, after the Second World War, as Tilmann Moser has pointed out, the Third Reich and the Holocaust, along with the other atrocities committed by Germans during the war, generally did not come up recognizably in psychoanalyses conducted during those years, not because they were unimportant but because they were too important and too traumatic both for the patients and for their analysts to face. Human beings live their lives outside the consulting room. It's important that psychoanalysts be aware of and sensitive to that fact. Also, it is difficult for me to imagine psychoanalysis generally and psychoanalytically oriented ("psychodynamic") psychology evolving and gaining new insights into human beings if psychoanalysts and psychologists ignore culture, society, and history. Many of the most profound insights into human psychology have come from psychoanalysts like my father, Erik Erikson, Kurt Eissler, and of course Anna and Sigmund Freud, who learned every bit as much from their study of society, culture, and history and from scholars of society, culture, and history as they did from their patients and from other psychoanalysts.

R.F.: One of the criticisms leveled at psychoanalysis, particularly by other disciplines in the humanities and social sciences, is that the psychoanalytic focus on the "inner self" leads to a neglect of the socio-cultural contexts of human experience. Thus I find it particularly important to take note of your essay "Psychoanalysis as psychohistory or why psychotherapists cannot afford to ignore culture," in which you state that

> "The mutual influence of history and psyche, so obvious to Freud and the generation that founded psychoanalysis in this country, is in danger of being forgotten today as analysts turn their eyes away from society, culture and history to rivet their gaze upon the clinical situation. Philosophically, a failure to appreciate the fact that psychoanalysis is historically determined and that analytic theory and practice reflect a particular cultural moment will render it unable to adapt to changing historical circumstances ... knowledge of history and culture exposes the psychoanalyst to the vast psychological universe beyond the consulting room, the world where people actually live out their lives." (T. A. Kohut, 2003, p. 235)

As you point out, the history of psychoanalysis, beginning with Freud, was rooted in an interdisciplinary approach and outlook. I wonder if you can expand on the important statement you make here, given its relevance to practicing psychoanalysts today?

T.K.: It's really a tough question to answer. I know somewhere deep down that one cannot understand human beings one-dimensionally or in one specific situation. I know somewhere deep down that one cannot be curious about human beings in one dimension or in one specific situation while being incurious about human beings in other dimensions and situations. On some basic level, psychoanalysts need to be curious about people, about what makes them tick, about who they are and where they come from. I cannot imagine restricting that curiosity to the clinical situation. Moreover, in regard to history, it is crucially important for psychoanalysts to appreciate historicity, to appreciate the fact of change in human psychology and in the effort to understand it. Particularly psychoanalysts who recognize the profound influence that the environment has on people psychologically, who appreciate that our selves are formed by internalizing and transforming or transmuting the responses to the environment to us, *have* to recognize that history, and culture, and society exert a decisive psychological influence on human beings. And that external historical, cultural, and social environment is constantly changing. As a result, people are changing, as are their psychological issues and the ways they attempt to come to terms with those issues. Clinicians need to appreciate that human beings are not the same psychologically, not the same psychologically from one individual to another, and not the same psychologically over time. People are psychologically different today than they were even a generation ago. Clinicians need to appreciate not only the consequences of those changes. Even more, they need to recognize the fact of those changes. A challenge faced by younger psychoanalysts and psychotherapists will be to deal with people who have grown up in an information age of constant communication and connectedness of a particular sort, who can see and know virtually anything that can be seen and known. The range of possibilities for good and for ill is relatively limitless. Nothing is impossible. That notion, "everything can be known and done, nothing is impossible," seems to me a scary notion and is perhaps one of the roots of contemporary terrorism. What people have been able to imagine doing, including to other human beings, has expanded exponentially. And the barrier between what one can imagine and what one can do seems to me to be breaking down as the boundary between virtual reality and reality breaks down as well.

In sum, what therapists can recognize and understand in their patients is increased with increased knowledge and understanding of the social, cultural, and historical environment. And therapists will develop a flexibility of mind, a readiness to appreciate the unfamiliar, the new, if they recognize the centrality of change in human life, of change in the human environment, change that is reflected in changes in the self and in its disorders. But that still feels to me a somewhat vague and facile response. Those of us who believe that a good psychoanalyst cannot afford to ignore culture, society, and history, cannot fail to learn about and from society, culture, and history and from others who study society, culture and history, need to face this issue head on and to think more and more rigorously about the relationship of the self to its context and about psychoanalytic clinical practice as connected with the social, cultural, and historical surround.

R.F.: I am reminded of Erich Fromm's statement in *Man for himself*, "Psychology cannot be divorced from philosophy and ethics nor from sociology and economics" (Fromm, 1947, p. ix). Clearly the discipline of history needs to be added to this list. Many psychoanalysts are very good at reconstructing their patients' histories in a way that is both nuanced and sophisticated. Yet they remain only novice students of history. This has always struck me as curious. Indeed, constructing a patient's history and being a student of history with a keen awareness of how we are all shaped by history's events seem inherently related. Yet the two are often kept separate. Do you think the way psychoanalysts are trained today can change to include other disciplines? Have you had the opportunity to work with psychoanalysts, and share your insights as a historian, given your involvement at the Austen Riggs Center or elsewhere?

T.K.: I've touched on this issue in my last responses. The emphasis you place on the connection between personal history and the history in which personal history is embedded seems important and fruitful. As far as Austen Riggs and psychoanalytic education generally is concerned, I've often fantasized about teaching the course I've taught at Williams and just last semester at the University of Vienna, "Victorian psychology: From the phrenologists to Freud," to the Riggs Fellows and/or to candidates in psychoanalysis. I think they'd find it fascinating. It would historicize their views of human psychology, showing not only how ideas about the psyche have changed over time but how the psyche itself has been transformed in tandem with social, cultural, and historical change. The Erikson Institute at Riggs, first under the leadership of Gerard Fromm and now of Jane Tillman, has organized numerous events, conferences, reading groups, and workshops that bring clinicians and scholars in the humanities and social sciences together. Indeed, Riggs has something called the Erikson Scholar program bringing scholars from the humanities and social sciences to Riggs for several months and integrating those scholars into the life of the institution, bringing them into contact with clinicians and patients, allowing them to participate in case conferences, bringing as it were the psychoanalytic treatment of people, often very troubled people, to life for those who normally only encounter psychoanalytic ideas on paper or on a computer screen. As I've considered elsewhere, I see real parallels between the way scholars in the humanities and social science, historians above all, approach their human subjects and the way psychoanalytically oriented psychotherapists approach their human patients. Those parallels should prompt scholars to be less reliant on psychological and psychoanalytic theory and more conscious of the centrality of empathy in their attempts to know and understand the people whom they study.

R.F.: When reading your work I am struck again and again by the remarkable parallels between the discipline of history and the practice of psychoanalysis. I'd like to quote another passage, this time from your recent essay "Reflections on empathy as a mode of observation in history":

"Knowing through empathic understanding involves reason and knowledge of course, but it also involves imagination, insight and intuition, sensitivity to people and emotional intelligence, even emotional resonance – qualities not generally associated with rationalistic social science … Although some may regard imagination, insight, intuition, sensitivity, emotional resonance, or feeling with skepticism, these are qualities that ultimately make the practice of history a fascinating, creative, fully human enterprise. Without those qualities, in fact, there could be no understanding of human motivation or of the events motivated by human beings in the past – or in the present for that matter." (T. A. Kohut, 2013, p. 194)

In this passage you suggest that psychoanalysts have much to teach historians and others in the social sciences. But another way of reading this passage would be in light of the changing field of clinical practice, which is increasingly shaped by manualized, short-term therapies, managed care, and a wholesale embrace of therapeutic technique over the therapeutic process. Do you think both fields are becoming increasingly instrumentalized with time? Given your interdisciplinary outlook as a historian and psychoanalyst, what suggestions would you have, be it for history or psychoanalysis?

T.K.: I always seem to anticipate your next question in my previous answer. As I suggested, I see history as increasingly open to new approaches generally and to psychological approaches particularly. I'm less well positioned to comment on the situation in psychoanalysis. There does seem to be a significant difference between North America and Europe in this regard. In the first place, psychoanalysts feel more embattled here I think, whereas I would describe psychoanalysis as more flourishing there. Also psychoanalysis is very much part of the public discourse in Europe in ways in which it is not here. A recent lead article in *Die Zeit*, the foremost German weekly newspaper, was by a psychoanalyst about the impact of the current refugee crisis on Germans, in which the author made specific reference to clinical material derived from working with his own patients. Such an article would be difficult to imagine in the United States. But in general, there is significantly greater public intellectual interest in Europe about social, cultural, and political developments generally as well as viewed from a psychoanalytic perspective. Historians, sociologists, political scientists, *and* psychoanalysts are regular commentators on current events and issues, and in a more thoughtful and sophisticated way than the expert commentators that one can view, say, on the PBS News Hour. Indeed, it would be quite incredible to imagine a psychoanalyst appearing on the News Hour to comment on the current world political situation. Europeans generally I think have a clearer conception of the need to incorporate psychology and history into public discourse because of the history they have lived through, because of the fact that social, cultural, and historical events have had a profound impact on people's lives, including on their inner lives. That awareness, the product of painful, even traumatic, history, makes them more receptive to academic and psychoanalytic approaches to people and to the world they live in. In North America, psychoanalysts are on the defensive. As I suggested, they are increasingly gun-shy about applying the word to themselves, preferring to talk about their "psychodynamic" approach. I sometimes feel that North American psychoanalysts are eager somehow to convince those skeptical about psychotherapy, in which speaking and listening and understanding are at the center of the therapeutic work, of the value of their approach, and in the process neglect their natural allies in the universities and abroad. Indeed, one of the advantages of clinicians collaborating with scholars in the humanities and social sciences who are generally not skeptical about psychoanalysis is that they will encounter a receptive and sympathetic audience, prepared to listen to and learn from them. And, given the time-consuming nature of psychoanalytic treatment (analysis or psychotherapy), it is important for its practitioners to take the insights gained from working intensively and over time with a handful of patients and engage with people concerned with the world beyond the consulting room. That engagement is not only interesting and potentially beneficial, it also seems to be something of an ethical imperative.

R.F.: I'd like to turn now to your specific focus on modern German history. You have argued convincingly that "history flows through us." Even when we conceive of ourselves as unique individuals, we are also historically determined beings. The determining impact of history is particularly evident in relation to historical traumas, above all, the Holocaust. Earlier you spoke of the traumatic history of your father's family, and in your essay "Psychoanalysis as psychohistory or why psychotherapists cannot afford to ignore culture" you state that

"The relatives of my father, his aunts and uncles who did not have his panic-stricken reaction and remained in Austria, were all exterminated … [this is] a dramatic example of the powerful influence of history on the psyche, an influence that exerts itself over generations … I have come to the conclusion that the influence of history on the psyche is at least as significant as the influence of the psyche on history." (T. A. Kohut, 2003, p. 22)

I wonder whether you might reflect on the impact of the Holocaust on your own life and work, given your father's experience as an Austrian-Jewish refugee?

T.K.: To expand on what I said earlier, although the Holocaust was a defining presence in my life, I was not fully aware or, better, not essentially aware of that fact until fairly recently. That seems almost unbelievable to me, but of course it's not unbelievable after all, since so many other people belonging to my generation have had great difficulty recognizing the central status of the Holocaust in their lives. As with Germans of my generation, certainly a large part of the need to be silent about the Holocaust was transmitted to us from our parents, and represents, I think, an effort to protect them from trauma. They didn't want to touch that subject, and so neither did we. But there is also an effort to protect oneself, I think. In the case of Germans of my generation, scholars like Gabriele Rosenthal have argued that the silence in families about the Holocaust is designed to protect the younger generation from learning things about the parents that might make it difficult for them to love their parents and/or is designed to protect the younger generation from having to imagine themselves in their parents' place during the Third Reich, thereby confronting themselves with their own fantasized reactions. In my case, at least, I suspect that there was something of both of these strategies at work. I think I sensed something shameful behind my father's silence about his life in Austria, particularly during the period after the Anschluss. My first attempt to identify what that shame might have been came only around 2012, I think, when I attended a conference in Hamburg on a project conducted by psychoanalysts and historians about the intergenerational transmission of trauma relating to the firebombing of that city by the Allies during the Second World War. I appreciated then, for some reason, that the incorporation of Austria into the Third Reich and with it the loss of my father's identity as a Viennese and as an Austrian had to have been a profound narcissistic injury, given my father's attempt to identify himself primarily as a Viennese and an Austrian as opposed to some other identity, most obviously as a Jew. There must have been something deeply shameful and degrading about being more or less suddenly told "you no longer belong in Vienna, in Austria, in Europe, perhaps even to the human race." Perhaps it's no accident that I arrived at this realization only in 2012, for my book *A German generation* had just appeared, and I had given a lecture at the Institut für Zeitgeschichte relating to the book just a day or two before. Perhaps I had managed to work through the personal issues that had prevented me from appreciating and understanding the place of the Holocaust in my father's life and especially in his work in writing my book. I was well aware, as I worked on it, that the book was definitely part of a process of personal development and of the personal working through of the place of Nazi Germany in the life of my father, in my life, in me. The second realization about the shame or secret bad feeling that I sensed in my father only came this past fall, when I spent five months in Vienna as the Fulbright Freud Visiting Scholar of Psychoanalysis. While there, I, and above all my wife, Susan, did a considerable amount of research into the history of my father's family in Vienna. With the help of others, above all of Thomas Aichhorn, the grandson of August Aichhorn, my father's analyst, we learned to appreciate more fully the degree of anti-Semitism in Austria before and, of course, especially after the Anschluss in March of 1938, we learned more about my relatives who died in the Holocaust, and we learned more about how my father was able to get out of Austria. Learning more about the extent and the nature of anti-Semitism in Vienna during the period that my father lived there increased my appreciation of the fact that being the target of racial prejudice can elicit feelings of shame and humiliation. Perhaps we all know that intellectually, but in exploring the Viennese past of my father, I was able for the first time to get a sense of what that shame and humiliation would feel like. It is difficult, when one is treated as an inferior, not to feel inferior, particularly when as a relatively powerless minority one simply has passively to "take it" and doesn't have the option of reacting with active rage and resistance. As self psychology makes clear, we internalize the responses of the environment to us, and therefore we may internalize the racial prejudice that is directed against us, at least to a degree. Indeed, one could argue that that the internalization of prejudice is one of its single worst aspects. Hence, for my father, recalling his life in Vienna, apart from his school experiences and immersion in Vienna's cultural life (which he did love to talk about), would very likely have reawakened the feelings of shame and humiliation in him that he must have experienced there. Perhaps I sensed those slumbering feelings in him as well. There was another, more specific, reason for my father to have felt ashamed about his experience in Austria. My father got out, as did my grandmother, Else Lampl Kohut, because he and she were incredibly well connected. In the first place, to the best of my understanding, my father was only able to get his medical degree from the University of Vienna at the last minute because his father, Felix, had fought in the First World War. Secondly, and more important and problematic, my father and grandmother were able to get out because of their close relationship with two leaders of the Viennese Jewish Community during the Third Reich, Joseph Löwenherz and Benjamin Murmelstein. I suspect that it was thanks to these well-connected leaders of the Jewish community (well connected with the Nazi authorities, that is) that my father and grandmother were able to get out and to take some of their possessions with them. Viennese Jews, like those on the Kohut side of my father's family, who were not so well connected did not survive the Holocaust. So in addition to a natural "survivor's guilt," my father may have felt guilt over the fact that family connections enabled him to survive when so many other Viennese Jews did not. I sensed somewhere, then, some shame and some guilt on the part of my father in relation to his Viennese past. Since learning more about anti-Semitism in Vienna during his lifetime, but particularly after the Anschluss, and about how my father and grandmother managed to get out of Austria, he in late March 1939, she in 1940, I for the first time feel a certain empathy for my father's silence about his Viennese past, a certain degree of understanding about why, as he once told me, he could not talk about that past because it made him "feel too sad."

R.F.: Your empathic understanding of your father's tragic experiences speaks to the issue of generations. Developed by the sociologist Karl Mannheim in the early 1920s, the concept of "generations" has become a central theme in the study of German and Jewish experience in the wake of the Holocaust and the notion of intergenerationally transmitted trauma more generally. It is also the title of your most recent book. Could you say more about your understanding of this notion and how it relates specifically to your recent scholarship on modern German history?

T.K.: Obviously, all human beings need to identify themselves, to orient themselves, and generation, along with occupation, nationality, ethnicity, region, family, kinship, religion, political orientation, gender, and other identities, gives people a sense of who they are and where they belong. Obviously, people have multiple identities, which are frequently called forth by the circumstances they find themselves in. Living in the United States, I don't generally think much about my identity as an American, but when I am in Europe faced with questions about Donald Trump, my American identity is more likely to come to the fore. Obviously, our identities are generated not only by our changing personal circumstances but also by the historical period in which we are living. It is my sense that "generation" may well be an identity that was particularly pronounced during the twentieth century. Certainly, before 1900 generation does not seem to have been a concept that people used to orient themselves and to understand others in the world. Despite the efforts launched primarily by people whose worldview was shaped in the twentieth century to identify twenty-first-century generations, "generation-X" or millennials, it is also my sense that generation as a form of identity plays today a less important role in people's lives who were born after, say, 1980 than for people my age. As you can tell from these comments, generation for me is an experiential and not an empirical concept. Generation exists for me when people experience themselves, and others, as belonging to a generation. It is not an objective criterion to be applied to people with no generational consciousness. In the same way, classes only exist when there is a consciousness of class. To speak of a class society in a society with no class consciousness or to speak of generations in history at a time when people had no sense of themselves or of others as belonging to a generation does not make sense from the perspective of my experiential approach to history, although it does make sense to historians who see themselves as empirical, more or less objective, outside observers of the people of the past who can see things in the past of which past people were largely or completely unaware. From an empathic historical perspective, from my historical perspective, generations only exist in history when they are experienced by past people as existing. To this day, I regret not articulating this notion in my first book, *Wilhelm II and the Germans: A study in leadership*. I would have avoided problems and misunderstandings had I defined what I meant by "Germans" as I used the term in my book. Given my empathic historical perspective, Germans were those people – people with multiple identities (e.g., father, baker, Berliner, Protestant, Socialist, left-handed, etc.) – who identified themselves as Germans at the moments when they did so. What in the book seemed like sweeping generalizations about a whole people would have become, with that definition of the "Germans," a specific response of a specific person, in a specific situation, and at a specific point in time. What I learned from that experience and sought to apply in my second book, *A German generation*, was to articulate at the outset my fundamental assumptions about history and about knowing history first to myself and then to my readers. Actually, I think that's a good thing for all scholars to do. So generation played an important role in my book because generation played an important role in the lives of the people I studied.

The second point I'd make about generations, both from an empathic and from an empirical standpoint, is that an awareness of generations on the part of historians brings with it, in a tangible, experience-near way, an appreciation of historicity, of historical change. When we talk, say, about "the Germans," it's easy to forget that we're frequently not talking about the same people. When we talk about "the Germans" in 1925, we're talking about completely different human beings for the most part as when we talk about "the Germans" in 1910. The concept of generation can help to bring that fact home, for the leading generation of Germans in 1910, those who set the tone and the agenda, who occupied positions of influence in communities, in institutions, in the nation, was a wholly different group of people from those who comprised the leading generation of Germans in 1925. Indeed, those comprising the leading generation in 1925 were frequently the children of those who comprised the leading generation in 1910. It's so easy to forget that historicity, the fact of change, that the actors on the historical stage are constantly different people, with different hopes and fears, different past histories, different "spaces of experience" and "horizons of expectation," to quote Reinhart Koselleck. The concept of generation applied to history helps us to appreciate that historicity, that change in personnel.

R.F.: What I so much appreciate about your book *A German generation* is the way in which you have integrated psychoanalytic ideas and thinking in a reader-friendly manner. Your discussion avoids psychoanalytic jargon so that your readers can appreciate the application of psychoanalytic ideas and insights without needing to consult a dictionary of psychoanalytic terms. This reminds me of the principle of "holding one's theories lightly" and staying true to the lived experience of the person, whether that person is a patient or a historical subject. Can you say more about your own approach to "lived experience," its relevance to the study of history and how it is psychoanalytically informed?

T.K.: When I was a research candidate at the Cincinnati Psychoanalytic Institute one of the real highlights for me was when my fellow candidates would present their control cases to the class. What struck me about the presentations was that when the analyst understood what was going on with his or her patient, the analyst would talk about the therapy in ordinary language, using ordinary, everyday terms, language and terms wholly in keeping with the patient's experience and way of talking about him- or herself. On rare occasions, however, psychoanalytic jargon would suddenly be introduced into the analyst's case report, where it seemed oddly jarring, indeed something of a foreign body. I soon concluded that when jargon reared its ugly head, the analyst actually didn't really know what was going on, couldn't really understand the patient in the patient's own terms, in terms of the patient's own life experience. Not knowing, not understanding, was difficult for the analyst to bear, in the setting of the case conference presentation at least, and so theory was introduced as a way to fill in effectively from without what was not being understood from within. I also noticed in my own training analysis that my analyst never talked about my "Oedipus complex" or my "defenses and resistances" or used terms like "reaction formation" or "displacement." He used ordinary language and talked about experience-near and wholly intelligible and ordinary feelings like "competitiveness" or "jealousy" or "anxiety." As my mother once put it to me when I began my brief career as a psychotherapist, it was far more important for me to listen to my patients than to Freud, Winnicott, Loewald, or Kohut. In my own work, I have tried to use theory in the way that my analyst used theory in my own analysis and in the way I used theory with my patients during the years I worked as a psychotherapist. The purpose of therapy is to a considerable degree to help patients understand themselves, to develop empathy with themselves, in their own terms, in the terms of their own life experiences. The purpose of the history I write is to help readers develop empathy with the people of the past I am presenting, to understand those people in ordinary terms, in terms of those past peoples' own life experiences. I think the most important thing I learned as a research candidate in Cincinnati is that psychoanalysis is less a body of theory, a general psychology, and more a clinical practice. In my *American Historical Review* article "Psychohistory as history" (T. A. Kohut, 1986), I tried to make the case that in their use of empathy historians and psychoanalysts approach their human subjects in much the same way. Indeed, given the central place of clinical practice in psychoanalysis, I see theory less as a compendium of universal laws of human psychology and more as an attempt to articulate and communicate the concrete clinical experiences of many different therapists working with many different patients. Theory in this sense is necessary in psychoanalysis since each analyst can only have clinical experience with a limited number of patients. Theory in this sense enables each individual therapist to come into contact with the life experiences of many different patients and with the clinical experiences of the many different psychotherapists who have treated them in a condensed, readily accessible, intelligible form. The role of theory is to expand one's ability to understand one's patients. But in analysis, theory should not intrude on the analyst's free-floating attention, should not interfere with his or her ability to *listen* to the patient. It should merely expand what the therapist is actually able to *hear*. In much the same way, the writing of other scholars, indeed theory, can help the historian understand his or her historical subject. In the end, however, the understanding of people needs to remain empathic and needs to be expressed in ordinary human terms, in terms of the patient's or the historical subject's own life experience. Theory, in psychoanalysis and in history, should expand and/or deepen empathic understanding, not substitute for it.

R.F.: In *A German generation*, you state that "psychologically we are constituted in no small measure through our experience of the environment" and that "That environment is constituted by history." You go on to describe the aim of your book as investigating "how the experience of a historically determined environment shapes the self" (T. A. Kohut, 2012, p. 1). Your book is a fascinating study of the way in which history flowed through the lives of 62 Germans, a group that for the most part were enthusiastic supporters of National Socialism, members of the generation of perpetrators and bystanders.

Reflecting on the idea that we are all shaped by history, I am struck by the challenges you must have faced in the process of researching and writing about this German generation. As you point out,

"These sixty-two Germans stood on one side of the Holocaust and my parents stood on the other. Although neither of my parents identified themselves as Jewish, both, according to Nazi racial criteria, would probably have been victims of the Final Solution had they been living in territory controlled by Germany during World War II." (T. A. Kohut, 2012, p. 16)

Can you describe what this experience was like for you? I can only imagine how challenging it must have been to engender empathy for these individuals, given their views and actions during the Third Reich. I wonder, moreover, whether you might comment on how the limits of sympathy might impact on our ability to empathize. Certainly the two concepts are often confused, even though they are very clearly related.

T.K.: Over the past year, I have been working on a manuscript with the working title "Empathy and the historical understanding of the human past." It still needs more work, rewriting, a bit more reading, and editing, but I think I've expressed the main ideas I wanted to express regarding empathy as a way of knowing other human beings. Clearly, the relationship between empathy and sympathy, the profound difference between empathy and sympathy, plays an important role in those reflections. There are numerous ways of defining "empathy," some incompatible, and I think it important to be clear about one's own definition. In my case, empathy is primarily a way of knowing more than it is affective sharing, although I do explore the relationship between affective sharing and empathic knowledge. For me, empathy is primarily a matter of observational position. When one empathizes, one leaves one's own observational position and seeks to imagine oneself, to think oneself, and perhaps even occasionally feel oneself, into the position of the other, into the experience of the other person, to see the world from his or her perspective, to enter into, cognitively, imaginatively, and perhaps even emotionally, their "space of experience" and "horizon of expectation." If empathy is understood in that way, the difference between empathy and sympathy becomes readily apparent. When I empathize, I seek to adopt the position of the other in my imagination; when I sympathize, I regard and react to the other from my own autonomous position. In a nutshell, empathy is feeling *with*; sympathy is feeling *for*. And of course, empathy can be used very unsympathetically to manipulate, exploit, and even destroy other human beings.

I have written so much about empathy, including its relation to sympathy, that it is difficult for me to restrain myself here. I will say, however, that I think we self-consciously empathize, we self-consciously seek to adopt the perspective of the other person, including other people in the past, when something about them does not make self-evident sense. For me at least, the reaction of Jews to their persecution, deportation, and extermination is not particularly puzzling. I don't find their reactions, their attitudes, their behavior, hard to understand, although I find their experiences difficult to imagine or share emotionally. By contrast, those who carried out or enabled the genocide seem especially worthy of empathic understanding because *their* reactions, attitude, and behavior do not make self-evident sense to me. In my book *A German generation*, I sought to empathize with Nazis and their supporters and to engender empathy for them on the part of readers, without my having much sympathy for them and without, I think, making them sympathetic to readers. So I resist the notion that I sought to engender "sympathy" for the Germans I studied in my book either in myself or in my readers. As I noted in the introduction to the book, I did not particularly like most of the interviewees based on their interviews. Nonetheless, I think I was able to empathize with them for the most part. As Alon Confino (2006, p. 10) elegantly put it: "One can understand without forgiving and forgive without understanding."

I think I've considered in some of my earlier answers the emotional difficulty I experienced in thinking and writing about the Third Reich in producing *A German generation*. But I think that difficulty had less to do with my efforts to empathize with the interviewees during that period of my life and more to do with the fact, as noted above, that I inhabited the Third Reich in my imagination and it inhabited me. I realized that had I been alive then, I would have been labeled as more than a "*Halbjude*" (given my mother's Jewish ancestors and my father's status as "*Volljude*"), and would have faced persecution and very likely deportation and extermination. That is, my most distressing experiences came not when I was occupying the position of the interviewees in my imagination; they came when I was occupying my own. Occupying my own position in my imaginary Third Reich was what was so profoundly unsettling.

R.F.: I would like to end by quoting a passage from the end of the Introduction to *A German generation*:

"Despite my abhorrence of National Socialism, I seek in this book to present and to understand its appeal to the interviewees and, ultimately, to other ordinary Germans during the 1930s and early 1940s. Specifically I seek to account for the attraction of what I regard to be Nazism's fundamental ideological tenet, the racial collective of the *Volksgemeinschaft*, or "community of the people" – reflecting in part the attraction that collective experiences exert on human beings more generally. My aim, then, is certainly not to engender sympathy for the interviewees or for Germans belonging to their generation but to reduce the intellectual and emotional distance separating us from them, in part by thinking our way inside their unique historical circumstances, in part by recognizing that on some level they were as we are and that we have within us the capacity to be as they were." (T. A. Kohut, 2012, p. 17)

This is a powerful statement on many levels. I am struck by the objective you set out for yourself and by the challenges involved in empathizing with individuals who were enthusiastic supporters of National Socialism. I think some readers may also struggle with the notion that we all have the capacity to be as these individuals were, a point of view you express in a significant and potentially controversial passage in your book:

"To be sure, the Holocaust occurred at a particular time and in a particular place. Nevertheless, not only were those who carried out genocide and those who simply acquiesced to it connected by a lack of empathy for Jewish people. There are also connections between them and us, connections we might prefer not to face. By splitting off Nazi perpetrators from ordinary Germans, we also split the perpetrators off from us. We can imagine ourselves in the place of – empathize with – the ordinary Germans perhaps, but we would prefer not to imagine ourselves in the place of – empathize with – the Nazi perpetrators and thus interpose "indifferent" bystanders to stand between us and the "hate-filled" killers. Paradoxically, through our unwillingness to think our way inside the experience of those who carried out the genocide, we demonstrate that the closing off of empathy, which made the genocide possible, is a universal (though [in this case wholly] ... "understandable") human response. If a shared lack of empathy brings Nazis and Germans, perpetrators and bystanders, closer together, it implicitly brings the Nazi perpetrators closer to us as well. For the Holocaust was not simply a dehumanizing and murderous German response; it was also a dehumanizing and murderous "all-too-human" response." (T. A. Kohut, 2012, p. 172)

I would be grateful if you could expand further. What do you envisage the lasting impact of this book to be?

T.K.: As far as I know this passage has only been noticed by one of my students, who read the book in a historical methods and philosophy of history course I taught at Williams College. The passage comes at the end of the essay "German anti-semitism during the Third Reich," and follows my critique of using the word "indifference" to characterize the attitude of ordinary Germans to the persecution, deportation, and extermination of the Jews. For a great many historians, whereas the "Nazis" were the hate-filled "perpetrators," ordinary "Germans" were the indifferent "bystanders." This distinction is problematic for several reasons: it is difficult to see how one can draw a clear line between "Nazis" and "Germans"; it is psychologically implausible to think that Nazi perpetrators passionately hated Jews whereas German bystanders had virtually no affective response to Jews at all; and, finally, it obscures the crucial role played by German society in carrying out the Final Solution. In the potentially controversial passage quoted above, I argued that we do not want to empathize with the hate-filled killers; indeed, we close off our empathy for them and interpose "indifferent" bystanders with whom we *can* experience empathy between them and us. I argued, then, that just as the Nazi bystanders and perpetrators closed off empathy for the Jews, we close off empathy for other human beings when we close off empathy for the Nazi perpetrators. Indeed, I think that historians like Ian Kershaw or Richard Evans, who see the German people as indifferent or even opposed to the violent exclusion of the Jews from the *Volksgemeinschaft* and see the German people as fundamentally at odds with National Socialism, avoid having to empathize with, to think and imagine their way inside, the Nazi experience of ordinary Germans by asserting that ordinary Germans did not by and large ever experience themselves as Nazis. I am convinced, as are many other historians, that National Socialism was in fact widely and deeply popular during most of the Third Reich, and it is our obligation to understand that popularity by thinking our way inside the "space of experience" and "horizon of expectation" of Germans during the 1930s and early 1940s. Not only in my scholarship but also in my teaching I seek to encourage my students to empathize with Nazis, to understand how human beings not wholly unlike themselves could have thought the things they thought and done the things they did, how, to cite but one example, someone could have been given the order to shoot helpless men, women, and children standing naked before a trench and thought that the order made sense. In doing that empathic work, German Nazis and Nazi Germans do not become monsters, expressions of a twisted German national character or the end product of a unique twisted German historical path. Instead, they become human beings, albeit human beings with different historical and psychologically determinative experiences. Those experiences are what ultimately distinguish us from them, not fundamentally different human natures. And, in the book, I concluded that there are two aspects of human nature that we may share with German Nazis and Nazi Germans. Although its intensity varies from person to person and from culture to culture, the first is the need to belong to a group and consequently to exclude others from it, a need that in my view motivated the creation of the racially exclusive collective of the *Volksgemeinschaft* and with it, in part, the extermination of the Jews. The second is the capacity to dehumanize others by closing off empathy for them, a capacity that we paradoxically, if wholly understandably, demonstrate when we close off empathy for those who carried out the extermination project. It was that capacity to close off empathy that enabled *human beings* to carry out the Holocaust. What separates us from the Nazis, both bystanders and perpetrators, is ultimately not a different human nature; it is, as I wrote in the book's conclusion, the "grace" of historical experience. It's a cliché I know, but history is characterized by change and by continuity. Viewing human beings as shaped psychologically by historical forces extends and deepens our appreciation of the power of change in human life. And yet there are some more or less universal human experiences that we can use to understand people in very different times and places, with historical experiences very different from our own. Those shared experiences coupled with the power of the imagination are what enable us to empathize and understand people in the past – and in the present – who seem different, alien, and at times even abhorrent to us.

References

Cocks, G. (2012). *The state of health: Illness in Nazi Germany*. Oxford, UK: Oxford University Press.

Confino, A. (2006). *Germany as a culture of remembrance: Promises and limits of writing history*. Chapel Hill, NC: University of North Carolina Press.

Confino, A. (2014). *A world without Jews: The Nazi imagination from persecution to genocide*. New Haven, CT: Yale University Press.

Daniel, U. (2001). *Kompendium Kulturgeschichte: Theorien, Praxis, Schlüsselwörter*. Frankfurt am Main, Germany: Suhrkamp.

Elovitz, P., & Cocks, G. (2005). Thomas A. Kohut: Historian with a psychoanalytic world view. *Clio's Psyche, 12*(1), 49–56.

Frie, R. (2014). Cultural psychoanalysis: Psychoanalytic anthropology and the interpersonal tradition. *Contemporary Psychoanalysis, 50*, 371–394.

Frie, R. (2017). *Not in my family: German memory and responsibility after the Holocaust*. New York, NY: Oxford University Press.

Frie, R., & Coburn, W. J. (eds.) (2010). *Persons in context: The challenge of individuality in theory and practice.* New York, NY: Routledge.

Fromm, E. (1947). *Man for himself: An inquiry into the psychology of ethics*. New York, NY: Rinehart & Company.

Garbarini, A. (2006). *Numbered days: Diaries and the Holocaust*. New Haven, CT: Yale University Press.

Gay, P. (1985). *Freud for historians*. New York, NY: Oxford University Press.

Kohut, H. (1985). *Self psychology and the humanities: Reflections on a new psychoanalytic approach*. C. B. Strozier (ed.). New York, NY: W. W. Norton.

Kohut, H. (2011). On leadership. In P. H. Ornstein (ed.). *The search for the self: Selected writings of Heinz Kohut*, 4 volumes (Vol. III, pp. 103–128). London, UK: Karnac Books.

Kohut, T. A. (1986). Psychohistory as history. *The American Historical Review, 91*, 336–354.

Kohut, T. A. (1991). *Wilhelm II and the Germans, A study in leadership*. New York, NY: Oxford University Press.

Kohut, T. A. (2000). The creation of Wilhelm Busch as a German cultural hero, 1902–1908. In M. Micale & R. Dietle (eds.), *Enlightenment, passion, modernity: Historical essays in European thought and culture* (pp. 286–304). Palo Alto, CA: Stanford University Press.

Kohut, T. A. (2003). Psychoanalysis as psychohistory or why psychotherapists cannot afford to ignore culture. *The Annual of Psychoanalysis, Psychoanalysis and History, 31*, 225–236.

Kohut, T. A. (2012). *A German generation: An experiential history of the twentieth century*. New Haven, CT: Yale University Press.

Kohut, T. A. (2013). Reflections on empathy as a mode of observation in history. In C. Frey, T. Kubetzky, K. Latzel, H. Mehrkens, & C. F. Weber (eds.), *Sinngeschichten: Kulturhistorische Beiträge für Ute Daniel* (pp. 190–197). Vienna, Austria: Böhlau.

Wierling, D. (2013). *Eine Familie im Krieg: Leben, Sterben und Schreiben, 1914–1918*. Göttingen, Germany: Wallstein.

Index